T0076287

# Get the eBook FREE!

(PDF, ePub, Kindle, and liveBook all included)

We believe that once you buy a book from us, you should be able to read it in any format we have available. To get electronic versions of this book at no additional cost to you, purchase and then register this book at the Manning website.

Go to https://www.manning.com/freebook and follow the instructions to complete your pBook registration.

That's it!
Thanks from Manning!

# Build a Frontend
# Web Framework
# (From Scratch)

ÁNGEL SOLA ORBAICETA

MANNING
SHELTER ISLAND

For online information and ordering of this and other Manning books, please visit www.manning.com. The publisher offers discounts on this book when ordered in quantity. For more information, please contact

Special Sales Department
Manning Publications Co.
20 Baldwin Road
PO Box 761
Shelter Island, NY 11964
Email: orders@manning.com

©2024 by Manning Publications Co. All rights reserved.

No part of this publication may be reproduced, stored in a retrieval system, or transmitted, in any form or by means electronic, mechanical, photocopying, or otherwise, without prior written permission of the publisher.

Many of the designations used by manufacturers and sellers to distinguish their products are claimed as trademarks. Where those designations appear in the book, and Manning Publications was aware of a trademark claim, the designations have been printed in initial caps or all caps.

♾ Recognizing the importance of preserving what has been written, it is Manning's policy to have the books we publish printed on acid-free paper, and we exert our best efforts to that end. Recognizing also our responsibility to conserve the resources of our planet, Manning books are printed on paper that is at least 15 percent recycled and processed without the use of elemental chlorine.

The authors and publisher have made every effort to ensure that the information in this book was correct at press time. The authors and publisher do not assume and hereby disclaim any liability to any party for any loss, damage, or disruption caused by errors or omissions, whether such errors or omissions result from negligence, accident, or any other cause, or from any usage of the information herein.

 Manning Publications Co.
20 Baldwin Road
PO Box 761
Shelter Island, NY 11964

| | |
|---|---|
| Development editors: | Toni Arritola and Ian Hough |
| Technical editor: | Arpit Sharma |
| Review editor: | Dunja Nikitović |
| Production editor: | Kathy Rossland |
| Copy editor: | Keir Simpson |
| Proofreader: | Mike Beady |
| Typesetter: | Dennis Dalinnik |
| Cover designer: | Marija Tudor |

ISBN: 9781633438064
Printed in the United States of America

*To my wife, Jen, for her unwavering love and support, and to my parents, who instilled in me the importance of hard work and dedication.*
*I also dedicate this book to the special family members and friends who support my technical writing, even when it's a world apart from their understanding.*

# contents

# *preface*

In 2007, when I began programming web applications, popular frameworks such as Vue, React, Svelte, and Angular didn't exist, and Node JS was a few years from its debut. To make a web application interactive back then, you had to attach event listeners to HTML elements manually and update the Document Object Model (DOM) through code. This approach often felt repetitive and cumbersome. Fortunately, innovators, including Miško Hevery at Google, recognized the need for a more efficient solution and introduced AngularJS, a groundbreaking framework designed to liberate developers from direct DOM manipulation. Around the same time, frameworks such as Backbone.js and Knockout emerged. In the years that followed, we witnessed the rise of Ember, Elm, and React, marking the beginning of a flourishing era in the world of web development frameworks.

It's 2023 at the time of this writing, and we still see new and innovative frameworks being released. Such is the example of Qwik, also made possible by Miško Hevery. (What a legend!)

My first encounter with Angular left me utterly astounded. I marveled at how, when the data within a component changed, the framework effortlessly updated the corresponding HTML. The speed at which this process occurred was nothing short of magical. It wasn't until I delved into Vue a few years later, however, that I felt burning curiosity to comprehend the mechanics behind this sorcery.

This experience occurred during my tenure as a frontend engineer at my current company. I decided to invest my learning time in dissecting Vue's source code and unraveling its inner workings. I embarked on this journey by cloning Vue's repository and meticulously traversing each commit, one step at a time. My objective was to comprehend how every subtle modification in the codebase contributed to the framework's functionality. I was captivated by the elegantly written source code, which remains easy to follow even today. My admiration for Evan You, a true frontend hero, grew with each insight I gained. Acquiring profound understanding of Vue's underlying mechanics proved to be invaluable for troubleshooting complex issues and making informed architectural decisions when crafting applications.

I repeated the same exercise with Svelte and Mithril, and I learned a lot from it. Svelte was particularly interesting, as its approach is quite different. That framework is a compiler that transforms your code into JavaScript components that update the DOM directly; no virtual DOM is involved. Rich Harris, the creator of Svelte, is a genius.

At one point, I posed a question to myself: Could I create a basic framework from scratch, not for the purpose of competing with industry giants or producing a production-ready solution, but solely for the sake of learning? Intrigued by the idea, I scoured the internet for resources, stumbling upon articles that discussed aspects such as the virtual DOM and rendering, but I found no comprehensive guide that would allow someone to build a framework entirely from the ground up. The thought struck me: "This would make an excellent book!" I would unquestionably purchase a book like that. So why not take on the challenge and write it myself?

Thus, I embarked on the journey of creating a simple framework—one that mirrors the tools you're accustomed to using in your daily work. I aimed to strike a balance between simplicity and real-world functionality. Although it may not have many advanced features or performance optimizations, this framework is a comprehensive one, offering insight into the core mechanics of frameworks. To ensure clarity, I dedicated myself to breaking intricate concepts into bite-size, understandable segments, supplementing the content with diagrams and detailed explanations when necessary, recognizing the intricate nature of frontend frameworks. Yet, as I delved deeper, I underestimated the enormity of the task, resulting in a book that is far more extensive than I initially envisioned. To keep it accessible, I pruned it down. After all, who wants to navigate an unwieldy 800-page tome? But I didn't want to deprive you of valuable insights into the advanced topics I had to omit, such as routing and creating a template loader plugin for Vite. Therefore, I decided to include these supplementary chapters in the wiki section of the book's GitHub repository, which you can find at http://mng.bz/gvYe.

I hope that you embark on this journey with me and enjoy the ride at least as much as I enjoyed writing the book. Learning how something works under the hood by doing it yourself, from scratch, is one of the most rewarding experiences you can have as a developer.

# *acknowledgments*

Writing a book is a very time-consuming task, and it's rarely the effort of a single person. Despite being the author of this book, I'm not the only one who contributed to it. Other great professionals helped me along the way, and they deserve to be mentioned here.

I'm very grateful to Manning's team of extraordinary professionals who have helped me in the process of writing this book. First, I'm thankful to Eric Pillar and Brian Sawyer for getting in touch with me and giving me the opportunity to write this book. They liked the idea from the beginning and decided to give it a go. Brian was especially helpful in the early stages of giving shape to the idea, turning what could have been an arid technical book into one that's more approachable and fun to read. If it weren't for him, this book would be more of a technical dissertation on the inner workings of frontend frameworks and less of a practical guide to building one.

I want to thank Toni Arritola, my development editor, for her patience and support. If this book does a good job of teaching you the concepts efficiently, it's all thanks to her. I learned a lot from her experience in teaching effectively, something for which I'm very grateful. Thanks for showing me your tricks, Toni! I also want to thank Ian Hough, who was the development editor in the last stages of the book, for the fantastic job he did.

I want to thank Arpit Sharma, my technical reviewer, for his invaluable feedback. Arpit is an engineer at OLX Group Berlin who has worked extensively on JavaScript and its related frameworks for the past 10 years in multiple organizations. He has a keen eye for JavaScript internals and web performance. Working with Arpit has been a pleasure.

I want to thank Ivan Martinović for his help with the technical aspects of the book. Thanks, Ivan, for helping me with finding the proper formatting for the code snippets. Without your expertise in AsciiDoc, the listings in this book wouldn't look as good as they do.

Thank you to all the reviewers: Andres Sacco, Andrew Judd, Chris Shin, David Cabrero, Fatih Ozer, Fernando Bernardino, Francisco Rivas, Frans Oilinki, Giampiero Granatella, Gregorio Piccoli, Ian De La Cruz, Jaume López, Javid Asgarov, Jeremy Chen, Jon Humphrey, Jonathan Reeves, Justin Kahn, Kamwa Fosso Arcel Raulain, Ken W. Alger, Lin Zhang, Luke Kupka, Manoj Kumar M. Reddy, Matteo Battista, Mladen Đurić, Muhammad Yousuf Tafhim, Nader Bahrami, Patrice Maldague, Petru Bocsanean, Prashant Sharma, Raul Ciotescu, Riccardo Marotti, Richard Meinsen, Rodney Weis, Rooparam Choudhary, and Stephan Max. Your suggestions helped make this book better.

Many other incredible professionals at Manning helped me in the process of writing this book. I want to thank them all for their support and encouragement.

Special thanks to my brother, Pablo (whose artistic name is *Paul Alone*), for his music, which has been the soundtrack of this book. I've listened to his songs on repeat for hours while writing. They helped me focus, and I found inspiration in them when I needed it most. (His song "Quería" is playing right now.)

Finally, I thank all my colleagues at Glovo, who were very supportive while I was writing this book. Thanks to all of you who bought the MEAP and gave me feedback about it. I appreciate it.

# about this book

*Build a Frontend Web Framework (From Scratch)* is a hands-on guide designed to lead you through the creation of your own frontend framework, closely mirroring the tools you routinely use in your professional life. My primary goal is to unveil the inner workings of frameworks, enabling you to harness their power more effectively. But the book isn't just about education; it's also about reveling in the journey!

Frontend frameworks are intricate pieces of software, and this book was crafted with your learning in mind. Each concept is methodically deconstructed into easily digestible segments, supplemented by diagrams and comprehensive explanations. I aim to equip you with everything you need to construct your own framework.

## Who should read this book

You may be a frontend developer (at any level of seniority) who's curious enough to want to understand how the tool they use every day works under the hood. Or you may be a coding enthusiast who wants to spend a few weekends using JavaScript to code a frontend framework for the fun of it—and for the learning experience, of course.

The book assumes that you have a basic understanding of JavaScript and HTML, as well as some experience with frontend frameworks. For the topics that are a bit more advanced, I've included links to external resources where you can learn more about them, as well as more detailed explanations. The book is written so that developers at all levels of experience should be able to follow along.

### *How this book is organized: A road map*

This book is divided into three parts. Part 1 introduces frontend frameworks and shows you how to code a simple application by using vanilla JavaScript.

- Chapter 1 covers how frontend frameworks work from 30,000 feet.
- Chapter 2 introduces the application you'll rewrite throughout the book. In this chapter, you start by coding the application with vanilla JavaScript.

Part 2 teaches you how to create the simplest possible frontend framework that renders components and handles the state of the application.

- Chapter 3 covers what the virtual DOM is and how it works. In this chapter, you implement the `h()` function to create virtual DOM nodes.
- Chapter 4 covers how to render the virtual DOM to the real DOM, creating the HTML elements and appending them to the browser's document. You implement the `mountDOM()` function for this task, and you use `destroyDOM()` to remove the elements from the DOM when the component is unmounted.
- Chapter 5 shows you how to implement a simple state management system that updates the DOM when the state of the application changes.
- Chapter 6 explains how to package and publish your framework's first version to NPM.
- Chapter 7 covers the first part of the reconciliation algorithm, comparing two virtual DOM trees to find out what changes need to be made in the real DOM to make it match the virtual DOM.
- Chapter 8 covers the second part of the reconciliation algorithm, updating the real DOM to make it match the virtual DOM. In this chapter, you implement the `updateDOM()` function to apply the changes to the real DOM.

In part 3, you make components manage their own state, communicate with other components, and run code as part of their lifecycle (when they're mounted and unmounted from the DOM).

- Chapter 9 explains how to define components that manage their own state and render themselves to the DOM. You implement the `defineComponent()` function to create component prototypes.
- Chapter 10 covers how components can implement functionality inside their prototype's methods.
- Chapter 11 covers how components can include other components inside their view and how they communicate with one another.
- Chapter 12 shows why it's so important to use a unique identifier when rendering lists of components and how to tweak your reconciliation algorithm to use hints that improve performance.
- Chapter 13 analyzes how asynchronous code executes in the browser and uses that knowledge to create a scheduler that executes the component's lifecycle methods (also known as hooks).

- Chapter 14 shows how to test components written with your framework, especially the ones that use asynchronous code.
- Appendix A covers configuring the NPM project where you'll be writing the code for your framework. I show you how to set it up yourself, but you can use a command-line-interface tool I created to scaffold the project.

Some extra chapters didn't fit into the book. You'll find this extra material in the wiki section of the book's GitHub repository: http://mng.bz/gvYe. The topics in that section are advanced ones that you may want to explore to continue improving your framework. The extra chapters cover topics such as creating slots to insert external content into components, creating a single-page application router, and writing a template compiler to transform HTML templates into render functions for your components. When you finish the chapters in this book, know that more content is waiting for you to help you continue learning.

### About the code

This book contains many examples of source code, both in numbered listings and inline with normal text. In both cases, source code is formatted in a `fixed-width font` like `this` to separate it from ordinary text. Sometimes, code is also in **bold** to highlight code that you need to add in an existing code fragment. Code that's ~~struck through like this~~ is code that you need to remove from an existing code fragment.

In this book, you'll create your framework's code incrementally. You'll modify the code you wrote in previous chapters, removing some parts and adding new ones. This is why using **bold** and strikethrough is so important: that formatting helps you identify what code you need to add and what code you need to remove. Suppose that you've written the following code for a function called `createTextNode()`:

```
function createTextNode(vdom, parentEl) {
  const textNode = document.createTextNode(vdom.value)
  vdom.el = textNode

  parentEl.append(textNode)
}
```

If I want you to modify that code so that the function accepts a third parameter called `index` and to modify the function's last line to call an `insert()` function instead of using the `append()` method of the `parentEl` element, this is how I'll format the code:

```
function createTextNode(vdom, parentEl, index) {
  const textNode = document.createTextNode(vdom.value)
  vdom.el = textNode

  parentEl.append(textNode)
  insert(textNode, parentEl, index)
}
```

As you can see, the first line includes the new `index` parameter in bold, meaning that you need to add it to the function's signature in your existing code. The previous last line is struckthrough, meaning that you need to remove it from your existing code and instead write the new line in bold.

Source code for the examples in this book is available for download from the publisher's website at https://www.manning.com/books/build-a-frontend-web-framework-from-scratch. You can also find it on the book's GitHub repository at https://github.com/angelsolaorbaiceta/fe-fwk-book. You can get executable snippets of code from the liveBook (online) version of this book at https://livebook.manning.com/book/build-a-frontend-web-framework-from-scratch.

### liveBook discussion forum

Purchase of *Build a Frontend Web Framework (From Scratch)* includes free access to live-Book, Manning's online reading platform. Using liveBook's exclusive discussion features, you can attach comments to the book globally or to specific sections or paragraphs. It's a snap to make notes for yourself, ask and answer technical questions, and receive help from the author and other users. To access the forum, go to https://livebook.manning.com/book/build-a-frontend-web-framework-from-scratch/discussion. You can also learn more about Manning's forums and the rules of conduct at https://livebook.manning.com/discussion.

Manning's commitment to our readers is to provide a venue where meaningful dialogue between individual readers and between readers and the author can take place. It isn't a commitment to any specific amount of participation on the part of the author, whose contribution to the forum remains voluntary (and unpaid). We suggest that you try asking the author some challenging questions lest their interest stray! The forum and the archives of previous discussions will be accessible on the publisher's website as long as the book is in print.

### Other online resources

Coding a frontend web framework from scratch is as complex as it is fun. Covering all the details in a single book of a reasonable size isn't an easy task, so I had to leave out some advanced topics. You'll find this extra material on the wiki space of the book's GitHub repository at http://mng.bz/gvYe.

The book contains exercises to test your knowledge and help you practice what you've learned. The answers to those exercises are also available in the wiki section of the book's GitHub repository at http://mng.bz/eoR9.

I suggest that as you read the book, you have the Mozilla Developer Network (MDN) documentation open in your browser. You'll need to refresh your knowledge of the Document API, and you'll probably need to look up some of the methods you'll be using to manipulate the DOM. You can find the documentation at http://mng.bz/ppE5.

Sometimes, you might want to dive deeper into a topic that I cover briefly in the book. When I want to learn how something related to HTML works or how JavaScript executes in the browser, my ultimate source is the HTML specification, which you can find at https://html.spec.whatwg.org. To learn specifics about the JavaScript language, I recommend the ECMAScript specification, which you can find at https://tc39.es/ecma262. As a frontend developer, you should always have these references at hand.

# *about the author*

**ÁNGEL SOLA ORBAICETA** is a senior software engineer with more than 10 years of experience building all kinds of software, from native desktop applications to backend services and frontend web applications. Mechanical engineer by training but software engineer by passion, Ángel is a curious person who loves to learn how things work from first principles and to share his knowledge with others. In his spare time, you'll likely find him hanging out with friends, cooking food from all over the world, or reading a book—most likely a popular science book or a dystopian novel.

# *about the cover illustration*

The figure on the cover of *Build a Frontend Web Framework (From Scratch)* is "Insulaire Nord Est de l'Asie" or "Islander North East Asia," taken from a collection by Jacques Grasset de Saint-Sauveur, published in 1788. Each illustration is finely drawn and colored by hand.

In those days, it was easy to identify where people lived and what their trade or station in life was just by their dress. Manning celebrates the inventiveness and initiative of the computer business with book covers based on the rich diversity of regional culture centuries ago, brought back to life by pictures from collections such as this one.

# Part 1

## No framework

This first part comprises two introductory chapters. The first chapter offers a high-level overview of frontend frameworks, providing a foundational understanding without delving into specifics.

In the second chapter, you'll embark on a hands-on journey to create a TODO application using vanilla JavaScript with no framework assistance. If you've never built an interactive frontend application without a framework, this exercise will provide insight into the intricacies of connecting the Document Object Model (DOM) and JavaScript code manually. You'll also appreciate the challenge of modifying the DOM programmatically whenever the application's state changes.

The essence of a framework lies in automating these tasks, which allows you to concentrate on your application's logic. By mastering the manual process, you'll gain a deeper appreciation of the indispensable role that a framework plays in your development workflow.

# Are frontend frameworks magic to you?

**This chapter covers**

- Why you should build your own frontend framework
- The features of the framework we'll build together
- How frontend frameworks work

Have you ever wondered how the frontend frameworks you use work internally? Are you curious about how they decide when to re-render a component and why they update only the parts of the Document Object Model (DOM) that change? Isn't it interesting that a single HTML page can change its content without reloading and that the URL in the browser's address bar changes without requesting the new page from a server? The inner workings of frontend frameworks are fascinating, and there's no better way to learn about them than to build one from scratch. But why would you want to learn how frontend frameworks work? Isn't it enough just to know how to use them?

Good cooks know their tools; they can use knives skillfully. Great chefs go beyond that skill, however: they know the different types of knives, when to use each type, and how to keep the blades sharp. Carpenters know how to use a saw to cut wood, but great carpenters also understand how a saw works and can fix it if it breaks. Electrical engineers not only understand that electricity is the flow of electrons through a conductor, but also deeply understand the instruments that they use to measure and manipulate it. They could build a multimeter, for example, and if their multimeter broke, they could disassemble it, figure out what went wrong, and repair it.

As a developer, you have a frontend framework in your toolbox. Do you know how it works, or is it magic to you? If the framework broke—say, you found a bug—would you be able to find its source and fix it? When a single-page application (SPA) changes the route in the browser's URL bar and renders a new page without requesting it from the server, do you understand how that happens?

## 1.1  Why build your own frontend framework?

The use of frontend frameworks is on the rise; it's uncommon to write pure-vanilla JavaScript applications nowadays, and rightly so. Modern frontend frameworks boost productivity and make building complex interactive applications a breeze. Frontend frameworks have become so popular that there are jokes about the unwieldy number of them at our disposal. (In the time it took you to read this paragraph so far, a new frontend framework was created.) Some of the most popular frontend frameworks even have their own fan groups, with people arguing about why theirs is the best. Let's not forget that frontend frameworks are tools—means to an end—and that the end is to build applications that solve real problems.

> **Framework vs. library**
>
> Frameworks and libraries are different. When you use a *library*, you import its code and call its functions. When you use a *framework*, you write code that the framework executes. The framework is in charge of running the application, and it executes your code when an appropriate trigger happens. Conversely, you call the library's functions when you need them.
>
> Angular is an example of a frontend framework, whereas React claims to be a library that you can use to build user interfaces (UIs). For convenience, I'll refer to both frameworks and libraries as *frameworks* in this book.

All of the most popular frameworks currently available—such as Vue, Svelte, Angular, and React—are exceptional. **Why should you create your own frontend framework when so many great options are already available?** Well, aside from the satisfaction and enjoyment of building a complex software piece from scratch, you have a few practical reasons to consider. Let me tell you a little story about a personal experience to illustrate this fact.

When I was little, I went to a cousin's house to hang out. He was a few years older than me, and he was a handyman, with cabinets full of cables, screwdrivers, and other tools. I'd spend hours observing how he fixed all kinds of appliances. Once, I brought a remote-control car along so we could play with it. He stared at it for some time and then asked a question that took me by surprise: "Do you understand how this thing works?" I didn't; I was just a kid with zero electronics knowledge. Then he said, "I like to know how the stuff I use works. So what do you say we take it apart and see what's inside?" I still think about that experience sometimes.

Now let me ask you a question similar to the one that my cousin asked me. You use frontend frameworks every day, but do you understand how they work? You write the code for your components and then hand it over to the framework, which does its magic. When you load the application into the browser, it works. It renders the views and handles user interactions, always keeping the page updated (in sync with the application's state). For most frontend developers—including me years ago—how this magic happens is a mystery. Is the frontend framework that you use a mystery to you?

Sure, most of us have heard about that thing called the "virtual DOM." We've heard about a "reconciliation algorithm" that selects the smallest set of changes required to update the browser's DOM. We also know that SPAs modify the URL in the browser's address bar without reloading the page, and if you're the curious kind of developer, you may have read about how the browser's history API (http://mng.bz/ZRdR) achieves this task. But do you understand how all these things work together? Have you disassembled and debugged the code of the framework you use? Don't feel bad if you haven't. Most developers haven't, including some very experienced ones. This reverse-engineering process isn't easy; it requires lots of effort (and motivation).

In this book, you and I—together as a team—will build a frontend framework from scratch. This framework will be simple but complete enough to demonstrate how frontend frameworks work. From then on, what the framework does will no longer be a mystery to you. This project will be lots of fun as well.

## 1.2 The framework we'll build

I like to set expectations early, so here goes: we won't build the next Vue or React in this book. After you finish the book, you may be able to do that yourself by filling in the missing details and optimizing a couple of things here and there. The framework we'll build can't compete with the mainstream frameworks, but that's not the objective anyway. The objective of this book is to teach you how these frameworks work in general so that what they do isn't magic to you anymore. You don't need to build the most advanced framework in the world to achieve this goal. You'd need a book four times as thick as this one, and writing that kind of framework wouldn't be as much fun. (Did I mention that writing your own framework is fun?)

The framework we'll build borrows ideas from a few existing frameworks, most notably Vue (https://vuejs.org), Mithril (https://mithril.js.org), Svelte (https://svelte.dev), React (https://react.dev), Preact (https://preactjs.com), Angular (https://angular.io), and Hyperapp (https://github.com/jorgebucaran/hyperapp). Our goal is to build a framework that's simple but includes the typical features of a frontend framework. I also want it to represent some of the relevant concepts behind the source code of the most popular frameworks.

Not all frameworks use the virtual DOM abstraction, but a big portion of them do. (Svelte in particular considers it to be pure overhead, and the reasons are simply brilliant; I recommend that you read their blog post at http://mng.bz/RmjZ). I chose our framework to implement a virtual DOM that's representative of the framework you're likely using today. In essence, I chose the approach that I thought would result in the greatest learning for you. I'll cover the virtual DOM in detail in chapter 3, but in a nutshell, it's a lightweight representation of the DOM that's used to calculate the smallest set of changes required to update the browser's DOM. The HTML markup

```
<div class="name">
  <label for="name-input">Name</label>
  <input type="text" id="name-input" />
  <button>Save</button>
</div>
```

would have a virtual DOM representation like figure 1.1, for example. (Note that the saveName() event handler in the figure doesn't appear in the HTML markup. Event handlers typically aren't shown in the HTML markup; they're added programmatically.) I'll be using figures a lot throughout the book to illustrate how the virtual DOM and the reconciliation algorithm work. The *reconciliation algorithm* is the process that decides what changes need to be made to the browser's DOM to reflect the changes in the virtual DOM, which is the topic of chapters 7 and 8.

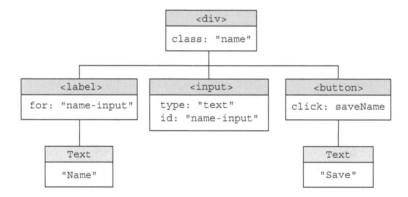

**Figure 1.1   A virtual DOM representation of HTML markup**

Your framework will have some shortcomings that make it a less-than-ideal choice for complex production applications, but it will still be a good fit for your latest side project. The framework will support only the standard HTML namespace (http://mng .bz/27Bg), which means that Scalable Vector Graphics (SVG) won't be supported. Most of the popular frameworks support this namespace, but we'll leave it out for simplicity.

### 1.2.1   *Features*

The framework you'll have by the time you finish the book will have the following features, which you'll build from scratch:

- A virtual DOM abstraction
- A reconciliation algorithm that updates the browser's DOM
- A component-based architecture in which each component does the following:
  - Holds its own state
  - Manages its own lifecycle
  - Re-renders itself and its children when their states change

If you decide that you want to continue learning, you can find extra chapters in the book's GitHub repository (appendix A). These chapters cover the following advanced features:

- An SPA router that updates the URL in the browser's address bar without reloading the page
- Slots for rendering content inside a component
- HTML templates that are compiled into JavaScript render functions
- Server-side rendering
- A browser extension that debugs the framework

As you can see, the framework will be a fairly complete framework—not a full-blown framework like Vue or React, but enough to demonstrate how those frameworks function. The neat thing is that you'll build the framework line by line, so you'll understand how everything fits together. I'll use lots of figures to help you understand concepts that may be hard to grasp. I recommend that you write the source code yourself as you read the book. Try to understand it line by line, take your time, debug it, and make sure that you understand the decisions and trade-offs that we'll make along the way.

Figure 1.2 shows the architecture of the framework we'll build. It depicts all the parts of the framework and shows how they interact.

I'll revisit this figure throughout the book, making sure to highlight each part of the framework as we build it. You don't need to understand all the details of the architecture right now, but it's good to have a high-level understanding. By the end of the book, this figure will make a lot of sense to you: you'll recognize every part because you'll have built each one yourself.

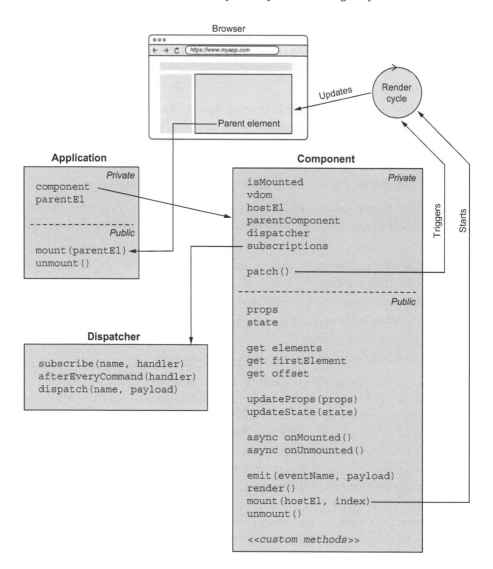

**Figure 1.2   Architecture of the framework we'll build**

### 1.2.2   *Implementation plan*

As you can imagine, you can't build everything in a single chapter. You want to break it down into smaller pieces so that you can focus on one thing at a time. Figure 1.3 shows the implementation plan for the framework; it resembles a kanban board, with each sticky note representing the work of one or more chapters. You'll pick up a sticky note in each chapter.

You'll start by implementing a simple example application using vanilla JavaScript, which will help you understand how frameworks can simplify the code of a frontend

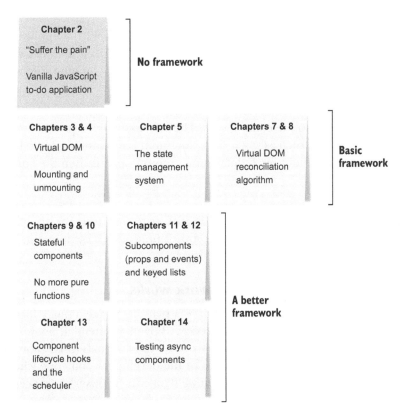

**Figure 1.3   Implementation plan for the framework we'll build**

app. (After you've suffered the "pain," you'll be in a better position to appreciate the benefits of a framework.)

### STATELESS COMPONENTS AND GLOBAL APPLICATION STATE

When you have a better understanding of the benefits of frameworks, you'll extract parts of the application's view to stateless components modeled by pure functions that return the virtual DOM representation of their view. The application will hold the entire state of the application and pass it to the components, which allows you to focus on the DOM reconciliation algorithm—likely the most complex part of the framework.

### STATEFUL COMPONENTS

Next, you'll allow components to have their own state, which makes state management much simpler. The application will no longer need to hold the entire state; state will be split among components instead. Pure functions will turn into classes that implement a `render()` method, and each component will be its own little application with its own lifecycle.

SUBCOMPONENTS

You'll add support for subcomponents, which allow you to split the application into smaller pieces. A component can pass information to its children via *props*, which are similar to the arguments of a function. Components can also communicate with their parents via *events* to which the parent can subscribe.

LIFECYCLE HOOKS

You'll add lifecycle *hooks* to the components. These hooks make it possible to execute code at certain moments, such as when the component is mounted into the DOM. An example lifecycle hook might fetch data from a remote server when the component is mounted.

TESTING

Every application must be tested, so how do you write unit tests for an application using our framework? You'll learn how to test the application's components and how to handle asynchronous events or lifecycle hooks.

## 1.3 Overview of how a frontend framework works

Now that you know what you'll build and have a plan, let's take a quick look at how frontend frameworks work. This section reviews how a frontend framework works when observed from the outside. (You'll learn about the internals throughout the rest of the book.) We'll start from the viewpoint of the developer—someone who's using the framework to build an application. Then we'll take the browser's perspective.

### 1.3.1 The developer's side

A developer starts creating a project by using the framework's command-line interface (CLI) tool or by installing the dependencies and configuring the project manually. Reading the framework's documentation is important, as every framework works differently.

In a web application, developers create components that define part of the application's view and how the user interacts with it. Components are written in HTML, CSS, and JavaScript code. Most frameworks use *single-file components* (SFCs), in which all the component's code (HTML, CSS, and JavaScript) lives in a single file. A notable exception is Angular, which uses three files for each component: one for the HTML, one for the TypeScript code, and one for the CSS. This arrangement allows the developer to keep the languages separate and potentially get better syntax support from their IDE, but it may be inconvenient to jump between files to see the entire component.

React and Preact use JSX—an extension of JavaScript—instead of writing HTML directly. Other frameworks (including Vue, Svelte, and Angular) use HTML templates with *directives* to add or modify the behavior of DOM elements, such as iterating over and displaying an array of items or showing specific elements conditionally. The following code snippet shows how you'd show a paragraph conditionally in Vue:

```
<p v-if="hasDiscount">
  You get a discount!
</p>
```

The v-if directive is a custom directive that Vue provides to show an element conditionally. Other frameworks use slightly different syntaxes, but all of them give the developer a way to show or hide elements based on the application's state. For the sake of comparison, here's how you'd do the same thing in Svelte

```
{#if hasDiscount}
<p>
  You get a discount!
</p>
{/if}
```

and in React

```
{hasDiscount && <p>You get a discount!</p>}
```

When the developer is satisfied with the application, they need to bundle the code into fewer files than originally written so that the browser can load the application by making fewer requests to the server. The files can also be *minified*—made smaller by removing whitespace and comments and by giving variables shorter names. The process of turning the application's source code into the files that are shipped to the users is called *building*.

Before we can deploy a frontend application to production, we need to build it. Most of the work of building an application with a specific framework is done by the framework itself. The framework typically provides a CLI tool that we can use to build the application by running a simple NPM script such as npm run build.

> **NOTE**  An application can be built in many ways, resulting in a wide variety of bundle formats. Here, I'll explain a build process that encapsulates some of the most common practices.

Building the application involves a few steps:

1  The template compiler transforms the template for each component into JavaScript code. This code, executed in the browser, creates the component's view.
2  The components' code, split into multiple files, is transformed and bundled into a single JavaScript file, app.bundle.js. (For larger applications, it's common to have more than one bundle and to *lazy-load* them—that is, load them only when they'll become visible to the user.)
3  The third-party code used by the application is bundled into a single JavaScript file, vendors.bundle.js. This file includes the code for the framework itself, along with other third-party libraries.
4  The CSS code in the components is extracted and bundled into a single CSS file: bundle.css. (As before, larger applications may have more than one CSS bundle.)

IO 825 5314

5  The HTML file that will be served to the user (index.html) is generated or copied from the static-assets directory.

6  The static assets (such as images, fonts, and audio clips) are copied to the output directory. Optionally, they can be preprocessed to optimize images or convert audio files to a different format.

A typical build process results in four files (or more, in the case of larger apps):

- *app.bundle.js* with the application's code
- *vendors.bundle.js* with the third-party code
- *bundle.css* with the application's CSS
- *index.html*—the HTML file that will be served to the user

These files are uploaded to a server, and the application is ready to be served to the user. When a user requests the website, the HTML, JS, and CSS files are statically served.

> **NOTE** When a file is *statically served*, the server doesn't need to do anything before sending it to the user. The server simply reads the file from disk and sends it. By contrast, when the application is rendered on the server, the server generates the HTML file before sending it to the user's browser.

Figure 1.4 shows a diagram of the build process. Note that a typical build process is more complex than the one shown in the figure, but this illustration is enough to explain the concepts. I've included a step that transforms the JavaScript code. This generic step applies to any transformation that needs to be made before the code is bundled, such as transpiling it by using Babel (https://babeljs.io) or TypeScript (https://www.typescriptlang.org).

Let's see what happens in the browser after these files are loaded. The flow is slightly different depending on whether the application server-side rendered (SSR) or statically served as an SPA. Let's start with the slightly simpler latter case.

### 1.3.2  *The browser side of an SPA*

In an SPA, the server responds with a mostly empty HTML file that's used to load the application's JavaScript and CSS files. Then the framework uses the Document API to create and update the application's view. A router makes sure that the entire application isn't reloaded when the user navigates to a different URL; rather, the view is updated to show the new content. The router also updates the URL in the browser's address bar to give the user a nice experience. The following sections describe this process step by step.

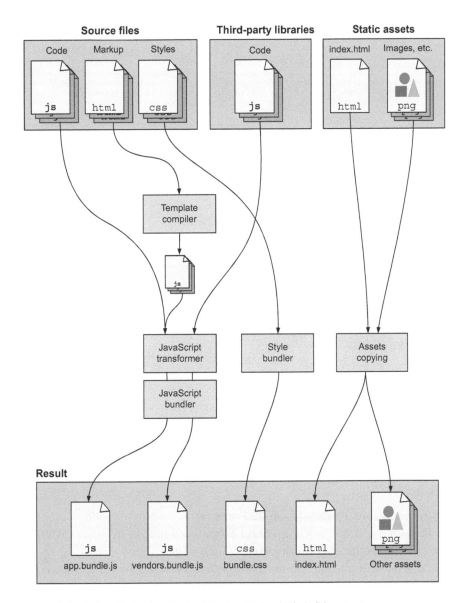

**Figure 1.4   A simplified diagram of a frontend application's build process**

### STEP 1: LOADING THE HTML FILE

When the user navigates to the application by writing its URL, the browser requests the page's HTML file (1), which is returned by the server (2), as illustrated in figure 1.5.

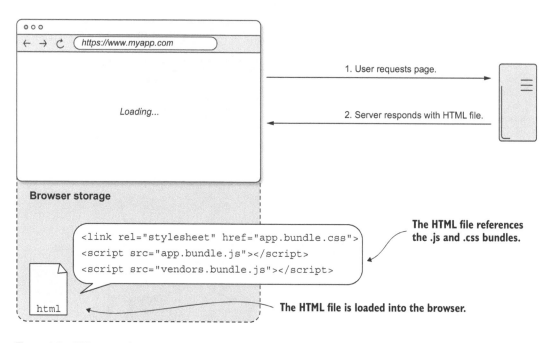

**Figure 1.5   SPA requesting the mostly empty HTML page**

The browser loads the HTML file and parses it. This HTML, which is mostly empty, is used to load the JavaScript and CSS bundles declared in the `<script>` and `<link>` tags. These bundles are the application and vendor bundles we talked about in the previous section.

### STEP 2: LOADING THE JAVASCRIPT AND CSS FILES

The browser loads the JavaScript and CSS files referenced in the HTML file (3) and parses the JavaScript code, as depicted in figure 1.6.

The browser is still blank at this point. It has rendered the HTML file, but this file's `<body>` element is mostly empty—except maybe for a `<div id="app">` tag that some frameworks use to render the app. The view of an SPA is created dynamically by the framework's JavaScript code.

### STEP 3: CREATING THE APPLICATION'S VIEW (MOUNTING THE APP)

The framework JavaScript code (living in the vendors bundle) finds the components defined in the application's code that need to be rendered (4) and creates the application's view (5), as depicted in figure 1.7. This initial rendering is called *mounting* the application.

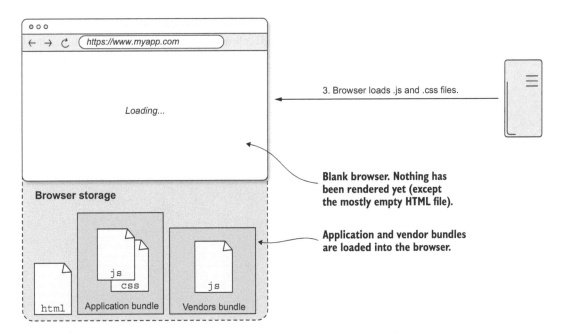

**Figure 1.6 The browser loads the JavaScript and CSS files referenced in the HTML.**

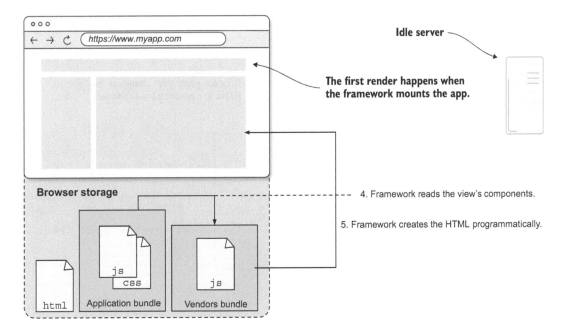

**Figure 1.7 The framework creates the application's view using the Document API.**

The framework uses the Document API to create the application's HTML programmatically. The Document API allows HTML elements to be created programmatically through JavaScript. Let's take a quick detour to see how this process works. Given an empty HTML <body> element like

```
<body></body>
```

a paragraph can be created programmatically and appended to the document like so:

```
const paragraph = document.createElement('p')
paragraph.textContent = 'Hello, World!'
document.append(paragraph)
```

This process results in the following HTML:

```
<body>
  <p>Hello, World!</p>
</body>
```

### STEP 4: HANDLING USER INTERACTIONS

Going back to how SPAs work, what happens when the user interacts with the application? When the user interacts with the application (6), the framework handles the event and updates the view accordingly, as depicted in figure 1.8. The framework han-

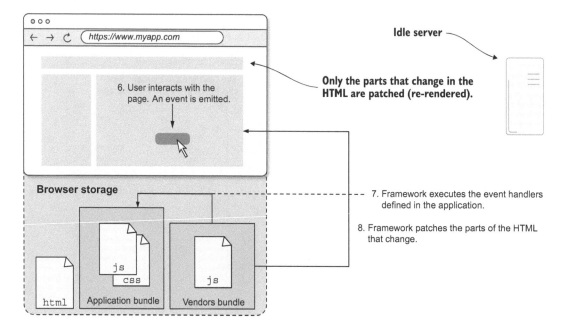

**Figure 1.8   SPA handling user interactions**

dles the event from the browser by executing the event handling code defined in the application's code (7) and then updating the view to reflect the changes in the application's state (8).

The framework is responsible for updating only the parts of the HTML that need to be updated. This process is called *patching* the DOM.

**DEFINITION**   A single change that the framework makes in the DOM is called a *patch*. The process of updating the view to reflect the changes in the application's state is called *patching the DOM*.

Making changes in the document is expensive, so a well-implemented framework minimizes the number of changes to the document required to make it reflect the updates. By *expensive*, I mean that the browser needs to repaint and reflow the document to reflect the changes—a process that consumes resources.

**TIP**   To better understand why changing the DOM is expensive in terms of computation, I recommend that you read "Render-tree Construction, Layout, and Paint" at http://mng.bz/1JlX. This article explains how the browser renders the document and gives you an overview of everything that happens under the hood.

How this task is achieved varies greatly across frameworks. Some frameworks use a virtual DOM (as ours will) to compare the current state of the document with the desired state and apply only the necessary changes; others take a completely different approach. To learn more about how some frameworks update the view, check the following sidebar.

### How some frameworks update the view

Svelte understands the ways in which the view can be updated at compilation time, and it produces JavaScript code to update the exact parts of the view that need to be patched for each possible state change. Svelte is remarkably performant because it does the least work in the browser to update the view.

Angular runs a change detection routine, comparing the last state it used to render the view with the current state, every time it detects that the state might have changed. Changes to the state of a component typically happen when an event listener runs, when data is requested from a server via an HTTP request, or when macrotasks (such as `setTimeout()`) or microtasks (such as `Promise.then()`) are executed. Angular makes this detection possible thanks to zone.js (https://angular .io/guide/zone), an execution context that's aware of the asynchronous tasks running at any given time. With zone.js, Angular can detect when a macrotask or microtask is executed and run the change detection routine. The web page "Event loops: microtasks and macrotasks" (https://javascript.info/event-loop) is a wonderful resource for learning more about the JavaScript event loop and the difference between the micro- and macrotask queues.)

**(continued)**

Most other widely used frameworks—including Vue, React, Preact, and Inferno—use a virtual DOM representation of the view. So by comparing the last-known virtual DOM with the virtual DOM after the state has changed, they compute the minimum changes required to update the HTML. React makes this virtual DOM comparison every time a component changes the state, using either `setState()` or the `useState()` hook's mechanism. Vue takes a remarkably smart approach, including a reactivity layer that the developer can use to define the application's state. These reactivity primitives wrap regular JavaScript objects (including arrays and sets) and primitives (such as `strings`, `numbers`, and `booleans`); they automatically detect when values change and notify the components that use those values that they need to re-render.

### STEP 5: NAVIGATING AMONG ROUTES

The last step we need to cover is how the framework handles navigation among routes. When the user clicks a link (9), the framework's router prevents the default behavior of reloading the page; instead, it renders the component that's configured for the new route (10 and 11). The router is also in charge of changing the URL (12) to reflect the new route. Figure 1.9 illustrates this process.

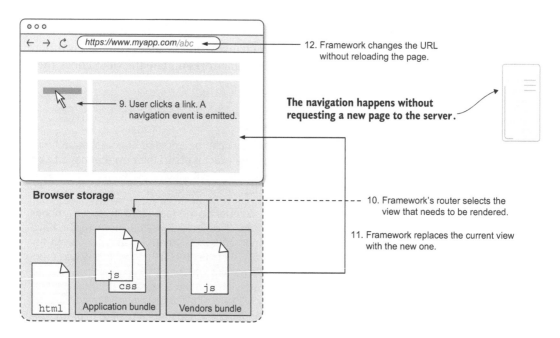

**Figure 1.9   SPA navigation among routes**

An SPA works with a single HTML file in which the HTML markup code is updated programmatically by the framework, so new HTML pages aren't requested to the server when the user navigates to a different route. SPAs are called *single-page applications* because a single HTML file is involved. The illusion of multiple pages is created by the framework, which renders the components that are configured for each route.

**THE COMPLETE FLOW OF AN SPA**

Figure 1.10 depicts the complete flow of an SPA, including all the steps described earlier but showing them more schematically.

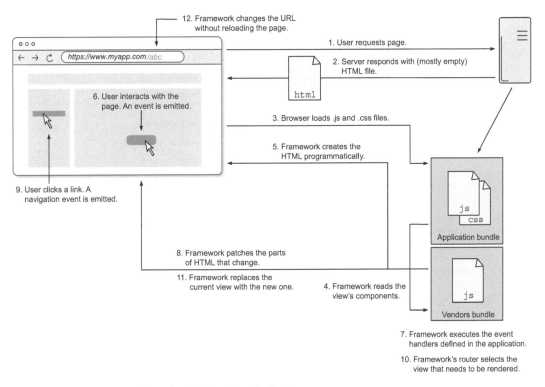

**Figure 1.10   The complete flow of an SPA rendered in the browser**

### 1.3.3   The browser and server sides of an SSR application

Now that you know how SPAs work, let's compare them with SSR applications. SSRs are web applications that render the HTML markup on the server and send it to the browser. Therefore, a backend is required to handle requests and render the HTML pages. In the browser, the frontend code is responsible for handling user interactions and updating the view to reflect the changes in the application's state, as in an SPA. But when the user navigates to a different route, the browser requests a new HTML page from the server instead of updating the HTML markup programmatically. Let's see how an SSR application works step by step.

### STEP 1: LOADING AN HTML PAGE

When the user types the application's URL into their browser, the browser asks the server for the HTML file (1). The server sends back a complete page that is created each time someone requests it. To create the page, the server uses the application's router to figure out which components to show based on the requested route; then it instantiates those components (2). Next, each component loads data from other servers or databases and executes its mounting code before being rendered. Finally, the components are turned into HTML (3) and sent to the user (4). Figure 1.11 illustrates this process.

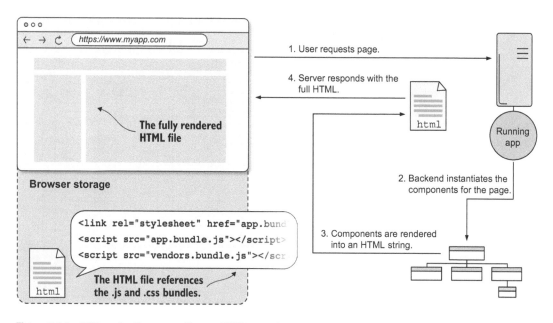

**Figure 1.11  SSR application requesting an HTML page from the server**

Even though the file looks like a static HTML file to the user, the server generates the page each time it's requested. The HTML file served to the user displays already-rendered HTML markup, so the framework doesn't need to use the Document API to generate it programmatically. But the HTML coming from the server lacks the event handlers defined in the application code, so the application doesn't respond to user interactions. This situation is where the hydration process comes into play.

> **DEFINITION**  *Hydration* is the process by which the framework matches HTML elements with their corresponding virtual DOM nodes and attaches event handlers to make the HTML markup interactive in the browser. The hydration algorithm binds the browser's HTML to each component's virtual DOM, allowing for dynamic updates.

### STEP 2: HYDRATING THE HTML PAGE

The HTML document instructs the browser to load the application JavaScript files and CSS stylesheets (5)—the same as in the case of an SPA. When the JavaScript code is parsed, the framework code needs to connect the existing HTML—produced in the server—to the component's virtual DOM, as well as attach event handlers (6). Figure 1.12 depicts the hydration process.

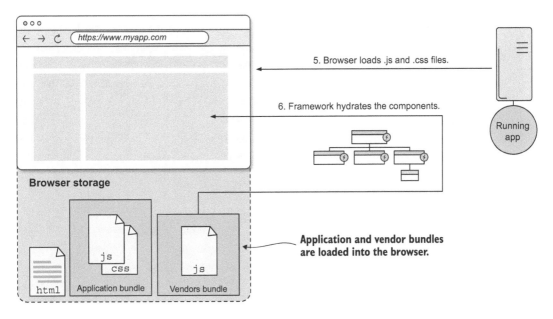

**Figure 1.12   The framework hydrates the HTML page.**

### STEP 3: HANDLING USER INTERACTIONS

After the framework's hydration process makes the page responsive, the user can interact with it. When the user interacts with the page (7), the framework's event handlers are triggered (8), and as in an SPA, the framework patches the parts of the HTML that need to be updated (9). All this processing happens in the browser, so the server isn't involved, as you can see in figure 1.13.

What happens when the user navigates to a different route? The flow is a bit different from flow in the case of SPAs.

### STEP 4: NAVIGATING BETWEEN ROUTES

When the user clicks a link (10), the browser changes the URL (the framework doesn't do anything on the browser side this time), and the page is reloaded (11). A new HTML page is requested from the server (12), and the process starts again from step 1 (figure 1.14).

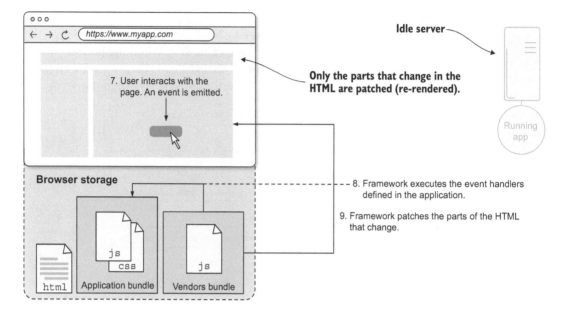

7. User interacts with the page. An event is emitted.

Idle server

Only the parts that change in the HTML are patched (re-rendered).

Running app

Browser storage

js
css
html    Application bundle

js
Vendors bundle

8. Framework executes the event handlers defined in the application.

9. Framework patches the parts of the HTML that change.

Figure 1.13   SSR application handling user interactions

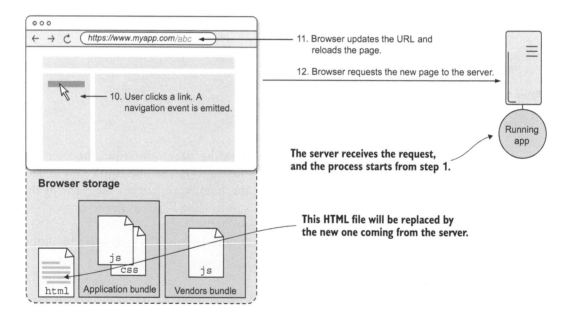

https://www.myapp.com/abc

10. User clicks a link. A navigation event is emitted.

11. Browser updates the URL and reloads the page.

12. Browser requests the new page to the server.

Running app

The server receives the request, and the process starts from step 1.

Browser storage

This HTML file will be replaced by the new one coming from the server.

js
css
html    Application bundle

js
Vendors bundle

Figure 1.14   SSR application navigating among routes

As you can see, navigating among pages is quite different in an SSR application than in an SPA. In the case of SPAs, the server isn't involved in the process. With SSRs, pages are generated in the server.

**THE COMPLETE FLOW OF AN SSR APPLICATION**

Figure 1.15 shows the complete flow of an SSR application, including all the steps described earlier but in a more schematic way.

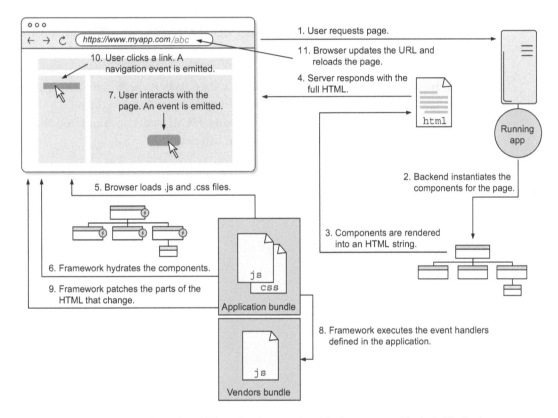

**Figure 1.15   The complete flow of an SSR application—rendered in the server and hydrated in the browser**

Now that you've seen how both SPAs and SSRs work, what about building a simple application yourself, without using a framework? That experience will show you what it was like to write web applications before frontend frameworks appeared.

WU 422 0672

## Summary

- Building a frontend framework from scratch is a great way to learn how frameworks operate.
- Frontend frameworks bundle the application's code into a single JavaScript file, the third-party dependencies into another file, and the CSS styles into yet another file. If the application is large, the framework might split the application's code into multiple bundles that are loaded lazily (as needed).
- The Document API allows HTML elements to be created programmatically, using JavaScript. Frontend frameworks use the Document API to create the application's view.
- SPAs consist of a single HTML file that's loaded by the browser and updated by the framework to reflect the application's state. When the route changes, the framework changes the view; the browser doesn't reload the page.
- The hydration process connects the existing HTML markup, rendered in the server, to the component's state and event listeners.

# Vanilla JavaScript— like in the old days

**This chapter covers**

- Building an application using vanilla JavaScript and HTML
- Creating DOM elements programmatically
- Using the Document API to manipulate the DOM

Before you can understand the benefits of using a frontend framework, you need to understand the problems that it solves, and there's no better way to gain this understanding than to write an application without a framework. That is, you should do the framework's job yourself. The objective of this chapter is to make you suffer the pain of writing applications without a framework so that you can build some appreciation for the job that frameworks do for you.

In the old days (I'm not *that* old, but technology evolves fast), developers wrote applications using only vanilla JavaScript and HTML. JQuery was the best we had; it provided a nice API to interact with the Document Object Model (DOM), hiding the browser differences. But we still had to write code down to the level of working with the DOM, and to be fair, the work wasn't that bad. That is, it wasn't bad until we used our first modern frontend framework (Angular, in my case). Now there's no going back. We've been there. We know how much simpler it's become to write JavaScript applications.

You're probably accustomed to writing applications that use the power of a framework—something you should keep doing if you get paid to ship applications quickly—so it may be hard for you to realize the problems that the framework solves. Or maybe, like me, you're from the pre-framework era but haven't written an application without a framework in a long time, in which case this chapter will be good for refreshing your memory. If your case is the former, I'm positive that when the framework is taken away from you, you'll quickly realize why you used it in the first place. Suppose that you always find your working space clean and tidy, but you rarely appreciate it because you're used to seeing it that way—until the cleaning personnel get sick and you have to clean up yourself. You suddenly realize that vacuuming every corner of the office is an arduous task and removing dust from the shelves and behind your computer—let alone cleaning the bathroom—is a pain. Only when you realize how much you value working in a clean, tidy environment do you start to truly appreciate the job that cleaning personnel do.

In this chapter, you'll do the cleaning yourself, so to speak. You'll build a simple application from scratch, using only vanilla JavaScript and HTML. The cleaning personnel—the existing frontend frameworks—will be on strike. Despite the simplicity of the app, you'll notice that the code operates at a low abstraction level by manipulating the DOM directly and that it's very imperative. You'll need to write code explicitly to update the HTML document with every change in the application state. It's evident that not using a framework becomes a challenge as the complexity and size of an application increase. The purpose of this chapter, however, is for you to realize this fact on your own by experiencing the process of creating an application without framework support.

> **NOTE**   Before you go any further, go to appendix A, and follow the instructions to set up the project for writing the code. Bear in mind that appendix A is a detour from the main topic of this chapter, but it's necessary for setting up the project. When you finish, and without further ado, you'll begin building the application. You can find the code you'll be writing in the GitHub repository, inside the examples/ch02 directory, at http://mng.bz/PRKw.

## 2.1   *The assignment: A TODOs app*

You're a developer in a consulting company, and your manager has assigned you a new project. A new client has an innovative idea for a new application, which they say has the potential to disrupt the market, and they want you to build it. The work might be interesting. Your manager sets up a meeting with the client to discuss the project. In the meeting, you make sure to understand the requirements, which you summarize as follows:

- Main idea: keep a list of the things I need to do (to-dos) in a day.
- A to-do can be marked as done so that it's removed from the list.

- A to-do can be modified when the user makes a typo or wants to change the description.

The idea is so simple that you're a bit wary of its being "super-mega revolutionary." (You wrote that phrase down; it's what the client said.) But your job is to build the app, not to question its disruptive potential.

---

**TODOs applications and frontend frameworks**

The TODOs application is a classic in the frontend-framework world (https://todomvc .com). It's the equivalent of "Hello World" for learning a new programming language. Framework authors like to use it as an example, both to test it and to show other developers how it's used. I don't want to break the tradition, so I'll use it as well.

Vue.js implemented one of these applications, which you can find in the examples directory of the framework's old repository at http://mng.bz/Jdpo. React did as well, as early as in its initial public release (v0.3.0), which you can find in the examples directory at http://mng.bz/vPj4. One more TODO application is Mithril's, which you can find in the examples directory of the framework's repository at http://mng .bz/wjKO.

---

Next, you talk with the design team to get the mockups for the application. The designers love the idea—although they swear that they've seen something similar— and they come up with a quick wireframe design that looks like figure 2.1. You show the design to the client, who loves it. It's time to get down to business.

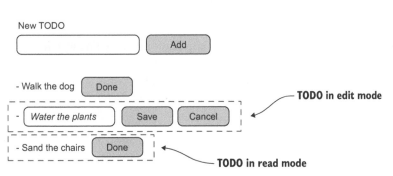

**Figure 2.1  Wireframe design for the TODOs app**

## 2.2 *Writing the application*

Now that you have the requirements and the design for the TODOs app, it's time to start writing the code. First, though, you decide to take some time to plan how you're going to tackle the task—as every good developer does. You realize that the application is a simple one; it doesn't have fancy features or complex requirements. So the first decision you make is to use plain JavaScript and HTML without any framework. You might use one later if the application grows in complexity, but for now, you want to keep things simple.

You figure out that part of the HTML markup is static—it won't change as the user interacts with the application—and that part of it needs to be generated dynamically because it depends on the application's current state. The list of to-dos, for example, will be generated from JavaScript programmatically because we can't know in advance what TODOs the user will write. By contrast, the title (My TODOs), the input box where the user enters a new to-do, that box's label, and the Add button will always be the same. Figure 2.2 shows the static and dynamic parts of the application.

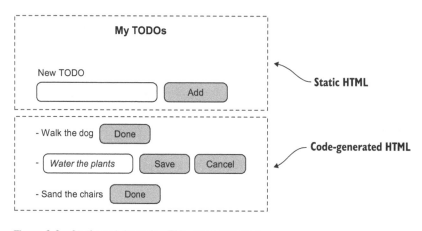

**Figure 2.2   Static and dynamic HTML of the TODOs app**

Then you think about what makes up the application's *state*. The application will look different when there are no to-dos than it does when there are to-dos, for example. This means that the list of to-dos is part of the application's state, so you'll need an array of strings to keep track of the existing to-dos. The strings represent the descriptions of the to-dos.

> **DEFINITION**   The *state* is the information the application keeps track of that makes it look and behave the way it does at a particular moment.

Last, before you start coding, you think about the application's behavior. Based on the requirements, the design, and a short conversation you had with the user-experience specialist, you decide that the application will behave as follows:

- When the user writes a new to-do and clicks Add, the to-do is added to the list of to-dos.
- If the user presses the Enter key while the input field is focused, the to-do is appended to the list of to-dos as well.

- The application won't allow the user to add to-dos that are shorter than three characters.
- To edit a to-do, the user has to double-click it.
- If the user discards the changes by clicking the Cancel button, the to-do is restored to its previous state; the changes are lost.
- When a to-do is marked as done, it's removed from the list of to-dos.

With these conditions in mind, it's time to start writing the code. Let's start by setting up the project.

### 2.2.1 Project setup

You'll write the vanilla JavaScript version of the TODOs application inside the *examples* directory in your project. (Make sure that you've completed the setup from appendix A.) First, create a new folder inside the examples directory for this chapter called ch02:

```
$ cd examples
$ mkdir ch02
```

Then create two new files inside the ch02 directory:

- *todos.html*, where you'll write the HTML markup for the application
- *todos.js*, where you'll write the JavaScript code for the application

Your examples directory should look like this:

```
examples/
    └── ch02/
            ├── todos.html
            └── todos.js
```

You want to move your terminal's working directory back to the project's root directory, so you can run the `serve:examples` script from there:

```
$ cd ..
$ npm run serve:examples
```

Your browser should open the examples directory and show the ch02 directory inside it. Click the todos.html file to open it. You should see an empty page because you haven't written any HTML markup yet. We'll write the static part of the HTML markup next.

### 2.2.2 The HTML markup

The static part of the HTML markup is fairly simple, consisting of a title (`<h1>`), an input field (`<input>`) with its label (`<label>`), and a button (`<button>`). There should also be a list, empty to start with, where the to-dos will be rendered programmatically

(`<ul>`). Finally, it's important for the HTML document to load the JavaScript file containing the application's code: todos.js.

The first task is to load the todos.js file as an ECMAScript (ES) module inside the `<head>` of the document, which you do by adding the `type="module"` attribute to the `<script>` element. All modern browsers support ES modules, and a neat feature is that they are deferred by default (https://v8.dev/features/modules#defer), which means that they won't start executing the JavaScript code until the HTML document has been parsed. That's why we can load the JavaScript file at the top of the document, the `<head>`, and still be sure the HTML markup will be available when the JavaScript code starts executing.

> **TIP**   Read more about how ES modules are different from classic scripts in the browser in the V8 blog at https://v8.dev/features/modules. The post is a good read that clarifies many concepts related to ES modules and their behavior in the browser; it's written by people who work on V8 itself.

Next, you'll add the input field, that field's label, and the Add button inside a `<div>` element. Note that you need to add `id` attributes to the input field and the button so that you can reference them from the JavaScript code. The same goes for the `<ul>` element that will contain the to-dos, which is below the `<div>` element and is empty at first. The JavaScript code will render the to-dos programmatically as `<li>` elements inside the `<ul>` element. Open the todos.html file, and add the markup in the following listing. If you refresh the browser window now, you should see something like figure 2.3.

**Listing 2.1   The static HTML markup for the TODOs app (todos.html)**

```
<!DOCTYPE html>
<html lang="en">
  <head>
    <meta charset="UTF-8" />
    <title>My TODOs</title>

    <script type="module" src="todos.js"></script>       ⟵  The todos.js
  </head>                                                     file loaded as
                                                              an ES module
  <body>
    <h1>My TODOs</h1>                                     ⟵  The input field, the
                                                              field's label, and
    <div>                                                     the Add button
      <label for="todo-input">New TODO</label>
      <input type="text" id="todo-input" />
      <button id="add-todo-btn" disabled>Add</button>
    </div>

    <ul id="todos-list"></ul>          ⟵  List where the
  </body>                                 to-dos will be
</html>                                   rendered
```

Figure 2.3 The HTML markup
for the TODOs app

The JavaScript code will generate the remaining HTML markup dynamically. This part is where the fun begins.

---

**Exercise 2.1**

Add some CSS styles to the title, the input field, and the button. Following are some suggestions:

- Use a nicer font than the default one. You can choose a free one from Google Fonts, such as Roboto (https://fonts.google.com/specimen/Roboto), and apply it to the document.
- Center the application in the middle of the page horizontally.
- Make the title bigger.
- Place the input field's label above the input field and make it italic.
- Give the input and button some padding.

Find the solution at http://mng.bz/qj9x.

---

### 2.2.3 The JavaScript code

You'll write the JavaScript code in the todos.js file, so make sure that you have it open in your editor. First, you want to define the application's state, which is a list of to-dos—an array of strings. You'll add some to-dos already populated in the array so that when you open the page in the browser, you'll see some to-dos already rendered. Then you want to grab references to the DOM elements that you need to interact with, using the `document.getElementById()` function from the Document API. Open the todos.js file, and write the code in the following listing.

Listing 2.2 The state and HTML element references (todos.js)

```
// State of the app
const todos = ['Walk the dog', 'Water the plants', 'Sand the chairs']

// HTML element references
const addTodoInput = document.getElementById('todo-input')
const addTodoButton = document.getElementById('add-todo-btn')
const todosList = document.getElementById('todos-list')
```

So far, your application doesn't do anything when you type a new to-do description in the input field and click the Add button. The to-do items in the state aren't rendered either. The reason is that you've neither added event listeners nor written the code that renders the to-dos.

### INITIALIZING THE VIEW

You want to initialize the view of the application—that is, dynamically generate the HTML markup that depends on the application's state—and attach event listeners to the DOM elements that need them. To initialize the view, iterate over the to-dos in the application's state and *render* each one, using a function that you'll call `renderTodoIn-ReadMode()`. Then append each element to the `<ul>` element, using the `todosList` element `append()` method.

> **DEFINITION**   To *render* means to transform some data into a visual representation—something we can see.

In this context, when we *render a to-do*, we're creating the HTML elements that represent the to-do in our application. The task of rendering a to-do—a JavaScript string—into an HTML representation is carried out by a function that you'll call `renderTodo-InReadMode()`. The name is important here: it says that the to-do is rendered in read mode. If you remember from your discussion with the client, the to-do can be edited, so you need to render it in edit mode as well. In short, a to-do can be rendered in two ways because it has two different visual representations. You'll write a `renderTodo-InEditMode()` function later in the chapter.

After rendering the to-dos in read mode, you need to add a few event listeners to the DOM elements. First, you add a listener to the `<input>` field's `input` event, which is fired every time the user types something in the input field. This handler function should check whether the input field has fewer than three characters, in which case the button is kept disabled to prevent the user from adding empty (or extremely short) to-do items. The button is enabled (that is, the `disabled` attribute is removed) when the to-do has at least three characters (figure 2.4). If you remember the HTML markup in listing 2.1, the Add `<button>` element is disabled by default.

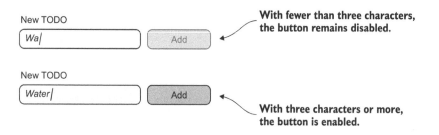

Figure 2.4   The field is disabled when the input field has fewer than three characters.

Next, you'll add a listener to the `<input>` field's `keydown` event, which fires every time the user presses any key. But you're not interested in responding to every key the user presses; only the Enter key is relevant. For this reason, you want to check whether the key pressed is Enter. If so, call a function named `addTodo()`, which you'll implement in the next listing; this function will add a new to-do to the application's state and render it in the HTML.

Finally, you need a listener for the Add `<button>` element's `click` event. The event handler is the same as the one for the `keydown` event: it calls the `addTodo()` function, clears the input field, and disables the Add button. In the todos.js file, write the code in listing 2.3.

**NOTE** A `// TODO` comment in the code means that you'll implement that part of the code later in the chapter. I'll add these comments sometimes to let you know that something is missing in the code and that you'll get to it soon.

**Listing 2.3  The initialization of the application (todos.js)**

```
// Initialize the view
for (const todo of todos) {                        To-dos rendered as <li>
  todosList.append(renderTodoInReadMode(todo))     items inside <ul>
}

addTodoInput.addEventListener('input', () => {          <button>
  addTodoButton.disabled = addTodoInput.value.length < 3  disabled until
})                                                      <input> has
                                                        at least three
addTodoInput.addEventListener('keydown', ({ key }) => {  characters
  if (key === 'Enter' && addTodoInput.value.length >= 3) {
    addTodo()
  }
})                                                 Pressing Enter
                                                   adds the to-do
                                                   written in the
addTodoButton.addEventListener('click', () => {    <input>.
  addTodo()
})

                                                   When <button> is
// Functions                                       clicked, the to-do in the
function renderTodoInReadMode(todo) {              <input> is added.
  // TODO: implement me!
}

function addTodo() {
  // TODO: implement me!
}
```

Figure 2.5 shows a visual representation of the events you've added to the static part of the HTML markup.

Now we're getting to the meat of the application: rendering to-dos. This task is one that a framework would do for you, but you're going to do it yourself in this chapter.

XC 459 0429

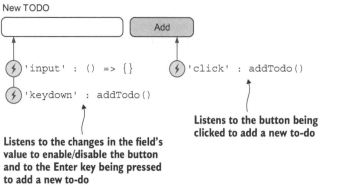

Figure 2.5   The event listeners added to the HTML elements

---

**Exercise 2.2**

Add a CSS transition to the `color` property of the button when it's enabled or disabled. This transition will make the button's color change smoothly when it's enabled or disabled. Following are some tips in case you get stuck:

- You can use the `transition` CSS property. Read about it in the MDN documentation (http://mng.bz/460j) if you need a refresher.
- You can use the `:disabled` pseudoclass to style the button when it's disabled.
- You can use the `:enabled` pseudoclass to style the button when it's enabled.

Find the solution at http://mng.bz/7vVQ.

---

### RENDERING TO-DOS IN READ MODE

To render a to-do in read mode, you need to use the `document.createElement()` method of the Document API to create some HTML elements:

- The to-do items are inside an unordered list element (`<ul>`), so each to-do should go inside a list item element (`<li>`).
- The to-do itself is simple text that you can render inside a `<span>` element.
- The user should be able to mark a to-do as done, so you need to provide a button for that purpose.

Figure 2.6 depicts the HTML markup for a to-do in read mode.

The to-do description can be added as the `textContent` property of the `<span>` element. We could have created a text node and appended it to the `<span>` element—using `span.append(todo)`, for example—but setting the `textContent` is a bit more concise.

The `<span>` element needs to have a listener attached to its `dblclick` event that will replace the to-do in read mode with the edit-mode version. To accomplish this

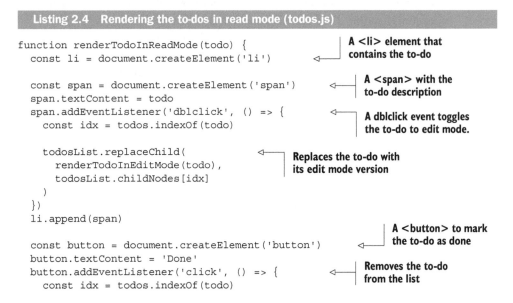

**Figure 2.6  A TODO in read mode is rendered as a `<li>` element containing a `<span>` element with the to-do text and a button to mark it as done.**

task, you'll call the `replaceChild()` method on the `<li>` DOM node. This method removes the entire `<li>` element and its children from the list of to-dos and renders the edit-mode version of the to-do in its place. To do the rendering, call the `render-TodoInEditMode()` function, which you'll implement in the next section.

---

**The `replaceChild()` method**

The `replaceChild()` method from the DOM API replaces a child node of a DOM node (the one on which the method is called) with another node. It accepts two arguments:

- `newNode`—The node that replaces the old node
- `oldNode`—The node to be replaced

---

Last, you attach an event listener to the `<button>` element's `click` event that will remove the to-do from the list of to-dos. For that purpose, you'll write a `removeTodo()` function, which you'll also need to fill in later. Now that you know what the plan is, fill in the `renderTodoInReadMode()` function as shown in the following listing.

**Listing 2.4  Rendering the to-dos in read mode (todos.js)**

```
function renderTodoInReadMode(todo) {
  const li = document.createElement('li')          ◁── A <li> element that
                                                        contains the to-do

  const span = document.createElement('span')      ◁── A <span> with the
  span.textContent = todo                              to-do description
  span.addEventListener('dblclick', () => {        ◁── A dblclick event toggles
    const idx = todos.indexOf(todo)                    the to-do to edit mode.

    todosList.replaceChild(                   ◁── Replaces the to-do with
      renderTodoInEditMode(todo),                 its edit mode version
      todosList.childNodes[idx]
    )
  })
  li.append(span)
                                                   ◁── A <button> to mark
  const button = document.createElement('button')     the to-do as done
  button.textContent = 'Done'
  button.addEventListener('click', () => {       ◁── Removes the to-do
    const idx = todos.indexOf(todo)                  from the list
```

```
      removeTodo(idx)
    })
    li.append(button)

    return li
}

function removeTodo(index) {
    // TODO: implement me!
}
```

Figure 2.7 is a visual representation of the events you've added to the to-dos in read mode.

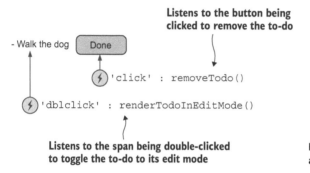

Figure 2.7   **The event listeners added to the to-dos in read mode**

### RENDERING TO-DOS IN EDIT MODE

Now let's implement the `renderInEditMode()` function. The to-do in edit mode is also part of the unordered list of to-dos, so it should also appear inside a `<li>` element. But this time, the `<li>` element should contain an `<input>` element instead of a `<span>` element so that the user can modify the to-do description. Also, instead of having one button, we need two: one to save the changes and another to cancel them. Figure 2.8 shows the HTML markup for a to-do in edit mode.

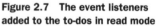

```
<li>
    <input type="text" />
    <button>Save</button>
    <button>Cancel</button>
</li>
```

Figure 2.8   **A TODO in edit mode is rendered as a `<li>` element containing an `<input>` element with the to-do text and two buttons to save or cancel the changes.**

When the user clicks the Save button, a function that you'll write later, `updateTodo()`, will modify the to-do description in the state and replace the to-do in edit mode with the read-mode version. (When the user is done editing the to-do, we want them to see the updated version in read mode.) When the user clicks the Cancel button instead, you need to call the `renderTodoInReadMode()` function. Write the code for the `renderTodoInEditMode()` function as shown in the following listing.

**Listing 2.5  Rendering the to-dos in edit mode (todos.js)**

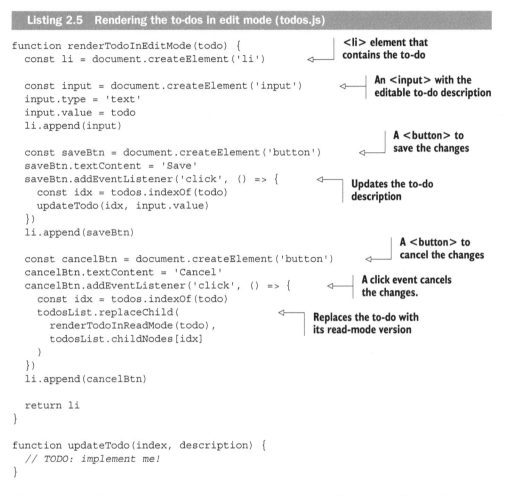

```
function renderTodoInEditMode(todo) {
  const li = document.createElement('li')          <li> element that
                                                    contains the to-do

  const input = document.createElement('input')     An <input> with the
  input.type = 'text'                               editable to-do description
  input.value = todo
  li.append(input)

  const saveBtn = document.createElement('button')   A <button> to
  saveBtn.textContent = 'Save'                        save the changes
  saveBtn.addEventListener('click', () => {          Updates the to-do
    const idx = todos.indexOf(todo)                  description
    updateTodo(idx, input.value)
  })
  li.append(saveBtn)

  const cancelBtn = document.createElement('button')   A <button> to
  cancelBtn.textContent = 'Cancel'                      cancel the changes
  cancelBtn.addEventListener('click', () => {          A click event cancels
    const idx = todos.indexOf(todo)                    the changes.
    todosList.replaceChild(                            Replaces the to-do with
      renderTodoInReadMode(todo),                      its read-mode version
      todosList.childNodes[idx]
    )
  })
  li.append(cancelBtn)

  return li
}

function updateTodo(index, description) {
  // TODO: implement me!
}
```

The code is similar to the one for the read-mode version of the to-do. Figure 2.9 shows the events you've added to the to-dos in edit mode.

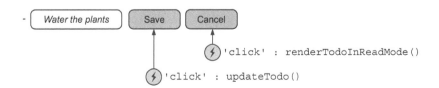

**Figure 2.9  The events added to the to-dos in edit mode**

The only things left to implement are the `addTodo()`, `removeTodo()`, and `update-Todo()` functions. Let's do that work now.

### ADDING, REMOVING, AND UPDATING TO-DOS

The functions to add, remove, and update to-dos are defined in our todos.js file, but they're not implemented yet. We left `TODO` comments (oh, the irony!) in the code to remind us of that fact. The implementation of these functions is straightforward, so let's see what each of them does.

The `addTodo()` function reads the description of the new to-do from the `<input>` element's `value` property, and pushes it into the array of to-dos. Then it calls the `renderTodoInReadMode()` function to render the HTML for the new to-do and appends it to the `todosList` element. Last, it clears the `<input>` element's `value` property so that the user can enter a new to-do description; then it disables the Add button.

The `removeTodo()` function removes the to-do from the array of to-dos and the `<li>` element from the document. To remove the `<li>` element from its parent `<ul>`, it calls the `remove()` method on the target node, which you can locate by index inside the `childNodes` array of the `<ul>` element.

The `updateTodo()` function needs to have two parameters passed to it: the index of the to-do to update and the new description of the to-do. The passed description overwrites whatever is in the array of to-dos at the given index. Then, using the `renderTodoInReadMode()` function, you can render the HTML for the updated to-do. Finally, you can replace the to-do at the given index inside the `todosList` element's `childNodes` array with the new HTML. The following listing shows the code for the `addTodo()`, `removeTodo()`, and `updateTodo()` functions.

> **Listing 2.6   Functions to add, remove, and edit to-dos (todos.js)**

```javascript
function addTodo() {                                        ⟵⎤ Adds a new to-do
  const description = addTodoInput.value

  todos.push(description)
  const todo = renderTodoInReadMode(description)
  todosList.append(todo)

  addTodoInput.value = ''
  addTodoButton.disabled = true
}
                                            ⎤ Removes a to-do
function removeTodo(index) {              ⟵⎦ at a given index
  todos.splice(index, 1)
  todosList.childNodes[index].remove()
}
                                             ⎤ Updates a to-do
function updateTodo(index, description) {  ⟵⎦ at a given index
  todos[index] = description
  const todo = renderTodoInReadMode(description)
  todosList.replaceChild(todo, todosList.childNodes[index])
}
```

If you refresh the page now, you should be able to add, remove, and update to-dos. Your application should look similar to figure 2.10. You've written a web application without a framework. The experience wasn't too painful, was it?

**Figure 2.10   The finished TODOs app**

Try to add a new to-do by typing something like *Sing a song* in the input field and clicking the Add button. Then click the Done button to remove the to-do from the list. Try clicking one of the to-dos to see how it's replaced by its edit-mode version, as in figure 2.11.

**Figure 2.11   The TODOs app in edit mode**

I hope you're excited about what you've built: an interactive web application made without a framework! But I also hope that you've realized how inefficient it would be to write a large application this way, which is why using a framework is a great idea. Operating at such a low level to generate the HTML markup for the DOM programmatically is tedious and error-prone.

**Exercise 2.3**

Suppose the customer says that they don't want done to-dos to be removed from the list; instead, they want those items to be crossed out. Can you implement this feature for them?

Find the solution at http://mng.bz/mjg8.

**Exercise 2.4**

The customer tried the application and loved it. But then they realized they could add the same to-do multiple times, which is unacceptable. Can you fix this bug so that if the user tries to add an existing to-do, the application doesn't add it and warns the user?

Find the solution at http://mng.bz/5oj7.

**Exercise 2.5**

The customer has a challenging request for you. To aid users with a hearing impairment, the customer wants the application to read each to-do aloud when it's added to the list. Can you implement this feature?

(Psst! Here's a little tip from a senior developer at your company: you may want to read about the Web Speech API at http://mng.bz/Xqva.)

Find the solution at http://mng.bz/6ngR.

The first thing we want our framework to take care of is the use of the Document API to create and manipulate the DOM—the part that's most burdensome to write. If we can abstract away the manipulation of the DOM, we can focus on the application logic, which makes our applications useful. Think about it: the time we spend working on manipulating the DOM doesn't add value for the user. We need to do this work to make the application interactive, but it's not what the user cares about. A good framework should allow us to forget about dealing with the DOM and focus on the application logic. That's exactly what we'll do in chapter 3.

## Summary

- Nothing prevents us from writing complete frontend applications without a framework, but doing so can easily result in code that's a mix of application logic and DOM manipulation, using the Document API to modify the browser's document.
- When we use vanilla JavaScript to write a fronted application, every event that changes the state of the application forces us to write the code that updates the DOM to reflect the new state. This code tends to be imperative and verbose.

# Part 2

# A basic framework

Get ready, because the real excitement begins now! You've already dabbled in the creation of a TODO application, using nothing but HTML and vanilla JavaScript. Part 1 gave you a glimpse of the challenges involved in developing large, complex web applications that require manual Document Object Model (DOM) manipulation and real-time synchronization between the view and the model as users interact with the app.

But don't worry; frontend frameworks were designed to make your life easier! We'll start by abstracting away the nitty-gritty DOM manipulation code required for view creation. Enter the concept of the virtual DOM. With a virtual DOM tree, you can define how a view should appear and let the framework handle the heavy lifting, using the DOM API to create its representation in the browser.

In chapter 5, you'll dive into crafting a state management system that communicates changes to your framework whenever the application state is altered. By bringing together the function responsible for rendering the virtual DOM and the state management system, you'll have the initial version of your own framework.

Chapter 6 takes you one step further as you publish your framework on NPM and use it to enhance your TODO application. That's exciting!

Before we conclude this part, we'll tackle a critical algorithm that underpins virtual-DOM-based frameworks: the reconciliation algorithm. Although the concept is complex, I'll guide you through it step by step. This algorithm ensures that only the portions of the DOM that require updates are modified, minimizing unnecessary changes.

An incredible adventure lies ahead—one that I embarked on with great enthusiasm. I hope that you'll find this journey as exhilarating as I did!

# Rendering and the virtual DOM

## 3

---

**This chapter covers**

- Defining the virtual DOM
- Understanding the problems the virtual DOM solves
- Implementing functions to create virtual DOM nodes
- Defining the concept of a stateless component

As you saw in chapter 2, mixing application and Document Object Model (DOM) manipulation code gets unwieldy quickly. If for every event resulting from the user's interaction with the application, we have to implement not only the business logic—the one that gives value to the application—but also the code to update the DOM, the codebase becomes a hard-to-maintain mess. We're mixing two different levels of abstraction: the application logic and the DOM manipulation. What a maintenance nightmare!

Manipulating the DOM results in *imperative code*—that is, code that describes how to do something step by step. By contrast, *declarative code* describes what to do without specifying how to do it; those details are implemented somewhere else. Also, manipulating the DOM is a *low-level* operation—that is, it requires considerable knowledge of the Document API and sits below the application logic. Contrast this operation with *higher-level* application code, which is framed in a language that is close to the business so that anyone working on the project can—and should—understand.

We would have a much cleaner codebase if we could describe in a more declarative manner how we want the view of our application to look and let the framework manipulate the DOM to create that view. What we need is similar to blueprints for a house, which describe what has to be built without specifying how to build it. The architect designs the blueprints and lets the construction company take care of building the house. Suppose that instead, the architect had to not only design the house, but also go to the construction site and build it—or at least tell the construction workers how they need to do their jobs step by step without missing a single detail. That approach would be a very inefficient way to build.

For the sake of productivity, the architect focuses on what needs to be built and lets the construction company take care of how it's built. Similarly, we want the application developer to focus on the "what" (what the view should look like) and let the framework take care of the "how" (how to assemble the view using the Document API).

> **NOTE**   You can find all the listings in this chapter in the listings/ch03 directory of the book's repository (http://mng.bz/qjpA). The code you write in this chapter is for the framework's first version, which you'll publish in chapter 6. Therefore, the code in this chapter can be checked out from the ch6 label (http://mng.bz/7vAm): $ `git switch --detach ch6`.

## 3.1   Separating concerns: DOM manipulation vs. application logic

In chapter 2, you wrote all the code together as part of the application, as you see in figure 3.1. That code is in charge of initializing the application and its state, programmatically building the view using the Document API, and handling the events that result from the user's interactions with the application by modifying the DOM accordingly.

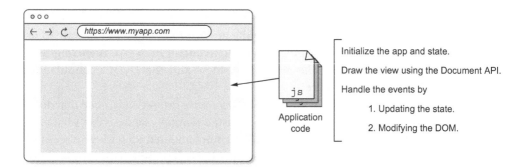

**Figure 3.1   So far, all the code is written together as part of the application.**

In this chapter, we want to separate the code that describes the view (the application's code) from the code that uses the Document API to manipulate the DOM and create the view (the framework's code). A term widely used in the software industry describes this process: *separation of concerns.*

> **DEFINITION**   *Separation of concerns* means splitting the code so that the parts that carry out different responsibilities are separated, which helps the developer understand and maintain the code.

Figure 3.2 shows the separation of concerns we want to achieve: splitting the application code from the framework code that deals with DOM manipulation and keeps track of the state. We'll focus on rendering the view in this chapter and chapter 4; we'll leave the state management for chapter 5.

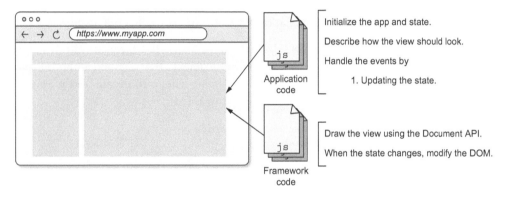

**Figure 3.2   By the end of chapter 4, you'll have separated the code that describes the view from the code that manipulates the DOM.**

The main objective of this separation of concerns is to simplify the application developer's job: they need to focus only on the application logic and let the framework take care of DOM manipulation. This approach has three clear benefits:

- *Developer productivity*—The application developer doesn't need to write DOM-manipulation code; instead, they can focus on the application logic. They have to write less code, which enables them to ship the application faster.
- *Code maintainability*—The DOM manipulation and application logic aren't mixed, which makes the code more succinct and easier to understand.
- *Framework performance*—The framework author, who's likely to understand how to produce efficient DOM-manipulation code better than the application developer does, can optimize how the DOM is manipulated to make the framework more performant.

Going back to the blueprints analogy, how do you define what the view should look like, as the architect does with blueprints? The answer is the *virtual DOM*.

## 3.2    *The virtual DOM*

The word *virtual* describes something that isn't real but mimics something that is. A *virtual machine* (VM), for example, is software written to mimic the behavior of a real machine—hardware. A VM gives you the impression that you're running a real machine, but it's software running on top of your computer's hardware.

> **DEFINITION**    The *virtual DOM* is a representation of the actual DOM (http://mng.bz/mjMP) in the browser. The DOM is an in-memory tree structure managed by the browser engine, representing the HTML structure of the web page. By contrast, the virtual DOM is a JavaScript-based in-memory tree of virtual nodes that mirrors the structure of the actual DOM. Each node in this virtual tree is called a *virtual node*, and the entire construct is the *virtual DOM*. I'll use vdom as an abbreviation of virtual DOM in the code listings.

The nodes in the actual DOM are heavy objects that have hundreds of properties, whereas the virtual nodes are lightweight objects that contain only the information needed to render the view. Virtual nodes are cheap to create and manipulate. Suppose that we want to produce the following HTML:

```
<form action="/login" class="login-form">
  <input type="text" name="user" />
  <input type="password" name="pass" />
  <button>Log in</button>
</form>
```

The HTML consists of a `<form>` with three child nodes: two `<input>` and a `<button>`. A virtual DOM representation of this HTML needs to contain the same information as the DOM:

- What nodes are in the tree and their attributes
- The hierarchy of the nodes in the tree
- The relative positions of the nodes in the tree

It's important that the virtual DOM includes the `<form>` as the root node, for example, and that the two `<input>` and `<button>` are its children. The form has `action` and `class` attributes, and the button has an `onclick` event handler, although it's not visible in the HTML. The `type` and `name` attributes of the `<input>` elements are crucial: an `<input>` of type `text` and an `<input>` of type `password` aren't the same; they behave differently. Also, the relative position of the form's children is important: the button should go below the inputs. The framework needs all this information to render the view correctly. Following is a possible virtual DOM representation of this HTML made of pure JavaScript objects:

```
{
  type: 'element',
  tag: 'form',
  props: { action: '/login', class: 'login-form' },
  children: [
    {
      type: 'element',
      tag: 'input',
      props: { type: 'text', name: 'user' }
    },
    {
      type: 'element',
      tag: 'input',
      props: { type: 'password', name: 'pass' }
    },
    {
      type: 'element',
      tag: 'button',
      props: { on: { click: () => login() } },
      children: [
        {
          type: 'text',
          value: 'Log in'
        }
      ]
    }
  ]
}
```

Each node in the virtual DOM is an object with a `type` property that identifies what kind of node it is. This example has two types of nodes:

- `element`—Represents a regular HTML element, such as `<form>`, `<input>`, or `<button>`
- `text`—Represents a text node, such as the `'Log in'` text of the `<button>` element in the example

We'll see one more type of node later in the chapter: the *fragment* node, which groups other nodes together but has no semantic meaning of its own. Each type of node has a set of properties to describe it. Text nodes, for example, have one property apart from the `type`: `value`, which is the string of text. Element virtual nodes have three properties:

- `tag`—The tag name of the HTML element.
- `props`—The attributes of the HTML element, including the event handlers inside an `on` property.
- `children`—The ordered children of the HTML element. If the `children` array is absent from the node, the element is a leaf node.

As we'll see, fragment nodes have a `children` array of nodes, similar to the `children` array of element nodes. Using this virtual DOM representation allows the developer to describe what the view of their application—the rendered HTML—should look like.

You, the framework author, implement the code that takes that virtual DOM representation and builds the real one in the browser. This way, you effectively separate the code that describes the view from the code that manipulates the DOM.

We can represent the virtual DOM in the previous example graphically as a tree, as shown in figure 3.3. The `<form>` element is the root node of the tree, and the two `<input>` and `<button>` elements are its children. The properties of each node, such as the `action` and `class` attributes of the `<form>` element, are inside the node's box. The `<button>` element has a child node—a text node with the text `"Log in"`.

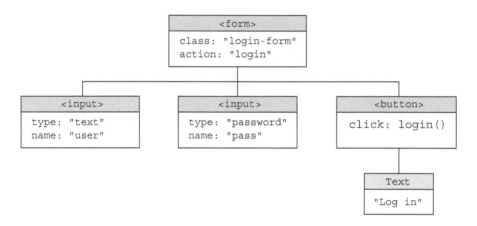

Figure 3.3   The virtual DOM is a representation of the DOM made of JavaScript objects.

> **NOTE**   As you can see in figure 3.3, the nodes of the tree have a title indicating their type. The HTML elements are written in lowercase letters and between angle brackets, such as `<form>` and `<input>`. Text nodes are inside a box whose title is simply `Text`.

This representation of an application's view holds all the information that we need to know to build the DOM. It maintains the hierarchy of the elements, as well as the attributes, the event handlers, and the positions of the child elements. If you are given such a virtual DOM, you can derive the corresponding HTML markup without ambiguity.

Creating virtual trees manually is a tedious task that can result in errors, such as misspelling property names. To simplify the process of defining an application's view, you write functions that generate each type of virtual node instead of have the developer do the work manually. Although using these functions makes the process of defining the virtual DOM less painful, it's still not as convenient as writing HTML templates or JSX, but it's a starting point.

### Exercise 3.1

Given the following HTML markup, can you draw the corresponding virtual DOM tree diagram (similar to figure 3.3)?

```html
<div id="app">
  <h1>TODOs</h1>
  <input type="text" placeholder="What needs to be done?">

  <ul>
    <li>
      <input type="checkbox">
      <label>Buy milk</label>
      <button>Remove</button>
    </li>
    <li>
      <input type="checkbox">
      <label>Buy eggs</label>
      <button>Remove</button>
    </li>
  </ul>
</div>
```

Find the solution at http://mng.bz/orpD.

## 3.3 Getting ready

Make sure that you've read appendix A and set up the project structure. All the code you'll write in this book will be part of the *runtime* package, which is the part of the framework that runs in the browser. So when I refer to the src/ directory, I mean that of the runtime package until further notice.

You want to create a file called h.js inside the src/ directory. This file is where you'll write most of the code in this chapter. Also create a utils/ directory inside src/, and add a file called arrays.js inside it. Here, you'll write a utility function to filter null and undefined values from an array. Your *runtime* package should look like this (with the configuration files omitted and the files you created in bold):

```
runtime/
└── src/
      ├──utils/
      │     └── arrays.js
      ├── h.js
      └── index.js
```

## 3.4 Types of nodes

Let's start writing some code. As you've seen, you can have three types of DOM nodes that need to be represented as virtual nodes:

- *Text nodes*—They represent text content.
- *Element nodes*—The most common type of node, they represent HTML elements that have a tag name, such as `'div'` or `'p'`.
- *Fragment nodes*—They represent a collection of nodes that don't have a parent node until they are attached to the DOM. (I haven't covered them yet but will in section 3.7.)

These nodes have different properties, so we need to represent them differently. In several chapters of the book, you'll have to write code that operates on the virtual nodes and do something different depending on the type of node. Therefore, it's a good idea to define a constant for each type to prevent typos. Inside the h.js file, write the following code:

```
export const DOM_TYPES = {
  TEXT: 'text',
  ELEMENT: 'element',
  FRAGMENT: 'fragment',
}
```

You've defined three constants, one for each type of node:

- `DOM_TYPES.TEXT`—The type for a text node, which is `'text'`
- `DOM_TYPES.ELEMENT`—The type for an element node, which is `'element'`
- `DOM_TYPES.FRAGMENT`—The type for a fragment node, which is `'fragment'`

Next, we'll implement the functions that create the virtual nodes, starting with element nodes.

## 3.5    *Element nodes*

*Element nodes* are the most common type of virtual node, representing the regular HTML elements that you use to define the structure of your web pages. To name a few, you have `<h1>` through `<h6>` for headings, `<p>` for paragraphs, `<ul>` and `<ol>` for lists, `<a>` for links, and `<div>` for generic containers. These nodes have a tag name (such as `'p'`), attributes (such as a class name or the `type` attribute of an `<input>` element), and children nodes (the nodes that are inside them between the opening and closing tags). In this section, you'll implement a function `h()` to create element nodes that take three arguments:

- `tag`—The element's tag name
- `props`—An object with its attributes (which we'll call *props*, for *properties*)
- `children`—An array of its children nodes

The name `h()` is short for *hyperscript*, a script that creates hypertext. (Recall that *HTML* is the initialism for *Hypertext Markup Language*.) The name `h()` for the function is a common one used in some frontend frameworks, probably because it's short and easy to type, which is important because you'll be using it often.

> **h(), hyperscript(), or createElement()**
>
> React uses the `React.createElement()` function to create virtual nodes. The name is a long one, but typically, you never call that function directly; you use JSX instead. Each HTML element you write in JSX is transpiled to a `React.createElement()` call.
>
> Other frameworks, such as Vue, name the virtual-node-producing function `h()`. Mithril, for example, gives the user a function called `m()` to create the virtual DOM, but the idea is the same. Internally, Mithril implements a virtual-node-creating function named `hyperscript()`. The user-facing function has a nice short name (`m()`), but the internal function has a more descriptive name.

The `h()` function should return a virtual node object with the passed-in tag name, props, and children, plus a `type` property set to `DOM_TYPES.ELEMENT`. You want to give default values to the `props` and `children` parameters so that you can call the function with only the tag name, as in `h('div')`, which should be equivalent to calling `h('div', {}, [])`.

Some child nodes might come as `null` (I'll explain why soon), so you want to filter them out. To filter `null` values from an array, in the next section you'll write a function called `withoutNulls()`. (That function is imported in listing 3.1 but not implemented yet.)

Some child nodes inside the passed-in `children` array may be strings, not objects representing virtual nodes. In that case, you want to transform them into virtual nodes of type `DOM_TYPES.TEXT`, using a function called `mapTextNodes()` that you'll write later.

Let's implement the `h()` function. In the h.js file, write the code shown in bold in the following listing.

**Listing 3.1    The `h()` function to create element virtual nodes (h.js)**

```
import { withoutNulls } from './utils/arrays'

export const DOM_TYPES = {
  TEXT: 'text',
  ELEMENT: 'element',
  FRAGMENT: 'fragment',
}

export function h(tag, props = {}, children = []) {
  return {
    tag,
    props,
    children: mapTextNodes(withoutNulls(children)),
    type: DOM_TYPES.ELEMENT,
  }
}
```

### 3.5.1  *Conditional rendering: Removing null values*

Now let's implement the `withoutNulls()` and `mapTextNodes()` functions. When we use *conditional rendering* (rendering nodes only when a condition is met), some children may be `null` in the array, which means that they shouldn't be rendered. We want to remove these `null` values from the array of children.

Let's use our TODO app from chapter 2 as an example. Recall that the Add to-do button is disabled when the input has no text or the text is too short. If instead of disabling the button, you decided to remove it from the page, you'd have a conditional like the following:

```
{
  tag: 'div',
  children: [
    { tag: 'input', props: { type: 'text' } },
    addTodoInput.value.length > 2
      ? { tag: 'button', children: ['Add'] }
      : null
  ]
}
```

When the condition `addTodoInput.value.length > 2` is `false`, a `null` node is added to the `div` node's `children` array:

```
{
  tag: 'div',
  children: [
    { tag: 'input', props: { type: 'text' } },
    null
  ]
}
```

This `null` value means that the button shouldn't be added to the DOM. The simplest way to make this process work is to filter out `null` values from the `children` array when a new virtual node is created so that a `null` node isn't passed around the framework:

```
{
  tag: 'div',
  children: [
    { tag: 'input', props: { type: 'text' } }
  ]
}
```

Inside the utils/arrays.js file, write a function called `withoutNulls()` that takes an array and returns a new array with all the `null` values removed:

```
export function withoutNulls(arr) {
  return arr.filter((item) => item != null)
}
```

Note the use of the `!=` operator, as opposed to `!==`. You use this operator to remove both `null` and `undefined` values. You aren't expecting `undefined` values, but this way, you'll remove them if they appear. Your linter might complain about this approach if you've enabled the eqeqeq rule (https://eslint.org/docs/latest/rules/eqeqeq), but you can disable the rule for this line. Tell the linter you know what you're doing.

### 3.5.2 Mapping strings to text nodes

After filtering out the `null` values from the `children` array, you pass the result to the `mapTextNodes()` function. Earlier, I said that this function transforms strings into text virtual nodes. Why do we want to do this? Well, we might do it as a convenience for creating text nodes, so instead of writing

```
h('div', {}, [hString('Hello '), hString('world!')])
```

we can write

```
h('div', {}, ['Hello ', 'world!'])
```

As you can anticipate, you'll use text children often, so this function will make your life easier—if only a little. Let's write that missing `mapTextNodes()` function now. In the h.js file, below the `h()` function, write the following code:

```
function mapTextNodes(children) {
  return children.map((child) =>
    typeof child === 'string' ? hString(child) : child
  )
}
```

You've used the `hString()` function to create text virtual nodes from strings, but that function doesn't exist yet. Next, you'll implement the function that creates text virtual nodes.

## 3.6 Text nodes

*Text nodes* are the nodes in the DOM that contain text. They have no tag name, no attributes, and no children—only text.

Text nodes are the simplest of the three types of virtual nodes to create. A text virtual node is simply an object with the `type` property set to `DOM_TYPES.TEXT` and the `value` property set to the text content. In the h.js file, write the `hString()` function like so:

```
export function hString(str) {
  return { type: DOM_TYPES.TEXT, value: str }
}
```

That was easy. Now you're missing only the `hFragment()` function to create fragment virtual nodes.

## 3.7     Fragment nodes

A *fragment* is a type of virtual node used to group multiple nodes that need to be attached to the DOM together but don't have a parent node in the DOM. You can think of a fragment node as being a container for an array of virtual nodes.

> **NOTE**  Fragments exist in the Document API; they're used to create subtrees of the DOM that can be appended to the document at the same time. They're represented by the `DocumentFragment` class (http://mng.bz/5oVz) and can be created by means of the `document.createDocumentFragment()` method. We won't be using the `DocumentFragment` to insert the virtual fragment nodes into the DOM, but it's good to know that `DocumentFragment`s exist.

### 3.7.1     Implementing fragment nodes

In this section, we'll implement the `hFragment()` function to create fragment virtual nodes. A fragment is an array of child nodes, so its implementation is simple. In the h.js file, write the `hFragment()` function as follows:

```
export function hFragment(vNodes) {
  return {
    type: DOM_TYPES.FRAGMENT,
    children: mapTextNodes(withoutNulls(vNodes)),
  }
}
```

Same as before, you filtered out the `null` values from the array of children and then mapped the strings in the `children` array to text virtual nodes. That's all!

### 3.7.2     Testing the virtual DOM functions

Now we'll use the `h()`, `hString()`, and `hFragment()` functions to create virtual DOM representations of the view of your application. We'll implement the code that takes in a virtual DOM and creates the real DOM for it, but first, we'll put the virtual DOM functions to the test. Use the `h()` function to define the view of a login form as follows:

```
h('form', { class: 'login-form', action: 'login' }, [
  h('input', { type: 'text', name: 'user' }),
  h('input', { type: 'password', name: 'pass' }),
  h('button', { on: { click: login } }, ['Log in'])
])
```

This code creates a virtual DOM, depicted in figure 3.4. Arguably, using the `h()` functions is more concise than defining the virtual DOM manually as a tree of JavaScript objects.

We'll use this virtual DOM, passed to the framework, to create the real DOM: the HTML code that will be rendered in the browser. In this case, the HTML markup is

```
<form class="login-form" action="login">
  <input type="text" name="user">
  <input type="password" name="pass">
  <button>Log in</button>
</form>
```

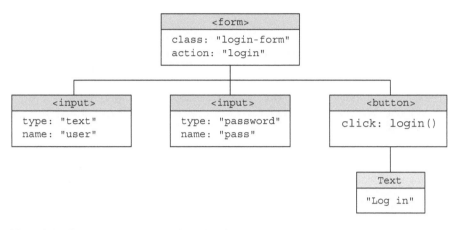

**Figure 3.4 Example of creating a virtual DOM tree**

**NOTE** The `<button>` element doesn't have a `click` event handler rendered in the HTML markup because the framework will add the event handler to the button programmatically when it's attached to the DOM. The event handlers added from JavaScript aren't shown in the HTML.

As you can imagine, you typically don't define the virtual DOM for your entire application in one place; that process can get unwieldy as the application grows. Instead, you split the view into parts, each of which we call a *component*. Components are the cornerstone of frontend frameworks; they allow us to break a large application into smaller, more manageable pieces, each of which is in charge of a specific part of the view.

**Exercise 3.2**

Using the `h()` function, define the virtual DOM equivalent to the following HTML markup:

```
<h1 class="title">My counter</h1>
<div class="container">
  <button>decrement</button>
  <span>0</span>
  <button>increment</button>
</div>
```

Find the solution at http://mng.bz/n1Md.

**Exercise 3.3**

Create a function, `lipsum()`, that takes in a number and returns a virtual DOM consisting of a fragment with as many paragraphs as the number passed to the function. Every paragraph should contain this text: *"Lorem ipsum dolor sit amet, consectetur adipiscing elit, sed do eiusmod tempor incididunt ut labore et dolore magna aliqua. Ut enim ad minim veniam, quis nostrud exercitation ullamco laboris nisi ut aliquip ex ea commodo consequat."*

This function might come in handy when you're building a user interface (UI) and need some placeholder text (https://www.lipsum.com) to fill in the space so you can see how the UI looks with real content.

Find the solution at http://mng.bz/vPza.

## 3.8   *Components: The cornerstone of frontend frameworks*

Let's see what makes a component in our early version of the framework. The component is the revolutionary concept that has made frontend frameworks popular. The ability to break a large application into smaller parts, each of which defines a specific part of the view and manages its interaction with the user, has been a game-changer (arguably; a good use of the MVC or MVVM pattern could already get us this far). Every frontend framework uses components, and ours will be no different.

First, we'll take a small detour from the implementation of the virtual DOM to understand how we'll decompose the view of our application into a hierarchy of components.

### 3.8.1   *What is a component?*

A component in your framework is a mini application of its own. It has its own internal state and lifecycle, and it's in charge of rendering part of the view. It communicates with the rest of the application, emitting events and receiving *props* (data passed to the component from the outside), re-rendering its view when a new set of props is passed to it. But we won't get to that process for a few chapters. Your first version of a component will be much simpler: a pure function that takes in the state of the whole application and returns the virtual DOM representing the view of the component. In chapter 9, you'll make components that have their own internal state and lifecycle. For now, start by breaking down the view of the application into pure functions that, given the state, return the virtual DOM representing part of it.

### 3.8.2   *The virtual DOM as a function of the state*

The view of an application depends on the state of the application, so we can say that the virtual DOM is a function of the state. Each time the state changes, the virtual DOM should be reevaluated, and the framework needs to update the real DOM accordingly. Figure 3.5 depicts this dependency between the state and the view. In the left column, the state consists of a list of to-dos with only one item: "Walk the dog." In the right column, the state changes to include a second to-do item: "Water the plants." Notice that the virtual DOM changes accordingly, and the HTML markup changes as well.

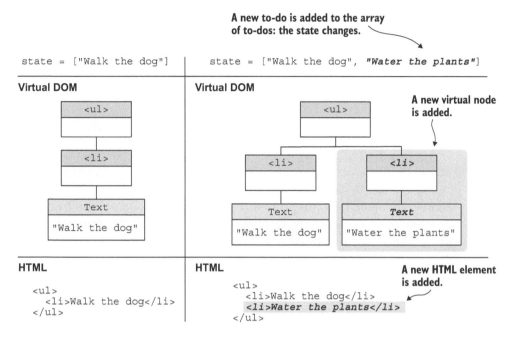

**Figure 3.5** The view of an application is a function of the state. When a new to-do item is added to the state, the virtual DOM is reevaluated, and the DOM is updated with the new to-do.

To produce the virtual DOM representing the view, we must take the current state of the application into account, and when the state changes, we must reevaluate the virtual DOM. If we generate the virtual DOM that represents the view of the application by calling a function that receives the state as a parameter, we can easily reevaluate it when the state changes. In the case of our TODOs application, the virtual DOM for the list of to-dos (consisting of only the to-do description for the sake of simplicity) could be generated by a function like this:

```
function TodosList(todos) {
  return h('ul', {}, todos.map((todo) => h('li', {}, [todo])))
}
```

If we call the `TodosList()` function with the following list of to-dos as an argument,

```
TodosList(['Walk the dog', 'Water the plants'])
```

the function would return the following virtual DOM (empty `props` objects omitted for brevity):

```
{
  tag: 'ul',
  type: 'element',
  children: [
    { tag: 'li', children: [{ type: 'text', value: 'Walk the dog' }] },
    { tag: 'li', children: [{ type: 'text', value: 'Water the plants' }] }
  ]
}
```

The framework would render the virtual DOM representing the list of to-dos into the following HTML:

```
<ul>
  <li>Walk the dog</li>
  <li>Water the plants</li>
</ul>
```

Figure 3.6 summarizes this process. The application code, written by the developer, generates the virtual DOM describing the view. Then the framework, which you wrote, creates the real DOM from the virtual DOM and inserts it into the browser's document.

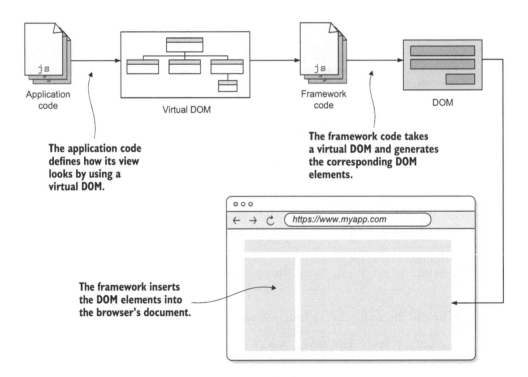

**Figure 3.6   The application creates the virtual DOM that the framework renders into the DOM.**

One nice benefit of using functions to produce the virtual DOM, receiving the application's state as an argument, is that we can break the view into smaller parts. We can easily compose *pure functions*—functions that don't produce any side effects and always return the same result for the same input arguments—to build more complex views.

---

### Exercise 3.4

Write a function called `MessageComponent()` that takes an object with two properties:

- `level`—A string that can be `'info'`, `'warning'`, or `'error'`
- `message`—A string with the message to display

The function should return a virtual DOM that represents a message box with the message and the corresponding CSS class depending on the level. The CSS classes are `message--info`, `message--warning`, and `message--error` for the different levels. The markup should look like this:

```
<div class="message message--info">
  <p>This is an info message</p>
</div>
```

Find the solution at http://mng.bz/46ZQ.

---

### 3.8.3 Composing views: Components as children

Pure functions can be composed nicely to build more complex functions. If we generate the virtual DOM to represent the view of the application by composing smaller functions, we can easily break the view into smaller parts. These subfunctions represent part of the view: the *components*. The arguments passed to a component are known as *props*, as I've already mentioned.

> **NOTE** In this first version of the framework, *components* are functions that generate the virtual DOM for part of the application's view. They take the state of the application or part of it as their argument. The arguments passed to a component, the data coming from outside the component, are known as *props*. This definition of a component changes in chapter 9, where components are more than pure functions and handle their own state and lifecycle.

Let's work on an example that uses the TODOs application view. If we don't break the view into smaller parts, we'll have a single function that generates the virtual DOM for the entire application. Such a function would be long and hard for other developers to understand—and probably hard for us to understand, too. But we can clearly distinguish two parts in the view: the form to add a new to-do item and the list of to-dos (figure 3.7), which be generated by two different functions. That is, we can break the view into two subcomponents.

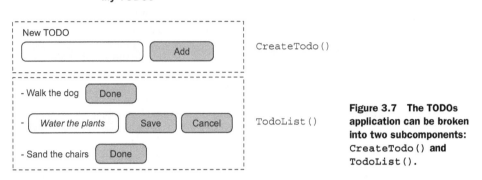

Figure 3.7  **The TODOs application can be broken into two subcomponents:** `CreateTodo()` **and** `TodoList()`.

So the virtual DOM for the whole application could be created by a component like the following:

```
function App(state) {
  return hFragment([
    h('h1', {}, ['My TODOs']),
    CreateTodo(state),
    TodoList(state)
  ])
}
```

Note that in this case, no parent node in the virtual DOM contains the header of the application and the two subcomponents; we use a fragment to group the elements. Also note the naming convention: the functions that generate the virtual DOM are written in PascalCase to signal that they're components that create a virtual DOM tree, not regular functions.

Similarly, the `TodoList()` component, as you've probably guessed, can be broken down into another subcomponent: the `TodoItem()`. You can see this subcomponent in figure 3.8.

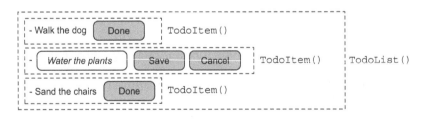

Figure 3.8  **The** `TodoList()` **component can be broken down into a** `TodoItem()` **subcomponent.**

Thus, the `TodoList()` component would look similar to the following:

```
function TodoList(state) {
  return h('ul', {},
    children: state.todos.map(
      (todo, i) => TodoItem(todo, i, state.editingIdxs)
    )
  )
}
```

The `TodoItem()` component would render a different thing depending on whether the to-do is in read or edit mode. Those components could be further decomposed into two different subcomponents: `TodoInReadMode()` and `TodoInEditMode()`. This split would be something like the following:

```
// idxInList is the index of this todo item in the list of todos.
// editingIdxs is a Set of indexes of todos that are being edited.
function TodoItem(todo, idxInList, editingIdxs) {
  const isEditing = editingIdxs.has(idxInList)

  return h('li', {}, [
    isEditing
      ? TodoInEditMode(todo, idxInList)
      : TodoInReadMode(todo, idxInList)
  ]
  )
}
```

Defining the views of our application by using pure functions—the components—allows you to compose them easily to build more complex views. This process probably isn't new to you; you've been decomposing your applications into a hierarchy of components when using frontend frameworks like React, Vue, Svelte, or Angular. We can visualize the hierarchy of components for the preceding example in a tree, as shown in figure 3.9.

In this figure, we see the view of the application as a tree of components with the virtual DOM nodes they generate below them. The `App()` component is the root of the tree, and it has three children: an `<h1>` element, the `CreateTodo()` component, and the `TodoList()` component. A component can return only a single virtual DOM node as its root, so the three children of `App()` are grouped in a fragment.

Then, following the hierarchy down, we see that the `TodoList()` component has a single child, the `<ul>` element, which in turn has a list of `TodoItem()` components. The ellipsis in the tree indicates that the `<ul>` element may have more children than the ones shown in the figure—a number that depends on how many to-dos are in the list. Finally, the `TodoItem()` component has two children: the `TodoInEditMode()` and `TodoInReadMode()` components. These components would render more virtual DOM nodes, but I don't show them in the figure for simplicity.

**NOTE** As you can see in figure 3.9, the component nodes have their titles written in PascalCase and include parentheses to indicate that they're functions. Each fragment is titled `Fragment`.

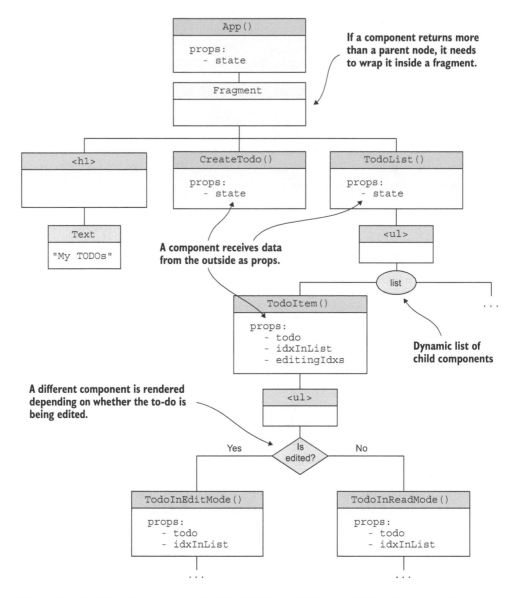

**Figure 3.9   The hierarchy of components of the TODOs application, in which each component has its child virtual DOM nodes below itself**

Now that you understand how to break the view of your application into components—pure functions that generate the virtual DOM given the state of the application—you're ready to implement the code in the framework, which is in charge of mounting the virtual DOM returned by the `h()` functions to the browser's DOM. You'll do exactly that in chapter 4.

## *Summary*

- The virtual DOM is the blueprint for the view of the application. It allows the developer to describe how the view should look in a declarative way (similar to what an architect does with the blueprints of a house) and moves responsibility for manipulating the DOM to the framework.

- By being able to use a virtual DOM to declare what the view should look like, the developer doesn't have to know how to manipulate the DOM by using the Document API and doesn't need to mix business logic with DOM-manipulation code.

- A component is a pure function—a function with no side effects—that takes the state of the application as input and returns a virtual DOM tree representing a chunk of the view of the application. In later chapters, the definition of a component will be extended to include the ability to have internal state and a lifecycle that's independent of the application's.

- The three types of virtual nodes are text, element, and fragment. The most interesting one is the element node, which represents the regular HTML elements that can have attributes, children, and event listeners.

- The `hString()`, `h()`, and `hFragment()` functions create text, element, and fragment virtual nodes, respectively. The virtual DOM can be declared directly as a tree of JavaScript objects, but calling these functions makes the process simpler.

- Fragment virtual nodes consist of an array of children virtual nodes.

- Fragment virtual nodes are useful when a component returns a list of virtual nodes without a parent node. The DOM—and, by extension, the virtual DOM—is a tree data structure. Every level of the tree (except the root) must have a parent node, so a fragment node can be used to group a list of virtual nodes.

# Mounting and destroying the virtual DOM

*4*

**This chapter covers**

- Creating HTML nodes from virtual DOM nodes
- Inserting HTML nodes into the browser's document
- Removing HTML nodes from the browser's document

In chapter 3, you learned what the virtual Document Object Model (DOM) is and how to create it. You implemented the `h()`, `hString()`, and `hFragment()` functions to create virtual nodes of type `element`, `text`, and `fragment`, respectively. Now it's time to learn how to create the real DOM nodes from the virtual DOM nodes and insert them into the browser's document. You achieve this task by using the Document API, as you'll see in this chapter.

When the view of your application is no longer needed, you want to remove the HTML nodes from the browser's document. You'll learn how in this chapter as well.

> **NOTE** You can find all the listings in this chapter in the listings/ch04 directory of the book's repository (http://mng.bz/6nxy). The code you write in this chapter is for the framework's first version, which you'll publish

in chapter 6. Therefore, the code in this chapter can be checked out from the ch6 label (http://mng.bz/orgM): $ `git switch --detach ch6`.

---

**Code catch-up**

In chapter 3, you implemented the `h()`, `hString()`, and `hFragment()` functions. These functions are used to create virtual nodes of type `'element'`, `'text'`, and `'fragment'`, respectively. You also defined the `DOM_TYPES` object containing the different types of virtual nodes.

---

## 4.1 Mounting the virtual DOM

Given a virtual DOM tree, you want your framework to create the real DOM tree from it and attach it to the browser's document. We call this process *mounting* the virtual DOM. You implement this code in the framework so that the developers who use it don't need to use the Document API themselves. You'll implement this process in the `mountDOM()` function.

Figure 4.1 is a visual representation of how the `mountDOM()` function works. You can see that the first argument is a virtual DOM, and the second argument is the parent element where we want the view to be inserted: the document's `<body>` element. The result is a DOM tree attached to the parent element, which is the `<body>` of the document.

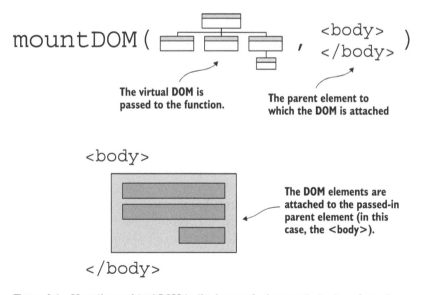

Figure 4.1 Mounting a virtual DOM to the browser's document `<body>` element

**WARNING**    In many examples in this book and the tests in the repository, I mounted the application inside the `<body>` element of the document. This approach is okay for the examples and tests, but you should avoid it in your applications. Some third-party libraries might attach elements to the `<body>` element, which might make your reconciliation algorithm work incorrectly.

When the `mountDOM()` function creates each DOM node for the virtual DOM, it needs to save a reference to the real DOM node in the virtual node under the `el` property (`el` for *element*), as you see in figure 4.2. The reconciliation algorithm that you'll write in chapters 7 and 8 uses this reference to know what DOM nodes to update.

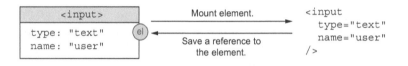

**Figure 4.2    The virtual node's `el` property keeps a reference to the real DOM node.**

Similarly, if the node includes event listeners, the `mountDOM()` function saves a reference to the event listener in the virtual node under the `listeners` property (figure 4.3).

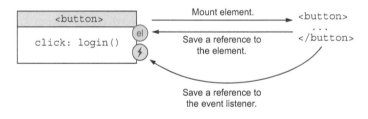

**Figure 4.3    The virtual node's `listeners` property keeps a reference to the event listener.**

Saving these references has a double purpose: it allows the framework to remove the event listeners and detach the element from the DOM when the virtual node is unmounted, and the reconciliation algorithm requires it to know what element in the DOM needs to be updated. This process will become clear in chapter 7; for now, bear with me. Using the example from earlier, the virtual DOM we defined as

```
const vdom = h('form', { class: 'login-form', action: 'login' }, [
  h('input', { type: 'text', name: 'user' }),
  h('input', { type: 'password', name: 'pass' }),
  h('button', { on: { click: login } }, ['Login'])
])
```

passed to the `mountDOM()` function as

```
mountDOM(vdom, document.body)
```

would result in the virtual DOM tree depicted in figure 4.4, where you can see the `el` and `listeners` references in the virtual nodes.

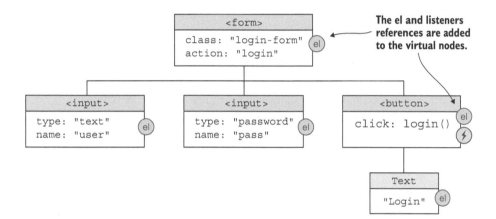

**Figure 4.4  The login form virtual DOM example mounted to the browser's document `<body>` element. The virtual nodes keep a reference to the real DOM nodes in the `el` property and to the event listeners in the `listeners` property (shown as a lightning-bolt icon).**

This HTML tree would be attached to the `<body>` element, and the resulting HTML markup would be

```
<body>
  <form class="login-form" action="login">
    <input type="text" name="user">
    <input type="password" name="pass">
    <button>Login</button>
  </form>
</body>
```

Different types of virtual nodes require different DOM nodes to be created:

- A virtual node of type `text` requires a `Text` node to be created (via the `document.createTextNode()` method).
- A virtual node of type `element` requires an `Element` node to be created (via the `document.createElement()` method).

The `mountDOM()` function needs to differentiate between the values of the `type` property of the virtual node and create the appropriate DOM node. With this fact in mind, let's implement the `mountDOM()` function.

### 4.1.1   *Mounting virtual nodes into the DOM*

Create a new file called mount-dom.js in the src/ directory. Then write the `mountDOM()` function as shown in the following listing. The listing includes some *TODO* comments toward the end of the file. You don't need to write those comments in your code; they're placeholders to show where you will implement the missing functions later.

---

**Listing 4.1   The `mountDOM()` function mounting the virtual DOM (mount-dom.js)**

```
import { DOM_TYPES } from './h'

export function mountDOM(vdom, parentEl) {
  switch (vdom.type) {
    case DOM_TYPES.TEXT: {
      createTextNode(vdom, parentEl)          ◁─┐ Mounts a text
      break                                        virtual node
    }

    case DOM_TYPES.ELEMENT: {
      createElementNode(vdom, parentEl)       ◁─┐ Mounts an element
      break                                        virtual node
    }
                                                 ┌ Mounts the children
                                                 │ of a fragment virtual
    case DOM_TYPES.FRAGMENT: {                   │ node
      createFragmentNodes(vdom, parentEl)     ◁─┘
      break
    }

    default: {
      throw new Error(`Can't mount DOM of type: ${vdom.type}`)
    }
  }
}

// TODO: implement createTextNode()

// TODO: implement createElementNode()

// TODO: implement createFragmentNodes()
```

The function uses a `switch` statement that checks the type of the virtual node. Depending on the node's type, the appropriate function to create the real DOM node gets called. If the node type isn't one of the three supported types, the function throws an error. If you made a mistake, such as misspelling the type of a virtual node, this error will help you find it.

### 4.1.2   *Mounting text nodes*

Text nodes are the simplest type of node to create because they don't have any attributes or event listeners. To create a text node, the Document API provides the `createTextNode()` method (http://mng.bz/n1aK). This method expects a string as an argument, which is the text that the text node will contain. If you recall, the virtual nodes created by the `hString()` function you implemented earlier have the following structure:

```
{
  type: DOM_TYPES.TEXT,
  value: 'I need more coffee'
}
```

These virtual nodes have a `type` property, identifying them as a text node, and a `value` property, which is set to the string that the `hString()` function receives as an argument. You pass this text to the `createTextNode()` method. After creating the text DOM node, you have to do two things:

1 Save a reference to the real DOM node in the virtual node under the `el` property.
2 Attach the text node to the parent element.

Inside the mount-dom.js file, write the `createTextNode()` function as follows:

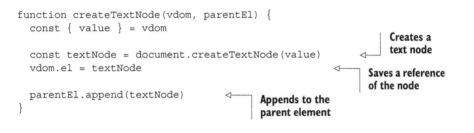

```
function createTextNode(vdom, parentEl) {
  const { value } = vdom

  const textNode = document.createTextNode(value)    ◁── Creates a text node
  vdom.el = textNode    ◁── Saves a reference of the node

  parentEl.append(textNode)    ◁── Appends to the parent element
}
```

> **Exercise 4.1**
>
> Using the `hString()` and `mountDOM()` functions, insert the text *OMG, so interesting!* below the headline of your local newspaper's website. (You'll need to copy/paste some of your code in the browser's console.)
>
> Find the solution at http://mng.bz/g7oG.

### 4.1.3 Mounting fragment nodes

Let's implement the `createFragmentNodes()` function. Fragment nodes are simple to mount; you simply mount the children of the fragment. It's important to remember that fragments aren't nodes that get attached to the DOM; they're an array of children. For this reason, the `el` property of a fragment virtual node should point to the parent element to which the fragment's children are attached (figure 4.5).

Note that if you have nested fragment nodes, all the fragment nodes' children will be appended to the same parent element. All the `el` references of those fragment virtual nodes should point to the same parent element, as shown in figure 4.6.

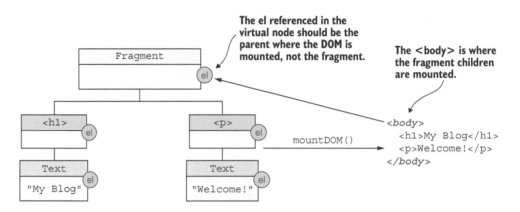

**Figure 4.5   A fragment's el should reference the parent element to which its children are attached.**

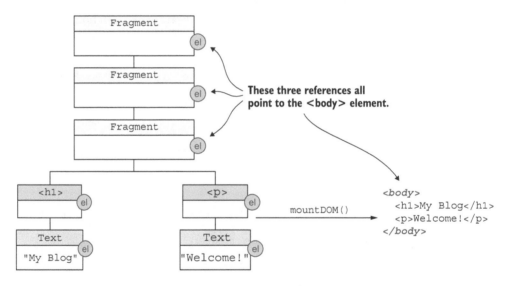

**Figure 4.6   All nested fragments point to the same parent element.**

Now that you have a good understanding of how fragments work, it's time to write some code. Write the `createFragmentNode()` function inside the mount-dom.js file as follows:

```
function createFragmentNodes(vdom, parentEl) {
  const { children } = vdom
  vdom.el = parentEl                                    Saves a reference of
                                                        the parent element

  children.forEach((child) => mountDOM(child, parentEl))    Appends each
}                                                           child to the
                                                            parent element
```

Great! Now you're ready to implement the `createElementNode()` function. This function is the most important one because it creates the element nodes—the visual bits of the DOM tree.

### 4.1.4 *Mounting element nodes*

To create element nodes (those regular HTML elements with tags like `<div>` and `<span>`), you use the `createElement()` method from the Document API (http://mng .bz/vP0M). You have to pass the tag name to the `createElement()` function. The Document API returns an element node that matches that tag or `HTMLUnknownElement` (http://mng.bz/46rV) if the tag is unrecognized. You can try this code yourself in the browser console:

```
Object.getPrototypeOf(document.createElement('foobar')) // HTMLUnknownElement
```

An obviously nonexistent tag such as `foobar` returns an `HTMLUnknownElement` node. So if a virtual node has a tag that the Document API doesn't recognize, the `document .createElement()` function returns an `HTMLUnknownElement` node. We're not going to worry about this case: if an `HTMLUnknownElement` results from the `createElement()` function, we'll assume an error on the developer's part.

If you recall, calling the `h()` function to create element virtual nodes returns an object with the `type` property set to `DOM_TYPES.ELEMENT`, a `tag` property with the tag name, and a `props` property with the attributes and event listeners. If the virtual node has children, they appear inside the `children` property. A `<button>` virtual node with a class of `btn` and an `onclick` event listener would look like this:

```
{
  type: DOM_TYPES.ELEMENT,
  tag: 'button',
  props: {
    class: 'btn',
    on: { click: () => console.log('yay!') }
  },
  children: [
    {
      type: DOM_TYPES.TEXT,
      value: 'Click me!'
    }
  ]
}
```

To create the corresponding DOM element from the virtual node, you need to do the following:

1 Create the element node using the `document.createElement()` function.
2 Add the attributes and event listeners to the element node, saving the added event listeners in a new property of the virtual node called `listeners`.
3 Save a reference to the element node in the virtual node under the `el` property.

4 Mount the children recursively into the element node.

5 Append the element node to the parent element.

As you can see, the props property of the virtual node contains the attributes and event listeners. But attributes and event listeners are handled differently, so you'll need to separate them.

Two special cases that are related to styling also need special handling: style and class. You'll extract them from the props object and handle them separately. Write the createElementNode() function inside the mount-dom.js file, as shown in the following listing.

**Listing 4.2  Mounting an element node into a parent element (mount-dom.js)**

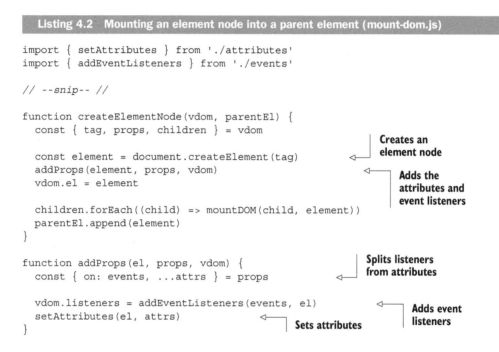

```
import { setAttributes } from './attributes'
import { addEventListeners } from './events'

// --snip-- //

function createElementNode(vdom, parentEl) {
  const { tag, props, children } = vdom

  const element = document.createElement(tag)          Creates an
  addProps(element, props, vdom)                       element node
  vdom.el = element                                    Adds the
                                                        attributes and
  children.forEach((child) => mountDOM(child, element)) event listeners
  parentEl.append(element)
}

function addProps(el, props, vdom) {                   Splits listeners
  const { on: events, ...attrs } = props               from attributes

  vdom.listeners = addEventListeners(events, el)       Adds event
  setAttributes(el, attrs)                             listeners
}                                        Sets attributes
```

Note that you're using two functions you haven't implemented yet: setAttributes() and addEventListeners(), imported from the attributes.js and events.js files, respectively. You'll write them soon.

Setting the attributes and adding event listeners is the part where the code differs from text nodes. With text nodes, you want to attach event listeners and set attributes to the parent element node, not to the text node itself.

**NOTE** The Text type defined in the Document API inherits from the Event-Target interface (http://mng.bz/QR9j), which declares the addEvent-Listener() method. In principle, you can add event listeners to a text node, but if you try to do that in the browser, you'll see that the event listeners are never called.

Next, we'll implement the addEventListeners() function, which is in charge of adding event listeners to an element node. Then we'll look at the setAttributes() function, and we'll be done with creating element nodes.

### 4.1.5 Adding event listeners

To add an event listener to an element node, you call its addEventListener() method (http://mng.bz/Xql6). This method is available because an element node is an instance of the EventTarget interface. This interface, which declares the addEventListener() method, is implemented by all the DOM nodes that can receive events. All instances returned by calling document.createElement() implement the EventTarget interface, so you can safely call the addEventListener() method on them.

Our implementation of the addEventListener() function in this chapter will be very simple: it will call the addEventListener() method on the element and return the event handler function it registered. You want to return the function registered as an event handler because later, when you implement the destroyDOM() method (as you can figure out, it does the opposite of mountDOM()), you'll need to remove the event listeners to avoid memory leaks. You need the handler function that was registered in the event listener to be able to remove it by passing it as an argument to the removeEventListener() method.

In chapter 9, when you make the components of your framework stateful (they'll be pure functions with no state for the moment), you'll also have references to the event listeners added to the components, which will behave differently from the event handlers of the DOM nodes. At that point in the book, you'll need to modify the implementation of the addEventListener() function to account for this new case. So if you wonder why we're implementing a function that does so little on its own, the reason is that it's a placeholder for the more complex implementation that you'll write later. Create a new file under the src/ directory called events.js, and add the following code:

```
export function addEventListener(eventName, handler, el) {
  el.addEventListener(eventName, handler)
  return handler
}
```

As promised, the addEventListener() function is simple. But if you recall, the event listeners defined in a virtual node come packed in an object. The keys are the event names, and the values are the event handler functions, like so:

```
{
  type: DOM_TYPES.ELEMENT,
  tag: 'button',
  props: {
    on: {
      mouseover: () => console.log('almost yay!'),
      click: () => console.log('yay!') ,
```

```
      dblclick: () => console.log('double yay!'),
    }
  }
}
```

It makes sense to have another function, if only for convenience, that allows you to add multiple event listeners in the form of an object to an element node. Inside the events.js file, add another function called addEventListeners() (plural):

```
export function addEventListeners(listeners = {}, el) {
  const addedListeners = {}

  Object.entries(listeners).forEach(([eventName, handler]) => {
    const listener = addEventListener(eventName, handler, el)
    addedListeners[eventName] = listener
  })

  return addedListeners
}
```

You may be tempted to simplify that function by removing the addedListeners variable and return the same listeners object that the function got as input:

```
export function addEventListeners(listeners = {}, el) {
  Object.entries(listeners).forEach( ... )

  return listeners
}
```

After all, the same event handler functions that we got as input, we're returning as output, so the refactor seems to be legit. But even though it may be legitimate now, that won't be the case later, when the components have their own state. You won't be adding the same functions as event handlers, but new functions created by the framework with some extra logic around them. This process might sound confusing, but stick with me, and you'll see how it makes sense.

Now that you've implemented the event listeners, let's implement the set-Attributes() function. We're getting closer to having a working mountDOM() function.

### 4.1.6  *Setting the attributes*

To set an attribute in an HTMLElement instance in code, you set the value in the corresponding property of the element. Setting the property of the element reflects the value in the corresponding attribute of the rendered HTML. It's important to understand that when you're manipulating the DOM through code, you're working with DOM nodes—instances of the HTMLElement class. These instances have properties that you can set in code, as with any other JavaScript object. When these properties are set, the corresponding attribute is automatically reflected in the rendered HTML. If you have a paragraph in HTML, such as,

```
<p id="foo">Hello, world!</p>
```

and assuming that you have a reference to the `<p>` element in a variable called `p`, you can set the `id` property of the `p` element to a different value, like so:

```
p.id = 'bar'
```

The rendered HTML reflects the change:

```
<p id="bar">Hello, world!</p>
```

In a nutshell, `HTMLElement` instances (such as the `<p>` element, which is an instance of the `HTMLParagraphElement` class) have properties that correspond to the attributes that are rendered in the HTML markup. When you set the value of these properties, the corresponding attributes in the rendered HTML are updated automatically. Even though the process is a bit more nuanced, this discussion gives you the gist.

---

### Caution on attributes

Some attributes work a bit differently. The `value` attribute of an `<input>` element, for example, isn't reflected in the rendered HTML. Suppose that you have the HTML

```
<input type="text" />
```

and programmatically set its value like so:

```
input.value = 'yolo'
```

You'll see the string `"yolo"` in the input, but the rendered HTML will be the same; no `value` attribute will be rendered. Even more interesting is the fact that you can add the attribute in the HTML markup:

```
<input type="text" value="yolo" />
```

The `"yolo"` string will appear in the input when it first renders, but if you type something different, the same value for the `value` attribute remains in the rendered HTML. You can read whatever was typed in the input by reading the `value` property of the input element. You can read more about this behavior in the HTML specification at http://mng.bz/yQ17.

---

Nevertheless, we'll handle two special attributes differently: `style` and `class`. We'll start by writing the `setAttributes()` function: the one used in listing 4.2 to set the attributes on the element node. The role of this function is to extract the attributes that require special handling (`style` and `class`) from the rest of the attributes and then call the `setStyle()` and `setClass()` functions to set those attributes. The rest of the attributes are passed to the `setAttribute()` function. You'll write the `setStyle()`, `setClass()`, and `setAttribute()` functions later. Start by creating the attributes.js file in the src/ directory and entering the code in the following listing.

Listing 4.3 Setting the attributes of an element node (attributes.js)

```
export function setAttributes(el, attrs) {
  const { class: className, style, ...otherAttrs } = attrs      ◁─┐ Splits the
                                                                   │ attributes
  if (className) {
    setClass(el, className)          ◁──────  Sets the class attribute
  }

  if (style) {
    Object.entries(style).forEach(([prop, value]) => {
      setStyle(el, prop, value)                                ◁─┐ Sets the style
    })                                                            │ attribute
  }

  for (const [name, value] of Object.entries(otherAttrs)) {
    setAttribute(el, name, value)                              ◁─┐ Sets the rest of
  }                                                               │ the attributes
}

// TODO: implement setClass

// TODO: implement setStyle

// TODO: implement setAttribute
```

Now you have the function that splits the attributes into ones that require special handling and the rest and then calls the appropriate functions to set them. The following sections discuss those functions separately.

### SETTING THE CLASS ATTRIBUTE

The setClass() function is in charge of setting the class attribute. Note that you've destructured the attrs property and aliased the class attribute to the className variable, as class is a reserved word in JavaScript. When you write HTML, you set the class attribute of an element node like this:

```
<div class="foo bar baz"></div>
```

In this case, the <div> element has three classes: foo, bar, and baz. Easy! But now comes the tricky part: a DOM element (an instance of the Element class; http://mng .bz/yZjq) doesn't have a class property. Instead, it has two properties, className (http://mng.bz/M9Gn) and classList (http://mng.bz/am2B), that are related to the class attribute.

The classList property returns an object—a DOMTokenList (http://mng.bz/ g7nE), to be specific—that comes in handy when you want to add, remove, or toggle classes on an element. A DOMTokenList object has an add() method (http://mng .bz/eE6v) that takes multiple class names and adds them to the element. If you had a <div> element like

```
<div></div>
```

and wanted to add the foo, bar, and baz classes to it, you could do it this way:

```
div.classList.add('foo', 'bar', 'baz')
```

This code would result in the following HTML:

```
<div class="foo bar baz"></div>
```

Next is the className property, a string that contains the value of the class attribute. Following the preceding example, if you want to add the same three classes to the <div> element, you could do it this way and get the same HTML:

```
div.className = 'foo bar baz'
```

You may want to set the class attribute both ways, depending on the situation. You should allow the developers who use your framework to set the class attribute either as a string or as an array of string items. So to add multiple classes to an element, a developer could define the following virtual node:

```
{
  type: DOM_TYPES.ELEMENT,
  tag: 'div',
  props: {
    class: ['foo', 'bar', 'baz']
  }
}
```

Alternatively, they could use a single string:

```
{
  type: DOM_TYPES.ELEMENT,
  tag: 'div',
  props: {
    class: 'foo bar baz'
  }
}
```

Both of these options should work. Thus, the setClass() function needs to distinguish between the two cases and handle them accordingly. With this fact in mind, write the following code in the attributes.js file:

```
function setClass(el, className) {
  el.className = ''                          ◁——— Clears the class attribute

  if (typeof className === 'string') {
    el.className = className                  ◁——— Class attribute as a string
  }

  if (Array.isArray(className)) {
    el.classList.add(...className)            ◁——— Class attribute as an array
  }
}
```

**SETTING THE STYLE ATTRIBUTE**

With the `setClass()` function out of the way, let's move to the `setStyle()` function, which is in charge of setting the `style` attribute of an element. The `style` property (http://mng.bz/p1e8) of an `HTMLElement` instance is a `CSSStyleDeclaration` object (http://mng.bz/OP0R). You can set the value of a CSS property by using conventional object notation, like this:

```
element.style.color = 'red'
element.style.fontFamily = 'Georgia'
```

Changing the `style` property key-value pairs of an `HTMLElement` instance is reflected in the value of the `style` attribute of the element. If the `element` in the preceding snippet were a paragraph (`<p>`), the resulting HTML would be

```
<p style="color: red; font-family: Georgia;"></p>
```

The `CSSStyleDeclaration` is converted to a `string` with a set of semicolon-separated key-value pairs. You can inspect this string representation of the `style` attribute by using the `cssText` property (http://mng.bz/YRBB) in the code:

```
element.style.cssText // 'color: red; font-family: Georgia;'
```

Using the `element` from the preceding snippet, you could remove the `color` style as follows:

```
element.style.color = null
element.style.cssText // 'font-family: Georgia;'
```

Now that you know how to work with the `style` property of an `HTMLElement` instance, write the `setStyle()` and `removeStyle()` functions. The first function takes an `HTMLElement` instance, the name of the style to set, and the value of the style, and it sets that style on the element. The second function takes an `HTMLElement` instance and the name of the style to remove, and it removes that style from the element. Inside the attributes.js file, write the following code:

```
export function setStyle(el, name, value) {
  el.style[name] = value
}

export function removeStyle(el, name) {
  el.style[name] = null
}
```

Note that you haven't used the `removeStyle()` function yet. The code you wrote before used only the `setStyle()` function. But because you'll need to remove styles later, now is a good time to write it.

You're almost done. You're missing only the `setAttributes()` function, which is in charge of setting the attributes other than `class` and `style`.

#### SETTING THE REST OF THE ATTRIBUTES

The `setAttribute()` function takes three arguments: an `HTMLElement` instance, the name of the attribute to set, and the value of the attribute. If the value of the attribute is `null`, the attribute is removed from the element. (Conventionally, setting a DOM element's property to `null` is the same as removing the attribute.) If the attribute is of the form `data-*`, the attribute is set using the `setAttribute()` function. Otherwise, the attribute is set to the given value using object notation (`object.key = value`). (In other words, the property of the DOM element is set to the given value, and the attribute in the HTML reflects that value.)

To remove an attribute, you want to both set it to `null` and remove it from the `attributes` object, using the `removeAttribute()` method. Inside the attributes.js file, write the following code:

```
export function setAttribute(el, name, value) {
  if (value == null) {
    removeAttribute(el, name)
  } else if (name.startsWith('data-')) {
    el.setAttribute(name, value)
  } else {
    el[name] = value
  }
}

export function removeAttribute(el, name) {
  el[name] = null
  el.removeAttribute(name)
}
```

With this last function, you're done implementing the `mountDOM()` function, which takes a virtual DOM and mounts it to the real DOM inside the passed-in parent element. Congratulations!

### 4.1.7 A mountDOM() example

Thanks to this function, you can define a view by using the virtual DOM representation of it and mount it to the real DOM. If you create a view like this,

```
const vdom = h('section', {} [
  h('h1', {}, ['My Blog']),
  h('p', {}, ['Welcome to my blog!'])
])

mountDOM(vdom, document.body)
```

the resulting HTML would be

```
<body>
  <section>
    <h1>My Blog</h1>
    <p>Welcome to my blog!</p>
```

```
  </section>
</body>
```

Now you want a function that, given a mounted virtual DOM, destroys it and removes it from the document. With this function, `destroyDOM()`, you'll be able to clear the document's body from the preceding example:

```
destroyDOM(vdom, document.body)
```

The work done by `mountDOM()` is undone by `destroyDOM()`. This code would make the document's body empty again:

```
<body></body>
```

---

**Exercise 4.2**

Using the `hFragment()`, `h()`, and `mountDOM()` functions, insert a new section below the headline of your local newspaper's website. The section should have a title, a paragraph, and a link to an article in Wikipedia. Be creative!

Find the solution at http://mng.bz/5oj8.

---

**Exercise 4.3**

Following up on exercise 4.2, inspect the virtual DOM tree in the browser's console. Check the `el` property of the fragment virtual node. What does it point to? What about the `el` property of the paragraph and link virtual nodes?

Find the solution at http://mng.bz/6ngp.

---

## 4.2   *Destroying the DOM*

Let's close this chapter by implementing the `destroyDOM()` function. Destroying the DOM is simpler than mounting it. Well, destroying anything is always simpler than creating it in the first place. Destroying the DOM is the process in which the HTML elements that the `mountDOM()` function created are removed from the document (figure 4.7).

To destroy the DOM associated with a virtual node, you have to take into account what type of node it is:

- *Text node*—Remove the text node from its parent element, using the `remove()` method.
- *Fragment node*—Remove each of its children from the parent element (which, if you recall, is referenced in the `el` property of the fragment virtual node).
- *Element node*—Do the two preceding things and remove the event listeners from the element.

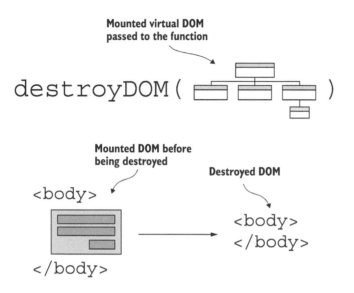

**Figure 4.7   Destroying the DOM**

In all cases, you want to remove the `el` property from the virtual node, and in the case of an element node, you also remove the `listeners` property so you can tell that the virtual node has been destroyed, allowing the garbage collector to free the memory of the HTML element. When a virtual node doesn't have an `el` property, you can safely assume that it's not mounted to the real DOM and therefore can't be destroyed. To handle these three cases, you need a `switch` statement that (depending on the `type` property of the virtual node) calls a different function.

You're ready to implement the `destroyDOM()` function. Create a new file inside the src/ directory called destroy-dom.js, and enter the code shown in the following listing.

**Listing 4.4   Destroying the virtual DOM (destroy-dom.js)**

```
import { removeEventListeners } from './events'
import { DOM_TYPES } from './h'

export function destroyDOM(vdom) {
  const { type } = vdom

  switch (type) {
    case DOM_TYPES.TEXT: {
      removeTextNode(vdom)
      break
    }

    case DOM_TYPES.ELEMENT: {
      removeElementNode(vdom)
      break
    }
```

```
      case DOM_TYPES.FRAGMENT: {
        removeFragmentNodes(vdom)
        break
      }

      default: {
        throw new Error(`Can't destroy DOM of type: ${type}`)
      }
    }

    delete vdom.el
  }

  // TODO: implement removeTextNode()

  // TODO: implement removeElementNode()

  // TODO: implement removeFragmentNodes()
```

You've written the algorithm for destroying the DOM associated with a passed-in virtual node: vdom. You've handled each type of virtual node separately; you'll need to write the missing functions in a minute. Finally, you've deleted the el property from the virtual node. Figure 4.8 depicts this process.

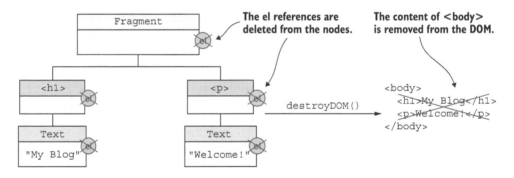

**Figure 4.8** Removing the el references from the virtual nodes

You've imported the removeEventListeners() function from the events.js file, but you haven't implemented that one yet. You will soon. Let's start with the code for destroying a text node.

### 4.2.1 Destroying a text node

Destroying a text node is the simplest case:

```
function removeTextNode(vdom) {
  const { el } = vdom
  el.remove()
}
```

### 4.2.2   Destroying an element

The code for destroying an element is a bit more interesting. To destroy an element, start by removing it from the DOM, similar to what you did with a text node. Then recursively destroy the children of the element by calling the destroyDOM() function for each of them. Finally, remove the event listeners from the element and delete the listeners property from the virtual node. First, implement the removeElement-Node() function in the destroy-dom.js file:

```
function removeElementNode(vdom) {
  const { el, children, listeners } = vdom

  el.remove()
  children.forEach(destroyDOM)

  if (listeners) {
    removeEventListeners(listeners, el)
    delete vdom.listeners
  }
}
```

Here's where you used the missing removeEventListeners() function to remove the event listeners from the element. You also deleted the listeners property from the virtual node.

Now write the removeEventListeners() function. This function, given an object of event names and event handlers, removes the event listeners from the element. Recall that the listeners property of the virtual node is an object that maps event names to event handlers. The following could be an example listeners object for a virtual node representing a button:

```
{
  mouseover: () => { ... },
  click: () => { ... },
  dblclick: () => { ... }
}
```

In this example, you'd have three event handlers to remove. For each of them, call the Element object's removeEventListener() method (http://mng.bz/z0WB), which it inherits from the EventTarget interface:

```
el.removeEventListener('mouseover', listeners['mouseover'])
el.removeEventListener('click', listeners['click'])
el.removeEventListener('dblclick', listeners['dblclick'])
```

Open the events.js file, and fill in the missing code:

```
export function removeEventListeners(listeners = {}, el) {
  Object.entries(listeners).forEach(([eventName, handler]) => {
    el.removeEventListener(eventName, handler)
  })
}
```

Great! You're missing only the code for destroying a fragment.

### 4.2.3 *Destroying a fragment*

Destroying a fragment is easy: simply call the `destroyDOM()` function for each of its children. But you have to be careful not to remove the `el` referenced in the fragment's virtual node from the DOM; that `el` references the element where the fragment children are mounted, not the fragment itself. If the fragment children were mounted inside the `<body>` and you called the `remove()` method on the element, you'd remove the whole document from the DOM. That's not what you want to do—or do you? Figure 4.9 shows the problem more graphically.

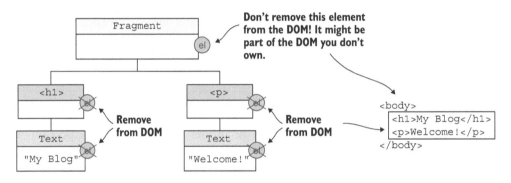

**Figure 4.9   When you're destroying a fragment, don't remove its referenced element from the DOM. That element might be the `<body>` or some other element that you didn't create and therefore don't own.**

The implementation of the `removeFragmentNodes()` is simple:

```
function removeFragmentNodes(vdom) {
  const { children } = vdom
  children.forEach(destroyDOM)
}
```

That's it! You've implemented the `mountDOM()` and `destroyDOM()` functions. These functions, together with the state management system that you'll implement in chapter 5, will be the core of the first version of your framework. You'll use the framework to refactor the TODOs application.

---

**Exercise 4.4**

Using the `destroyDOM()` function, remove the section that you added to your local newspaper's website (exercise 4.2) from the DOM. Make sure that the fragment's referenced element isn't removed from the DOM because it was created by the newspaper's website, not by you. Then check the `vdom` tree you used to create the section and make sure that the `el` property has been removed from all the virtual nodes.

Find the solution at http://mng.bz/orpy.

The first version won't be very sophisticated—it'll destroy the entire DOM using `destroyDOM()` and mount it from scratch using `mountDOM()` every time the state changes—but it will be a great starting point. By the end of the next chapter, you'll have a working framework, so I hope you're excited. See you in chapter 5!

## Summary

- Mounting a virtual DOM means creating the DOM nodes that represent each virtual node in the tree and inserting them into the DOM, inside a parent element.
- Destroying a virtual DOM means removing the DOM nodes created from it, making sure to remove the event listeners from the DOM nodes as well.

# 5

# State management and the application's lifecycle

**This chapter covers**

- Understanding state management
- Implementing a state management solution
- Mapping JavaScript events to commands that change the state
- Updating the state using reducer functions
- Re-rendering the view when the state changes

Some time ago, I went to the coast in the south of Spain, to a small village in Cadiz. One restaurant was so popular that it ran out of food quickly; it served a limited quantity of the dishes on the menu. As waiters took orders from customers, they updated a chalkboard with the number of servings the restaurant had left, and when no more of a particular dish was left, they crossed it out. The customers could easily tell what they could order by looking at the chalkboard. But from time to time, due to the workload, a waiter might forget to update the chalkboard, and customers would find out that the dish they'd been waiting in line so long to order was sold out. You can picture the drama. Clearly, it was important for the restaurant to have an updated chalkboard that matched the remaining servings of each dish.

To have a working framework, you're missing a key piece that does a job similar to that of a waiter in that restaurant: a *state manager*. In the restaurant, a waiter is in charge of keeping the chalkboard in sync with the state of the restaurant: the number of servings of each dish still available. In a frontend application, the state changes as the user interacts with it, and the view needs to be updated to reflect those changes. The state manager keeps the application's state in sync with the view, responding to user input by modifying the state accordingly and notifying the renderer when the state has changed. The *renderer* is the entity in your framework that takes the virtual Document Object Model (DOM) and mounts it into the browser's document.

In this chapter, you'll implement both the renderer—using the `mountDOM()` and `destroyDOM()` functions from chapter 4—and the state manager entities, and you'll learn how they communicate. By the end of the chapter, you'll have your first version of the framework, the architecture of which (figure 5.1) is the state manager and renderer glued together. (The state manager is displayed with a question mark in the figure because you'll discover how it works in this chapter.)

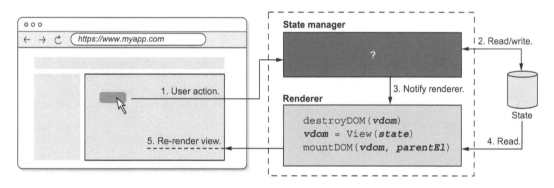

**Figure 5.1 Your first framework is a state manager and a renderer glued together.**

The framework you'll have at the end of the chapter is rudimentary. To ensure that the view reflects the current state, its renderer destroys and mounts the DOM every time the state changes. As you can see in figure 5.1, the renderer draws the view in a three-step process:

1  Destroy the current DOM (calling `destroyDOM()`).
2  Produce the virtual DOM representing the view given the current state by calling the `View()` function, the top-level component.
3  Mount the virtual DOM into the real DOM by calling `mountDOM()`.

Destroying and mounting the DOM from scratch is far from ideal, and we'll discuss why in chapter 7. In any case, re-rendering the entire application is a good starting point. You'll improve the rendering mechanism in chapters 7 and 8, where (thanks to the reconciliation algorithm) your framework can update the DOM more efficiently. You have to walk before you can run, they say.

How does implementing a renderer and state manager fit into the bigger picture of your framework? Let's take a step back. If you recall from chapter 1, when the browser loads an application, the framework code renders the application's view (step 5 in figure 5.2, reproduced from chapter 1 for convenience). The renderer can do this job alone; the state manager doesn't intervene. (It might, but let's leave that case for now.)

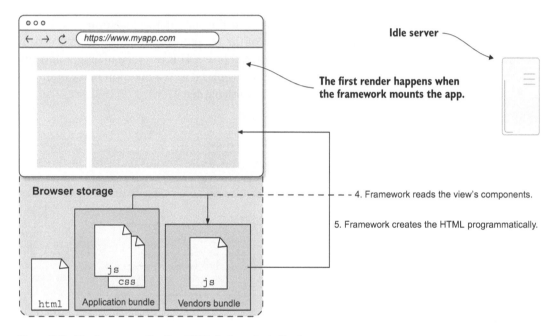

**Figure 5.2   Single-page application (SPA) first render in the browser**

When the user interacts with the application (step 6 in figure 5.3, reproduced from chapter 1), the state manager updates the state and notifies the renderer to re-render the view. This dynamic is a bit more complex and requires the state manager and renderer to work together.

The state manager somehow needs to be aware of the events that the user interactions can trigger, such as clicking a button or typing in an input field, and it must know what to do with the state when those events take place. In a way, it needs to know everything the user might do with the application beforehand and how those actions will affect the state.

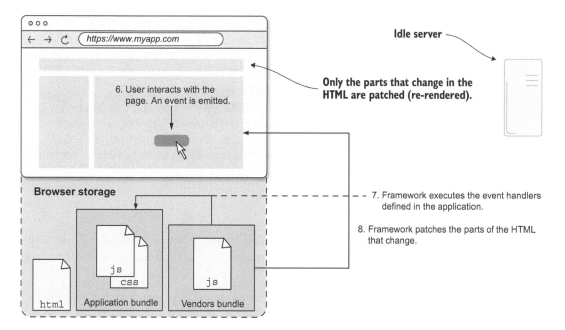

**Figure 5.3  SPA responding to events**

In this chapter, you'll learn how to handle state changes in response to user input. With the big picture in mind, let's start working on the state manager.

> **NOTE**  You can find all the listings in this chapter in the listings/ch05 directory of the book's repository (http://mng.bz/qjKw). The code you write in this chapter is for the framework's first version, which you'll publish in chapter 6. Therefore, the code in this chapter can be checked out from the ch6 label (http://mng.bz/7vo9): `$ git switch --detach ch6`.

## Code catch-up

In chapter 4, you implemented the `mountDOM()` and `destroyDOM()` functions.

`mountDOM()` takes a virtual DOM tree and a parent DOM element, and mounts the virtual DOM into the parent element. Its implementation is broken into a few subfunctions:

- `createTextNode()`—To create HTML text nodes.
- `createElementNode()`—To create HTML element nodes. This function uses two subfunctions: `addEventListeners()` and `setAttributes()`.
- `createFragmentNodes()`—To create lists of nodes that have a common parent.

**(continued)**

destroyDOM() takes a DOM element and removes it from the DOM. Its implementation is also broken down into a few subfunctions:

- removeTextNode()—To remove HTML text nodes.
- removeElementNode()—To remove HTML element nodes. This function uses another function to remove the element's event listeners: removeEventListeners().
- removeFragmentNodes()—To remove lists of nodes that have a common parent.

## 5.1    The state manager

Let's study the chronology of everything that happens between the user's interacting with the application and the view's being updated. In the following list, the actor goes first, followed by the action it performs:

1  *The user*—Interacts with the application's view (clicks a button, for example).
2  *The browser*—Dispatches a native JavaScript event (http://mng.bz/mjYr), such as MouseEvent (http://mng.bz/5o5B) or KeyboardEvent (http://mng.bz/6n6o).
3  *The application developer*—Programmed the framework to know how to update the state for each event.
4  *The framework's state manager*—Updates the state according to the application developer's instructions.
5  *The framework's state manager*—Notifies the renderer that the state has changed.
6  *The framework's renderer*—Re-renders the view with the new state.

This list isn't exactly a chronology because the application developer doesn't intervene between the user's interaction with the application and the state manager's update of the state. Instead, the developer gives instructions on updating the state during application development (not at run time). Still, this list is a good way to describe the flow of events. Figure 5.4 illustrates this pseudochronology in the architectural diagram of the framework I presented in figure 5.1.

This pseudochronology gives rise to two key questions: how does the application developer instruct the framework how to update the state when a particular event is dispatched, and how does the state manager execute those instructions? The answers to both questions are the keys to understanding the state manager.

### 5.1.1    From JavaScript events to application domain commands

The first thing you need to notice is that the JavaScript events dispatched by the browser don't have a concrete meaning in the application domain on their own. The user clicked this button; so what? The application developer is the one who translates

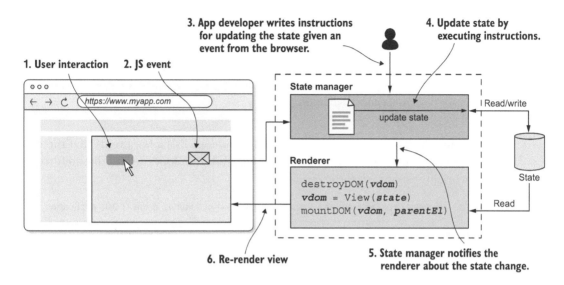

**Figure 5.4   The pseudochronology of events in a frontend application**

user actions into something meaningful for the application. Think about the TODOs application:

- When the user clicked the *Add* button or pressed the *Enter* key, they wanted to add a new TODO item to the list.
- "*Adding a to-do*" is framed in the language of the application, whereas "*clicking a button*" is a generic thing to do. (You click buttons in all sorts of applications, but that action translates to *adding a to-do* only in the TODOs application.)

If the application developer wants to update the state when a particular event is dispatched, first they need to determine what that event means in terms of the application domain. Then the developer maps the event to a command that the framework can understand. A *command* is a request to do something, as opposed to an *event*, which is a notification of something that has happened. These commands ask the framework to update the state; they are expressed in the domain language of the application.

### Events vs. commands

An *event* is a notification of something that has happened. "A button was clicked," "A key was pressed," and "A network request was completed" are examples of events. Events don't ask the framework or application to do anything; they're simply notifications with some additional information. Event names are usually framed in past tense: `'button-clicked'`, `'key-pressed'`, `'network-request-completed'`, and so on.

**(continued)**

A *command* is a request to do something in a particular context. "Add todo," "Edit todo," and "Remove todo" are three examples of commands. Commands are written in imperative tense because they're requests to do something: `'add-todo'`, `'edit-todo'`, `'remove-todo'`, and so on.

Continuing the TODOs application example, table 5.1 lists a few events that the user can trigger and the commands that the application developer would dispatch to the framework in response to those events.

**Table 5.1    Mapping between browser events and application commands in the TODOs application**

| Browser event | Command | Explanation |
|---|---|---|
| Click the Add button. | `add-todo` | Clicking the *Add* button adds a new to-do item to the list. |
| Press the Enter key (while the input field is focused). | `add-todo` | Pressing the *Enter* key adds a new to-do item to the list. |
| Click the Done button. | `remove-todo` | Clicking the *Done* button marks the to-do item as done, removing it from the list. |
| Double-click a to-do item. | `start-editing-todo` | Double-clicking a *to-do* item sets the to-do item in edit mode. |

In figure 5.5, you see the same mapping. In it, you can establish a link between the browser events and the application commands, which the application developer dispatched to the framework by using the `dispatch()` function. You'll learn more about this function in section 5.1.3.

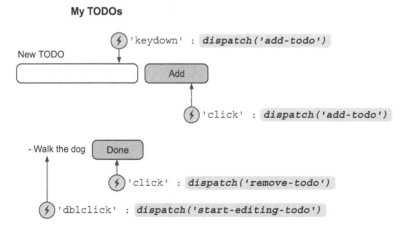

**Figure 5.5    The mapping between browser events and application commands**

How does this figure answer the preceding questions? After the application domain commands are identified, the application developer can supply functions that update the state as a response to those commands. The state manager executes those functions to update the state. In section 5.1.2, we'll look into what these functions are and how they're executed.

> ### Exercise 5.1
> Imagine an application that consists of a counter and two buttons: one to increment the counter and another one to decrement it. Its HTML could look like this:
>
> ```
> <button>-</button>
> 0
> <button>+</button>
> ```
>
> When each button is clicked, what commands would you dispatch to the framework? Can you draw a diagram similar to the one in figure 5.5 that maps browser events to application commands?
>
> Find the solution at http://mng.bz/n1MV.

### 5.1.2 The reducer functions

*Reducer* functions can be implemented in a few ways. But if we decide to stick to the functional programming principles of using pure functions and making data immutable, instead of updating the state by mutating it, these functions should create a new one (figure 5.6).

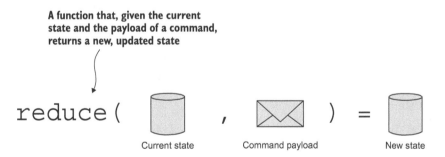

Figure 5.6 A reducer function takes the current state and a payload and returns a new state.

> **NOTE** This process may sound familiar if you've used Redux (https://redux .js.org): these functions are the reducers. (The term *reducer* comes from the *reduce* function in functional programming.) A *reducer*, in our context, is a function that takes the current state and a payload (the command's data) and returns a new updated state. These functions never mutate the state that's

passed to them (mutation would be a side effect, so the function wouldn't be pure); instead, they create a new state.

Consider an example based on the TODOs application. To create a new version of the state when the user removes a to-do item from the list (recall from chapter 2 that the state was the list of to-dos), the reducer function associated with this `'remove-todo'` command would look like this:

```
function removeTodo(state, todoIndex) {
  return state.toSpliced(todoIndex, 1)
}
```

If we had the state

```
let todos = ['Walk the dog', 'Water the plants', 'Sand the chairs']
```

and wanted to remove the to-do item at index 1, we would compute the new state by using the `removeTodo()` reducer, as follows:

```
todos = removeTodo(todos, 1)
// todos = ['Walk the dog', 'Sand the chairs']
```

In this case, the payload associated with the `'remove-todo'` command is the index of the to-do item to remove. Note that the original array is not mutated; a new one is created instead. The `toSpliced()` method of an array returns a new array.

---

### Exercise 5.2: Challenge

Suppose that you're building a tic-tac-toe game (https://playtictactoe.org) as a web application. You have a 3x3 grid of squares, and when one of the two players clicks one of them, you want to mark it with an x (cross) or an o (nought). The player who places three of their marks in a horizontal, vertical, or diagonal row wins the game.

How would you design the state of the application? What commands would you dispatch to the framework in response to the user's clicking a square? What reducer functions would you implement to update the state? Here are some tips to help you get started:

- The state needs to have at least four pieces of information: the grid of squares, the player whose turn it is, the winner of the game (if any), and whether the game ended in a draw.
- To design what commands are needed, think about what actions the user can perform in the application.
- You can deduce the reducers from the commands, as well as how the state needs to be updated in response to them.

Find the solution at http://mng.bz/vPzm.

Let's do a quick recap. We've seen that the application developer translates browser events into application domain commands and that the state manager executes the reducer functions associated with those commands to update the state. But how does the state manager know which reducer function to execute when a command is dispatched? Something has to map the commands to the reducer functions. We'll call this mechanism a *dispatcher*; it's the state manager's central piece.

### 5.1.3  The dispatcher

The association between commands and reducer functions is performed by an entity we'll call the *dispatcher*. The name reflects the fact that this entity is responsible for dispatching the commands to the functions that handle the command—that is, for executing the corresponding handler functions in response to commands. To do this, the application developer must specify which handler function (or functions) the system should execute in response to each command.

These command handler functions are consumers. *Consumer* is the technical term for a function that accepts a single parameter—the command's payload, in this case—and returns no value, as figure 5.7 shows.

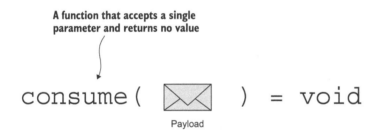

**Figure 5.7   A consumer function takes a single parameter and returns no value.**

A consumer that handles a command can easily wrap a reducer function, as the following example shows:

```
function removeTodoHandler(todoIndex) {
  // Calls the removeTodo() reducer function to update the state.
  state = removeTodo(state, todoIndex)
}
```

As you can see, the command-handler function that removes a to-do from the list receives the to-do index as its single parameter and then calls the `removeTodo()` reducer function to update the state. The handler simply wraps the reducer function; it's the dispatcher's responsibility to execute the handler function in response to the `'remove-todo'` command. But how do you tell the dispatcher which handler function to execute in response to a command?

**ASSIGNING HANDLERS TO COMMANDS**

Your dispatcher needs to have a subscribe() method that registers a consumer function—the handler—to respond to commands with a given name. The same way that you can register a handler for a command, you can unregister it when it doesn't need to be executed anymore (because the relevant view has been removed from the DOM, for example). To accomplish this task, the subscribe() method should return a function that can be called to unregister the handler.

Your dispatcher also needs to have a dispatch() method that executes the handler functions associated with a command. Figure 5.8 shows how the dispatcher works.

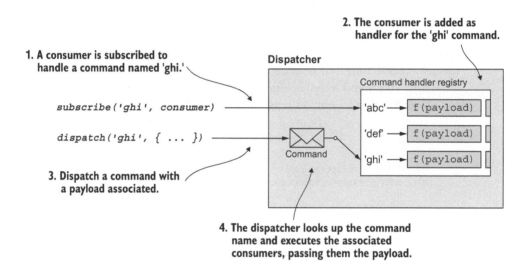

**Figure 5.8   The dispatcher's** subscribe() **method registers handlers to respond to commands with a given name, and** dispatch() **executes the handlers associated with a command.**

It's time to implement the dispatcher. Create a new file called dispatcher.js in the src/ directory. Your runtime/src/ directory should look like this (new file in bold):

```
src/
├── utils/
│    └── arrays.js
├── attributes.js
├── destroy-dom.js
├── dispatcher.js
├── events.js
├── h.js
├── index.js
└── mount-dom.js
```

Now write the code in listing 5.1.

**NOTE** The hash (#) in front of the variable name is the ES2020 way to make the variable private inside a class. Starting with ES2020, any variable or method that starts with a hash is private and can be accessed only from within the class.

---

**Listing 5.1   Registering handlers to respond to commands (dispatcher.js)**

```
export class Dispatcher {
  #subs = new Map()
                                        Creates the array of subscriptions
  subscribe(commandName, handler) {     if it doesn't exist for a given
    if (!this.#subs.has(commandName)) { command name
      this.#subs.set(commandName, [])
    }

    const handlers = this.#subs.get(commandName)
    if (handlers.includes(handler)) {    Checks whether the
      return () => {}                    handler is registered
    }

    handlers.push(handler)         Registers the handler

    return () => {
      const idx = handlers.indexOf(handler)   Returns a function to
      handlers.splice(idx, 1)                 unregister the handler
    }
  }
}
```

The `Dispatcher` is a class with a private variable called `subs` (short for *subscriptions*): a JavaScript map (http://mng.bz/orzd) to store the registered handlers by event name. Note that more than one handler can be registered for the same command name.

The `subscribe()` method takes a command name and a handler function as parameters, checks for an entry in `subs` for that command name, and creates an entry with an empty array if one doesn't exist. Then it appends the handler to the array in case it wasn't already registered. If the handler was already registered, you simply return a function that does nothing because there's nothing to unregister.

If the handler function was registered, the `subscribe()` method returns a function that removes the handler from the corresponding array of handlers, so it's never notified again. First, you look for the index of the handler in the array; then you call its `splice()` method to remove the element at that index. Note that the index lookup happens only when the returned function—the unregistering function—is called. This detail is very important because if you did the lookup outside that function—inside the `subscribe()` method body—the index that you'd get might not be valid by the time you want to unregister the handler. The array might have changed in the meantime.

**WARNING** When the handler is already registered, instead of returning an empty function, you may be tempted to return a function that unregisters the existing handler. But returning an empty function is a better idea because it prevents the side effects that result when a developer inadvertently calls the returned function twice—once for each time they called `subscribe()` using the same handler. In this case, when the same handler is unregistered for the second time, `indexOf()` returns `-1` because the handler isn't in the array anymore. Then the `splice()` function is called with an index of `-1`, which removes the last handler in the array—not what you want. This *silent failure* (something going wrong without throwing an exception) is something you want to avoid at all costs, as debugging these kinds of problems can be a nightmare.

Now that you've implemented the dispatcher's first method, `subscribe()`, how does the dispatcher tell the renderer about state changes? We'll try to find the answer in the next section.

### NOTIFYING THE RENDERER ABOUT STATE CHANGES

At the beginning of this chapter, I said that the state manager is in charge of keeping the state in sync with the views. It does so by notifying the renderer about state changes so that the renderer can update the views accordingly. Then how does the dispatcher notify the renderer?

You know that the state can change only in response to commands. A command triggers the execution of one or more handler functions, which execute reducers, which in turn update the state. Therefore, the best time to notify the renderer about state changes is after the handlers for a given command have been executed. You should allow the dispatcher to register special handler functions (we'll call them *after-command handlers*) that are executed after the handlers for any dispatched command have been executed. The framework uses these handlers to notify the renderer about potential state changes so that it can update the view.

Figure 5.9 shows the `afterEveryCommand()` method as part of the dispatcher's architecture. The functions registered with this method are called after every command is handled; you can use them to notify the renderer about state changes.

In the following listing, write the code in bold inside the `Dispatcher` class to add the `afterEveryCommand()` method.

**Listing 5.2    Registering functions to run after commands (dispatcher.js)**

```
export class Dispatcher {
  #subs = new Map()
  #afterHandlers = []

  // --snip-- //

  afterEveryCommand(handler) {
    this.#afterHandlers.push(handler)              ⟵— Registers the handler

    return () => {                                 ⟵┐ Returns a function to
      const idx = this.#afterHandlers.indexOf(handler)  │ unregister the handler
      this.#afterHandlers.splice(idx, 1)
    }
  }
}
```

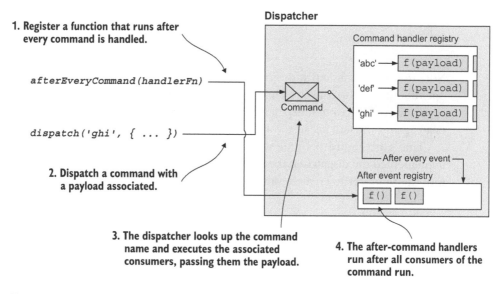

**Figure 5.9**   The dispatcher's `afterEveryCommand()` method registers handlers to run after every command is handled.

This method is similar to the `subscribe()` method except that it doesn't take a command name as a parameter: these handlers are called for all dispatched commands. This time, we're not checking for duplicates; we're allowing the same handler to be registered multiple times. After-command handlers don't modify the state; they're a notification mechanism, so delivering notifications of the same event multiple times might be a valid use case. The last part that's missing is the `dispatch()` method, which dispatches a command and calls all the registered handlers.

**DISPATCHING COMMANDS**

A dispatcher wouldn't be much of a dispatcher if it didn't have a `dispatch()` method, would it? This method takes two parameters: the name of the command to dispatch and its payload. It looks up the handlers registered for the given command name and calls them one by one, in order, passing them the command's payload as a parameter. Last, it runs the after-command handlers, as in the following listing.

**Listing 5.3   Dispatching a command given its name and payload (dispatcher.js)**

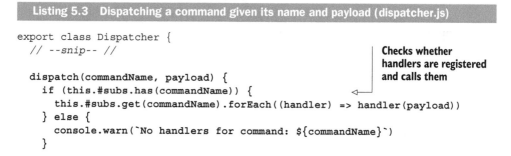

```
    this.#afterHandlers.forEach((handler) => handler())
  }
}
```
⟵┐ **Runs the**
   **after-command**
   **handlers**

Note that if a command with no handlers associated is dispatched, we warn the developer about it in the console. This approach will be handy when you write your example applications. It's easy to misspell a command name without noticing and then bang your head against the wall because you don't understand why your code isn't working.

That's it! Figure 5.10 shows the framework's first-version architecture. You've implemented the dispatcher: the state manager. Now it's time to integrate the dispatcher with the renderer to create a working framework.

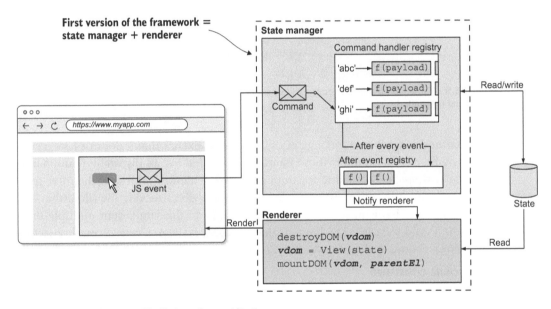

**Figure 5.10   The framework's first-version architecture**

Before integrating the dispatcher with the rendering system, make sure that the code you wrote matches the one in listing 5.4 in section 5.1.4. If you need to copy and paste to compare, you can find the complete listing in the book's GitHub repository; see appendix A for more information.

### 5.1.4 Result

For your reference, the following listing shows the complete `Dispatcher` class implementation.

> **Listing 5.4 Complete `Dispatcher` implementation (dispatcher.js)**

```
export class Dispatcher {
  #subs = new Map()
  #afterHandlers = []

  subscribe(commandName, handler) {
    if (!this.#subs.has(commandName)) {
      this.#subs.set(commandName, [])
    }

    const handlers = this.#subs.get(commandName)
    if (handlers.includes(handler)) {
      return () => {}
    }

    handlers.push(handler)

    return () => {
      const idx = handlers.indexOf(handler)
      handlers.splice(idx, 1)
    }
  }

  afterEveryCommand(handler) {
    this.#afterHandlers.push(handler)

    return () => {
      const idx = this.#afterHandlers.indexOf(handler)
      this.#afterHandlers.splice(idx, 1)
    }
  }

  dispatch(commandName, payload) {
    if (this.#subs.has(commandName)) {
      this.#subs.get(commandName).forEach((handler) => handler(payload))
    } else {
      console.warn(`No handlers for command: ${commandName}`)
    }

    this.#afterHandlers.forEach((handler) => handler())
  }
}
```

Make sure that you wrote the code correctly and that your implementation matches the one in listing 5.4. If so, let's move on to the next section.

**Exercise 5.3**

To put your newly implemented `Dispatcher` class to use, paste the code in listing 5.4 into the browser's console. (Remember to leave out the `export` statement.) Then create a new instance of the `Dispatcher` class and register a handler for a command called `'greet'`. This command's payload should be a string with the name of the person to greet. When the command is dispatched, the handler should log a greeting to the console: `'Hello, <name>!'` (where `<name>` is the name of the person in the payload). You also want to have an after-command handler that logs a message to the console: `Done greeting!`

When the command `'greet'` is dispatched with the payload `'John'`, for example,

```
dispatcher.dispatch('greet', 'John')
```

the console should log the following:

```
Hello, John!
Done greeting!
```

Find the solution at http://mng.bz/46Z5.

## 5.2 Assembling the state manager into the framework

Merriam-Webster defines *assemble* as bringing together (as in a particular place or for a particular purpose). To assemble the state manager and renderer, you need a particular place to bring them together. This place is an object that contains and connects them so that they can communicate. If you think about it, this object represents the running application that uses your framework, so we can refer to it as the *application instance*. Let's think about how you want developers to create an application instance in your framework.

### 5.2.1 The application instance

The *application instance* is the object that manages the lifecycle of the application. It manages the state, renders the views, and updates the state in response to user input. Developers need to pass three things to pass to the application instance:

- The initial state of the application
- The reducers that update the state in response to commands
- The top-level component of the application

Your framework can take care of the rest: instantiating a renderer and a state manager and wiring them together. (Remember that your initial version of the framework won't be much more than these two things glued together.) The application instance can expose a `mount()` method that takes a DOM element as a parameter, mounts the application in it, and kicks off the application's lifecycle. From this point on, the application instance is in charge of keeping the state in sync with the views, like the waiters in the restaurant at the beginning of this chapter.

This process may sound a bit abstract at the moment, but it'll become clear when you rewrite the TODO application by using your framework. For now, bear with me. Let's move on to implementing the application instance, starting with the renderer.

### 5.2.2 *The application instance's renderer*

First, implement a function called `createApp()` that returns an object with a single method, `mount()`, which takes a DOM element as a parameter and mounts the application in it. This object is the application instance inside which you implement the renderer and the state manager.

The `createApp()` function takes an object with two properties: `state` and `view`. The `state` property is the initial state of the application, and the `view` property is the top-level component of the application. You'll add the reducers later.

You need two variables in the closure of the `createApp()` function: `parentEl` and `vdom`. These variables keep track of the DOM element where the application is mounted and the virtual DOM tree of the previous view, respectively. Both should be initialized to `null` because the application hasn't been mounted yet.

Then comes the renderer, which is implemented as a function: `renderApp()`. This function, as previously discussed, renders the view by destroying the current DOM tree (if one exists) and then mounting the new one. At this point, this function is called only once: when the application is mounted by the `mount()` method, the only method exposed to the developer. It takes a DOM element as a parameter and mounts the application in it. Note that you save the DOM element in the `parentEl` variable so that you can use it later to unmount the application.

Create a new file inside the src/ directory called app.js, and write the code in the following listing. The listing shows the implementation of the `createApp()` function that returns the application instance.

---

**Listing 5.5  The application instance with its renderer (app.js)**

```
import { destroyDOM } from './destroy-dom'
import { mountDOM } from './mount-dom'                    ◁─┐ The function
                                                            that creates the
export function createApp({ state, view }) {           ◁─┘ application object
  let parentEl = null
  let vdom = null

  function renderApp() {
    if (vdom) {                         ◁─┐ If a previous view
      destroyDOM(vdom)                     exists, unmounts it
    }

    vdom = view(state)                  ◁─┐ Mounts the
    mountDOM(vdom, parentEl)               new view
  }
```

```
    return {
      mount(_parentEl) {              ◁────┐ Method to mount
        parentEl = _parentEl                │ the application in
        renderApp()                         │ the DOM
      },
    }
}
```

Okay, you've got the renderer; you could already render an application in the browser, but it wouldn't respond to user input. For that purpose, you need the state manager, which tells the renderer to re-render the application when the state changes.

### 5.2.3 The application instance's state manager

The state manager is a bit more complex than a function. The `Dispatcher` class that you implemented in section 5.2.2 is the central piece of the state manager, but you have to hook some things up. Most notably, you need to wrap the state reducers—given by the developer—in a consumer function that the dispatcher will call every time a command is dispatched. Let's see how this is done.

Write the code in bold in the following listing. Note that part of the code you wrote earlier is omitted for clarity.

---

**Listing 5.6   Adding the state manager to the application instance (app.js)**

```
import { destroyDOM } from './destroy-dom'
import { Dispatcher } from './dispatcher'
import { mountDOM } from './mount-dom'

export function createApp({ state, view, reducers = {} }) {
  let parentEl = null                              Re-renders the
  let vdom = null                                  application after
                                                   every command
  const dispatcher = new Dispatcher()
  const subscriptions = [dispatcher.afterEveryCommand(renderApp)]  ◁────

  for (const actionName in reducers) {
    const reducer = reducers[actionName]

    const subs = dispatcher.subscribe(actionName, (payload) => {   ◁────┐
      state = reducer(state, payload)                                   │ Updates the
    })                                                                  │ state calling the
    subscriptions.push(subs)  ◁────┐ Adds each command                 │ reducer function
  }                                 │ subscription to the
  // --snip-- //                    │ subscriptions array
}
```

---

Let's unpack what you've done here. First, you added a `reducers` property to the `createApp()` function parameter. This property is an object that maps command names to reducer functions—functions that take the current state and the command's payload and return a new state.

Next, you created an instance of the `Dispatcher` class and saved it in the `dispatcher` variable. The next line is crucial: you subscribed the `renderApp()` function to be an after-command handler so that the application is re-rendered after every command is handled. Not every command necessarily changes the state, but you don't know in advance, so you have to re-render the application after every command.

> **NOTE** To avoid re-rendering the application when the state didn't change, you could compare the state before and after the command was handled. This comparison can become expensive if the state is a heavy and deeply nested object and the commands are frequent. In chapters 7 and 8, you'll improve the performance of the renderer by patching the DOM only where necessary, so re-rendering the application will be a reasonably fast operation. Not checking whether the state changed is a tradeoff we're making to keep the code simple.

Can you see now why after-command handlers are a good idea? The `afterEvery-Command()` function returns a function that unsubscribes the handler, so you saved it in the `subscriptions` array—an array that you initialized to have this function as its first element.

Next, you iterated the `reducers` object, wrapped each of the reducers inside a handler function that calls the reducer and updates the state, and subscribed that handler to the dispatcher. You were careful to save the subscription functions in the `subscriptions` array so that you can unsubscribe them when the application is unmounted.

Great—you've got the state manager hooked up to the renderer. But we haven't talked about one thing yet: how the components dispatch commands.

### 5.2.4 *Components dispatching commands*

If you recall from chapter 3, your virtual DOM implementation allows you to attach event listeners to DOM elements:

```
h(
  'button',
  { on: { click: () => { ... } } },
  ['Click me']
)
```

If you want to dispatch commands from within those event listeners, you need to pass the dispatcher to the components. In a way, you can imagine the dispatcher as being a remote control; each button dispatches a command whose handler function can modify the state of the application (figure 5.11). By passing the dispatcher to the components, you give it the capability to dispatch commands in response to user input.

The dispatcher in the application instance has the command handlers that the developer has provided. The component can dispatch those commands using the `dispatch()`

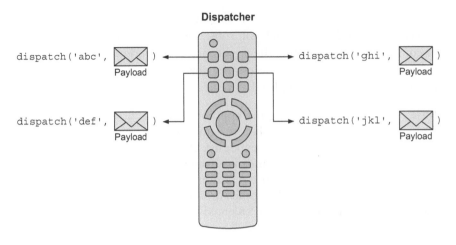

**Figure 5.11   The dispatcher is like a remote control: each button dispatches a command whose handler function can modify the state of the application.**

method of the dispatcher. To remove a to-do item from the list, for example, the component can dispatch a `remove-todo` command this way:

```
h(
  'button',
  {
    on: {
      click: () => dispatcher.dispatch('remove-todo', todoIdx)
    }
  },
  ['Done']
)
```

To allow the components to dispatch commands, change your code in app.js, adding the code shown in bold in the following listing.

**Listing 5.7   Allowing components to dispatch commands (app.js)**

```
export function createApp({ state, view, reducers = {} }) {
  let parentEl = null
  let vdom = null

  const dispatcher = new Dispatcher()
  const subscriptions = [dispatcher.afterEveryCommand(renderApp)]

  function emit(eventName, payload) {
    dispatcher.dispatch(eventName, payload)
  }

  // --snip-- //
```

```
function renderApp() {
  if (vdom) {
    destroyDOM(vdom)
  }

  vdom = view(state, emit)
  mountDOM(vdom, parentEl)
}

// --snip-- //
}
```

To allow components to dispatch commands more conveniently, you implemented an
`emit()` function. So instead of writing `dispatcher.dispatch()`, you can write `emit()`
inside the components, which is a bit more concise. Then you passed the `emit()` function to the components as a second argument.

Bear in mind that from now on, components will receive two arguments: the state
and the `emit()` function. If a component doesn't need to dispatch commands, it can
ignore the second argument.

You're almost done! There's one thing left to do: unmount the application.

### 5.2.5   *Unmounting the application*

When an application instance is created, the state reducers are subscribed to the dispatcher, and the `renderApp()` function is subscribed to the dispatcher as an after-command handler. When the application is unmounted, apart from destroying the view, you
need to unsubscribe the reducers and the `renderApp()` function from the dispatcher.
To clean up the subscriptions and destroy the view, you need to add an `unmount()`
method to the application instance, as shown in bold in the following listing.

> **Listing 5.8  Unmounting the application (app.js)**

```
export function createApp({ state, view, reducers = {} }) {
  let parentEl = null
  let vdom = null

  // --snip-- //

  return {
    mount(_parentEl) {
      parentEl = _parentEl
      renderApp()
    },

    unmount() {
      destroyDOM(vdom)
      vdom = null
      subscriptions.forEach((unsubscribe) => unsubscribe())
    },
  }
}
```

The unmount() method uses the destroyDOM() function from chapter 4 to destroy the view, sets the vdom property to null, and unsubscribes the reducers and the render-App() function from the dispatcher.

That's it! Now is a good time to review the code you wrote in app.js to make sure that you got it right.

### 5.2.6 Result

Your app.js should look like the code in the following listing.

**Listing 5.9  The application instance (app.js)**

```
import { destroyDOM } from './destroy-dom'
import { Dispatcher } from './dispatcher'
import { mountDOM } from './mount-dom'

export function createApp({ state, view, reducers = {} }) {
  let parentEl = null
  let vdom = null

  const dispatcher = new Dispatcher()
  const subscriptions = [dispatcher.afterEveryCommand(renderApp)]

  function emit(eventName, payload) {
    dispatcher.dispatch(eventName, payload)
  }

  for (const actionName in reducers) {
    const reducer = reducers[actionName]

    const subs = dispatcher.subscribe(actionName, (payload) => {
      state = reducer(state, payload)
    })
    subscriptions.push(subs)
  }

  function renderApp() {
    if (vdom) {
      destroyDOM(vdom)
    }

    vdom = view(state, emit)
    mountDOM(vdom, parentEl)
  }

  return {
    mount(_parentEl) {
      parentEl = _parentEl
      renderApp()
    },

    unmount() {
      destroyDOM(vdom)
      vdom = null
```

```
        subscriptions.forEach((unsubscribe) => unsubscribe())
      },
    }
}
```

That's the first version of your framework, put together in fewer than 50 lines of code. The framework is fairly simple, but it's good enough to build simple applications. In chapter 6, you build and publish your framework to NPM and refactor the TODOs application to use it.

## Summary

- Your framework's first version is made of a renderer and a state manager wired together.
- The renderer first destroys the DOM (if it exists) and then creates it from scratch. This process isn't very efficient and creates problems with the focus of input fields, among other things.
- The state manager is in charge of keeping the state and view of the application in sync.
- The developer of an application maps the user interactions to commands, framed in the business language, that are dispatched to the state manager.
- The commands are processed by the state manager, updating the state and notifying the renderer that the DOM needs to be updated.
- The state manager uses a reducer function to derive the new state from the old state and the command's payload.

# Publishing
# and using your
# framework's first version

**This chapter covers**

- Publishing the first version of your framework to NPM
- Refactoring the TODOs application to use your framework

In chapter 5, you implemented a state manager and assembled it, together with a renderer, to build the first version of your frontend framework. In this chapter, you'll publish the first version of your framework and then refactor the TODOs application you built using vanilla JavaScript.

> **NOTE** You can find all the listings in this chapter in the listings/ch06 directory of the book's repository (http://mng.bz/n1Ga). The code in this chapter can be checked out from the ch6 label (http://mng.bz/vPE7):
> ```
> $ git switch --detach ch6.
> ```

> **Code catch-up**
>
> In chapter 5, you implemented the `Dispatcher` class, used to dispatch commands from the application and subscribe handler functions to those commands. You also implemented the `createApp()` function, which takes in the state of the application, reducer functions to update the state, and a view function to render the application and then wires everything together.

## 6.1 Building and publishing the framework

The first thing you want to do to build your framework is export the functions that you want to expose to the developer using it from the src/index.js barrel file. Whatever you export from this file makes the public API of the framework. The src/index.js file is the entry point of the build process, so everything that's exported from this file will be made available in the final bundle.

You want developers to use the `h()`, `hString()`, and `hFragment()` functions to create virtual Document Object Model (DOM) nodes and the `createApp()` function to create an application. You don't need to export the `mountDOM()` and `destroyDOM()` functions because they're used internally by the framework. Open the src/index.js file, delete whatever is in there, and add the following lines:

```
export { createApp } from './app'
export { h, hFragment, hString } from './h'
```

Now run the `build` script inside the runtime workspace to build the framework:

```
$ npm run build
```

As you see in appendix A, this script bundles the JavaScript code into a single ESM file: dist/*<fwk-name>*.js. (*<fwk-name>* is the name of your framework, as named in the package.json file's `name` property.)

> **NOTE** Before you proceed, make sure that you follow the instructions in appendix A and set up your NPM account to publish your package.

You can import this file directly from packages/runtime/dist/*<fwk-name>*.js in your examples to use the framework. But you can also publish it to NPM so that you and other developers can install it in their projects using NPM like so:

```
$ npm install <fwk-name>
```

You want the `version` field in your package.json file to be `1.0.0`, which is the first version of your framework, but you'll be publishing more versions later:

```
"version": "1.0.0",
```

To publish the package to https://www.npmjs.com, make sure that your terminal's working directory is the runtime workspace and then run the `publish` NPM script as follows:

```
$ npm publish
```

That's it. You've published the first version of your frontend framework to NPM. You can find it at https://www.npmjs.com/package/ followed by the name of your framework (the `name` field in your package.json file), and you can install it in your projects through NPM by running the command `npm install <fwk-name>`. You can also find it at https://unpkg.com followed by the name of your package, where you can import it directly into your HTML files. We'll use the latter method in most of the examples in the book.

## 6.2    *A short example*

You're probably excited to start using your framework and seeing how it works. You'll rewrite your TODOs app to use the framework in the next section, but first, I want to help you make sense of everything you've done so far. To that end, you might appreciate a short example that shows how the framework works.

You don't need to write the code in this section (unless you want to try it); just read it to see how the framework works. You'll get your hands dirty in section 6.3.

I can't think of anything simpler than a button that counts how many times you click it. This application's view is a button, but it's interactive; it renders something different based on the state, which is a number representing a count. You can implement this simple application with the following few lines of code:

```
createApp({
  state: 0,

  reducers: {
    add: (state, amount) => state + amount,
  },

  view: (state, emit) =>
    h(
      'button',
      { on: { click: () => emit('add', 1) } },
      [hString(state)]
    ),
}).mount(document.body)
```

This code is all you need to make a simple application with the framework. No DOM manipulation drama is involved; the framework handles that work now. You can focus on the important stuff: the application's logic.

This application renders as a single button with the number 0 on it (you haven't clicked it yet):

```
<body>
  <button>0</button>
</body>
```

When you click the button, the number it displays increments by 1 and the button renders the new number:

```
<body>
  <button>1</button>
</body>
```

The framework removes the `<button>` element from the DOM and creates a new one every time the state changes—that is, when you click the button. This change happens in a fraction of a millisecond, so you won't even notice it. To you, the button appears to be updating its number, but in reality, you never click the same button twice. (How philosophical is that?)

---

**Exercise 6.1**

Using your framework, implement a counter application that allows the user to increment and decrement a counter. The counter should start at 0, and the user should be able to increment it by clicking a button with a + (plus sign) label. The user should also be able to decrement it by clicking another button, this one with the – (minus sign) label. The counter should be displayed between the two buttons. You can create the application inside the examples/ directory.

Find the solution at http://mng.bz/QRm1.

---

## 6.3 Refactoring the TODOs app

Now let's take the TODOs application you built without a framework and refactor it to use the framework you've built. You'll see how much simpler the code becomes (except for the nuances of writing virtual DOMs instead of HTML), and you'll be in a good position to assess the benefits of using a frontend framework versus writing your own DOM-manipulation code.

The first step in refactoring the TODOs application is cleaning up the `<body>` tag in the todos.html file. Your framework creates all the HTML markup this time, so the `<body>` tag should be empty. Your todos.html file should look like the following listing.

**Listing 6.1  Removing all the markup from the HTML file (todos.html)**

```
<!DOCTYPE html>
<html lang="en">
  <head>
    <meta charset="UTF-8" />
    <script type="module" src="todos.js"></script>
    <title>My TODOs</title>
  </head>

  <body></body>          ⟵⊣  Removes everything
</html>                        inside the <body> tag
```

Do the same thing with the todos.js file; you'll be writing all the code from scratch. Then import the functions exported by the framework from the dist/ directory or (preferably) unpkg.com. (I'll be using unpkg.com in this book, but you can use whichever method you prefer.) Here's what your todos.js file should look like:

```
import { createApp, h, hFragment } from 'https://unpkg.com/<fwk-name>@1'
```

> **NOTE**   Please recall (and this is the last time I'll mention it to avoid sounding repetitive) that *<fwk-name>* is the name of your framework, as named in the package.json file's name property.

Next, you want to define the application's state. This time, the state will be a bit more nuanced than a simple array of to-do items.

### 6.3.1   Defining the state

The state of the TODOs application, when you wrote it using vanilla JavaScript, was simply an array of strings, with each string being a to-do item. You didn't need to keep other pieces of information as part of the state, such as the text of the new to-do item that the user was typing in the input field, because you could grab it from the DOM, like so:

```
const addTodoInput = document.getElementById('todo-input')

// The text of the new to-do item
addTodoInput.value
```

The point of using a framework is to abstract away the manipulation of the DOM, so we want to avoid accessing the DOM. Any piece of information that's relevant to the application should be part of the state. The value of the input field in which the user writes the new to-do item's text has to be part of the state, and it must be up to date with what the user is typing. You'll need to keep three pieces of information in the state this time:

- todos—The array of to-do items (same as before)
- currentTodo—The text of the new to-do item that the user is typing in the input field
- edit—An object containing information about the to-do item being edited by the user:
  - idx—The index of the to-do item in the todos array that's being edited
  - original—The original text of the to-do item before the user started editing it (in case the edition is canceled and you need to bring back the original value)
  - edited—The text of the to-do item as the user is editing it

With these requirements in mind, use the code in the following listing to define the new state.

**Listing 6.2   The state for the TODOs application (todos.js)**

```
import { createApp, h, hFragment } from 'https://unpkg.com/<fwk-name>@1'

const state = {
  currentTodo: '',
  edit: {
    idx: null,
    original: null,
    edited: null,
  },
  todos: ['Walk the dog', 'Water the plants'],
}
```

Next, let's think about the actions that the user can perform on the application and how they affect the state.

### 6.3.2   *Defining the reducers*

This seemingly simple application has a few actions that the user can perform on it. We need to write a reducer function to update the state for each of these actions. If you think about the different ways in which a user can interact with the application, you'll come up with a list similar to the following:

- *Update the current to-do.* The user types a new character in the input field, so the current to-do needs to be updated.
- *Add a new to-do.* The user clicks the Add button to add a new to-do to the list.
- *Start editing a to-do.* The user double-clicks a to-do item to start editing it.
- *Edit a to-do.* The user types a new character in the input field while editing a to-do item.
- *Save an edited to-do.* The user finishes editing a to-do and saves the changes.
- *Cancel editing a to-do.* The user cancels editing a to-do and discards the changes.
- *Remove a to-do.* The user marks a to-do as completed so that it can be removed from the list.

Write a reducer function for each of these actions below the state definition, as shown in the following listing. Recall from section 5.1.2 that a reducer must be a pure function, so it can't have side effects or mutate its arguments; it has to return a new state object, not a modified version of the current state.

**Listing 6.3   The reducer functions of the state (todos.js)**

```
const reducers = {
  'update-current-todo': (state, currentTodo) => ({        ⟵┐  The reducer receives the
    ...state,                                                   current TODO as payload.
    currentTodo,                               ⟵┐  Updates the current TODO in the state
  }),

  'add-todo': (state) => ({
    ...state,                                         Sets an empty string as the
    currentTodo: '',                            ⟵┘   current TODO (to clean the field)
```

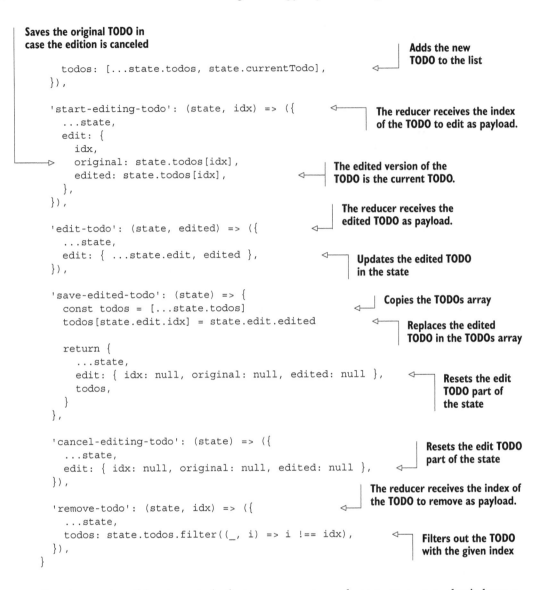

```
                                                              Adds the new
                                                              TODO to the list
        todos: [...state.todos, state.currentTodo],
    }),

    'start-editing-todo': (state, idx) => ({            The reducer receives the index
      ...state,                                         of the TODO to edit as payload.
      edit: {
        idx,
        original: state.todos[idx],                 The edited version of the
        edited: state.todos[idx],                   TODO is the current TODO.
      },
    }),
                                                      The reducer receives the
    'edit-todo': (state, edited) => ({                edited TODO as payload.
      ...state,
      edit: { ...state.edit, edited },            Updates the edited TODO
    }),                                           in the state

    'save-edited-todo': (state) => {              Copies the TODOs array
      const todos = [...state.todos]
      todos[state.edit.idx] = state.edit.edited   Replaces the edited
                                                  TODO in the TODOs array
      return {
        ...state,
        edit: { idx: null, original: null, edited: null },   Resets the edit
        todos,                                               TODO part of
      }                                                      the state
    },

    'cancel-editing-todo': (state) => ({                  Resets the edit TODO
      ...state,                                           part of the state
      edit: { idx: null, original: null, edited: null },
    }),
                                                      The reducer receives the index of
    'remove-todo': (state, idx) => ({                 the TODO to remove as payload.
      ...state,
      todos: state.todos.filter((_, i) => i !== idx),   Filters out the TODO
    }),                                                  with the given index
}
```

Saves the original TODO in case the edition is canceled

One interesting thing to note is that some events, such as `'add-todo'`, don't have a payload associated with them. A payload isn't necessary because now the new to-do description is part of the state, so the reducer can access it directly:

```
'add-todo': (state) => ({
  ...state,
  currentTodo: '',
  todos: [...state.todos, state.currentTodo],
})
```

Now that you have the state and the reducers, you can define the view.

### 6.3.3 Defining the view

Let's break the application into small components, starting with the top-level component, which we'll call `App()`. This component consists of a fragment containing the title (an `<h1>` element), a `CreateTodo()` component, and a `TodoList()` component. Write the code in the following listing.

**Listing 6.4  The `App()` component, top-level view (todos.js)**

```
function App(state, emit) {
  return hFragment([
    h('h1', {}, ['My TODOs']),
    CreateTodo(state, emit),
    TodoList(state, emit),
  ])
}
```

As you recall from section 5.2.4, the components are now functions that take in not only the state, but also the `emit()` function to dispatch events to the application's dispatcher. Implement the `CreateTodo()` component next, as shown in the following listing. This component is equivalent to the static HTML markup you had in the todos.html file: the `<label>`, `<input>`, and `<button>` elements.

**Listing 6.5  The `CreateTodo()` component (todos.js)**

```
function CreateTodo({ currentTodo }, emit) {          ⟵  Destructures the currentTodo
  return h('div', {}, [                                   from the state object
    h('label', { for: 'todo-input' }, ['New TODO']),   ⟵  The input's label
    h('input', {
      type: 'text',
      id: 'todo-input',                                    The input field's value is the
      value: currentTodo,                              ⟵  currentTodo in the state.
      on: {
        input: ({ target }) =>
          emit('update-current-todo', target.value),
        keydown: ({ key }) => {                                Checks whether
          if (key === 'Enter' && currentTodo.length >= 3) {  ⟵ the user pressed
            emit('add-todo')                                   the Enter key and
          }                                                    the input field
        },                                                     has at least three
      },                                                       characters
    }),
    h(
      'button',
      {                                                     Disables the button if
        disabled: currentTodo.length < 3,               ⟵  the input field has fewer
        on: { click: () => emit('add-todo') },          ⟵  than three characters
      },
      ['Add']                                               Dispatches the 'add-todo'
    ),                                                      command when the user
  ])                                                        clicks the button
}
```

Updates the field's value when the user types in it

Dispatches the 'add-todo' command

This code is the first time you see the emit() function being used inside a component, so a few words of explanation are in order. The case of the <input> is particularly interesting because you've set up a two-way binding between the input field and the state. A *two-way binding* reflects the changes in the state in the input field, and anything typed in the input field is set in the state. Whatever side changes (the state or the DOM), the other is updated. You've accomplished this two-way binding by using the value attribute of the <input> element and by setting an event listener on the input event:

```
h('input', {
  type: 'text',
  value: state.currentTodo,
  on: {
    input: ({ target }) => emit('update-current-todo', target.value)
  }
})
```

This way, when the currentTodo in the state changes its value, this change is reflected in the input field. When the user types a new character in the input field, the input event is triggered and the update-current-todo event is dispatched, so the reducer updates the state. This flow is a beautiful use of your renderer and state manager working together, as you can see in figure 6.1.

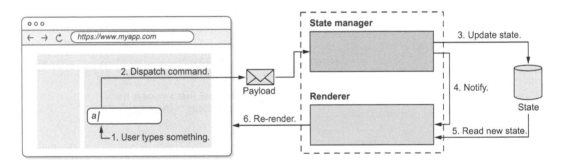

**Figure 6.1   A two-way binding between the state and the DOM**

Next, we'll implement the TodoList() component, which is the list of to-do items. Write the following code below the CreateTodo() component.

**Listing 6.6   The TodoList() component (todos.js)**

```
function TodoList({ todos, edit }, emit) {
  return h(
    'ul',
    {},
    todos.map((todo, i) => TodoItem({ todo, i, edit }, emit))
  )
}
```

The TodoList() component is a simple one: a `<ul>` element with a list of TodoItem() components. Implement the missing TodoItem() component to finish the application, as shown in the following listing.

---

**Listing 6.7** The `TodoItem()` **component (todos.js)**

```
function TodoItem({ todo, i, edit }, emit) {
  const isEditing = edit.idx === i

  return isEditing                                    The item in edit mode
    ? h('li', {}, [
        h('input', {                                  The input field's value is the
          value: edit.edited,                         edited TODO's description.
          on: {
            input: ({ target }) => emit('edit-todo', target.value)
          },                                          Updates the field's value
        }),                                           when the user types in it
        h(
          'button',
          {
            on: {
              click: () => emit('save-edited-todo')   Saves the edited TODO
            }                                          by dispatching the
          },                                           'save-edited-todo'
          ['Save']                                    command
        ),
        h(
          'button',
          {                                            Cancels the
            on: {                                      edit mode by
              click: () => emit('cancel-editing-todo') dispatching the
            }                                          'cancel-editing-
          },                                           todo' command
          ['Cancel']
        ),
      ])
    : h('li', {}, [            The item in read mode
        h(                                             Starts editing the
          'span',                                      TODO by dispatching
          {                                            the 'start-editing-
            on: {                                      todo' command
              dblclick: () => emit('start-editing-todo', i)
            }
          },
          [todo]                    The TODO's description
        ),                          coming from the state
        h(
          'button',
          {                                            Removes the
            on: {                                      TODO by
              click: () => emit('remove-todo', i)      dispatching the
            }                                          'remove-todo'
          },                                           command
          ['Done']
```

```
      ),
   ])
}
```

You're passing the to-do item's index because some of the dispatched events need to know it, such as when you want to edit or remove a to-do. That index is known by the parent component, `TodoList()`, so it needs to pass it to the child component as a prop. This index isn't part of the application's state—what we typically pass as the first argument to the component—but it's relevant to the component.

The last task is putting everything together. Write the last line of the todos.js file as follows:

```
createApp({ state, reducers, view: App }).mount(document.body)
```

Now if you run the `serve:examples` script, you'll see the application running in your browser:

```
$ npm run serve:examples
```

At this point, you can add new to-do items, edit them, and remove them. Everything works the same way as before, but this time, you wrote no DOM manipulation code. You should be proud of yourself for having built your first frontend framework. Congratulations!

You probably noticed one thing when you attempted to add a new to-do item: every keystroke you type in the input field removes the focus from the input field, so you have to click it again to type the next character. Can you guess why? Every time the state changes, your framework is destroying the DOM and re-creating it from scratch. As a result, the field where you wrote the last character is no longer in the DOM; you're writing in a new input field. (You never write two characters in the same input field. Oh, philosophy!) This situation is far from ideal, but worry not: you'll fix the problem in chapter 7.

---

**Exercise 6.2: Challenge**

Write the tic-tac-toe game using your framework. If you need a refresher on how the game works, you can find the rules at http://mng.bz/oe4p. The game should have the following features:

- The game should start with an empty board. (You can use a `<table>` element to represent the board.)
- The first player is always the X player. A title should say whose turn it is: "It's X's turn" or "It's O's turn."
- When a player clicks a cell, the cell should be filled with the player's symbol (X or O), and the turn should be passed to the other player.
- When a player wins the game, a message should say who won the game: "Player X wins!" or "Player O wins!" The remaining cells should be disabled.
- When all the cells are filled and neither player has won, a message should say that the game ended in a draw: "It's a draw!".

You can use the same state and reducer you used in exercise 5.2, but this time, you'll need to write the logic to determine whether a player has won the game (the `checkWinner()` function).

Find the solution at http://mng.bz/Xqdl.

The next two chapters are among the most challenging in the book. You'll write the reconciliation algorithm, thanks to which your framework can update the DOM when the state changes, without needing to destroy and re-create it. The reconciliation algorithm is complex, but it's also lots of fun to write, so I hope you'll enjoy it.

Be sure to grab a cup of coffee and maybe go out for a relaxing walk before you move on to chapter 7. If you're into yoga, you might want to do a couple of Sun Salutations. Whatever you do, come back refreshed and ready to write some code!

## Summary

- To publish your framework on NPM, first bundle it by using `npm run build`; then publish it by using the `npm publish` command.
- Whatever you export from the src/index.js file is what's going to be available to the users of your framework. (You configure it this way in appendix A.)
- In a two-way binding, the state and the DOM are synchronized. Whatever changes on one side is reflected on the other.
- Using the first version of your framework, you've rewritten the to-do application you wrote in chapter 2. This time, you didn't have to worry about DOM manipulation—only about the application's logic.

# The reconciliation algorithm: Diffing virtual trees

**This chapter covers**

- Comparing two virtual DOM trees
- Finding the differences between two objects
- Finding the differences between two arrays
- Finding a sequence of operations that transforms one array into another

Picture this: you're in the supermarket, using the shopping list your partner gave you. You walk around the aisles, picking up the items one by one and putting them in the cart. When you're done, you head to the checkout counter, but at that very moment your phone vibrates in your pocket; it's a message from your partner. She realized that there are already a dozen eggs in the fridge; what's missing is a bottle of wine for that fancy dinner you're going to have tonight with some friends. She's texted you the updated shopping list. Now you have two lists: the original one (whose items are already in your cart) and the updated one, as you can see in figure 7.1.

**Figure 7.1  The two shopping lists: the original one and the updated one**

You have two options:

- You can start over, emptying the cart by putting back the items on the shelves and then picking up the items in the updated list. This way, you'll be sure that you have the right items—the ones on the updated list—in your cart.
- You can pause for a minute to compare the two lists and figure out which items were removed and which items were added. Then you can get rid of the items that were removed from the original list and pick up the items that were added to the updated list.

You're a smart person (after all, you're reading this book), so you choose the second option, which requires some extra brainpower but is less labor-intensive. It takes you only a few seconds to realize that if you take the original list, strike out the egg carton, and add the bottle of wine, you'll have the updated list (figure 7.2). You figured out the minimum number of operations you need to put the items on the new list in your cart.

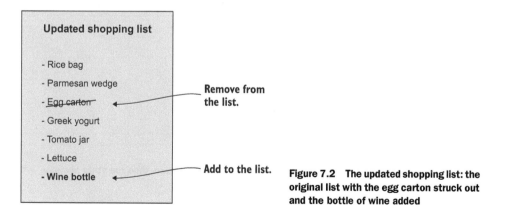

**Figure 7.2  The updated shopping list: the original list with the egg carton struck out and the bottle of wine added**

This analogy perfectly illustrates what the reconciliation algorithm does: compares two virtual Document Object Model (DOM) trees, figures out the changes, and applies those changes to the real DOM. Destroying the entire DOM and re-creating it from scratch every time the state changes would be like emptying the cart and starting from scratch every time you get a new shopping list: you don't need to think, but the process is laborious. You want your framework to be smart enough to figure out the minimum number (or at least a reasonably small number) of operations to apply to the real DOM to make it reflect the new state.

Figure 7.3 shows how your framework currently renders the view when the state changes. Destroying and re-creating the DOM every time the state changes is an expensive operation. In a frontend application, the state can change a couple of times every second. Suppose that your shopping list changed that often and that you had to empty your cart and start over every time your partner sent you an updated list.

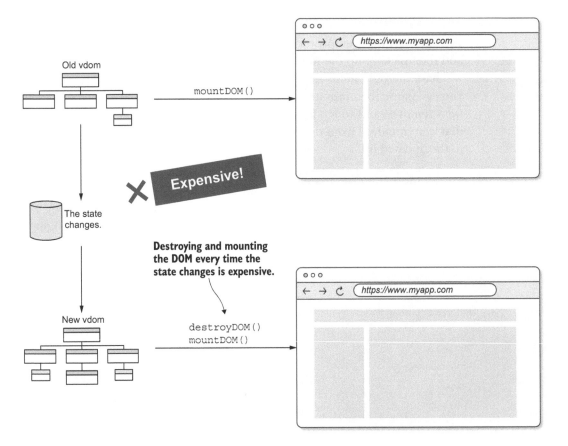

**Figure 7.3   The current framework destroys and re-creates the DOM every time the state changes, which is an expensive operation.**

The objective of this chapter is to implement the first half of the reconciliation algorithm; you'll implement the rest in chapter 8. This algorithm does two things:

- Figures out the differences between two virtual DOM trees (this chapter)
- Applies those differences to the real DOM so that the framework can update it more efficiently (chapter 8)

The process is the same as getting a new shopping list, comparing it with the original one, finding the differences, and then changing the items in your cart. You have to compare the old virtual DOM with the new virtual DOM, find the differences, and then apply those differences to the real DOM. You'll focus on the first part in this chapter. In chapter 8, you'll write a `patchDOM()` function to implement the algorithm, putting all the pieces together. Then your framework will update the view much more efficiently, as you can see in figure 7.4.

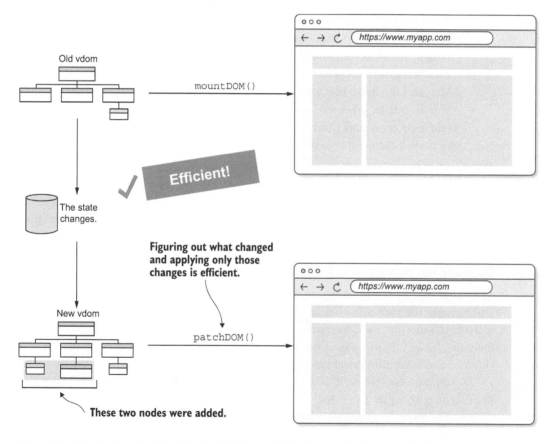

Figure 7.4 The framework will update the DOM more efficiently by using the reconciliation algorithm written in the `patchDOM()` function.

**NOTE**  You can find all the listings in this chapter in the listings/ch07 directory of the book's repository (http://mng.bz/46ww). The code you'll write in this chapter is for the framework's second version, which you'll publish in chapter 8. Therefore, the code in this chapter can be checked out from the ch8 label (http://mng.bz/QRBG): $ git switch --detach ch8.

---

**Code catch-up**

In chapter 6, you rewrote the TODOs application using the framework you built in the previous chapters.

---

## 7.1 The three key functions of the reconciliation algorithm

Believe it or not, finding the differences between two virtual DOMs, which is the most complex part of the reconciliation algorithm, can be solved with three functions:

- A function to find the differences between two objects, returning the keys that were added, the keys that were removed, and the keys whose associated values changed (used to compare the attributes and CSS style objects)
- A function to find the differences between two arrays, returning the items that were added and the items that were removed (used to compare two CSS classes' arrays)
- A function that, given two arrays, figures out a sequence of operations to apply to the first array and transform it into the second array (used to turn the array of a node's children into its new shape)

The two first functions are somehow straightforward, but the third is a bit more complex; I'd say it's where 90 percent of the complexity of the reconciliation algorithm lies. In this chapter, you'll write these functions, which you'll use in chapter 8 to implement the patchDOM() function. Let's start by exploring how to figure out what changed from one virtual DOM tree to another and how to apply those changes to the real DOM.

## 7.2 Comparing two virtual DOM trees

As we've seen, the view is a function of the state: when the state changes, the virtual DOM representing the view also changes. The reconciliation algorithm compares the old virtual DOM—the one used to render the current view—with the new virtual DOM after the state changes. Its job is to *reconcile* the two virtual DOM trees—that is, figure out what changed and apply those changes to the real DOM so that the view reflects the new state.

To compare two virtual DOM trees, start comparing the two root nodes, checking whether they're equal (we'll see what it takes for two nodes to be equal) and whether their attributes or event listeners have changed. If you find that the node isn't the same, you look no further. First, you destroy the subtree rooted at the old node and replace it with the new node and everything under it. (We'll explore this topic in detail in chapter 8.) Then you compare the children of the two nodes, traversing the trees recursively in a depth-first manner. When you compare two arrays of child nodes, you need to figure out whether a node was added, removed, or moved to a different position. In a sense, depth-first traversal is the natural order in which the DOM is modified.

> **NOTE**   By traversing the tree in a depth-first manner, you ensure that the changes are applied to a complete branch of the tree before moving to the next branch. Traversing the tree this way is important in the case of fragments because the children of a fragment are added to the fragment's parent, and if the number of children changes, that change could potentially alter the indices where the siblings of the fragment's parent are inserted.

### 7.2.1   *Finding the differences*

Let's look at an example. Suppose that you're comparing the two virtual DOM trees in figure 7.5: the old virtual DOM tree at top and the new virtual DOM tree at the bottom.

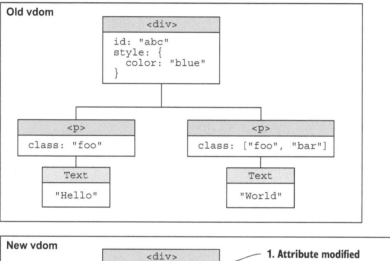

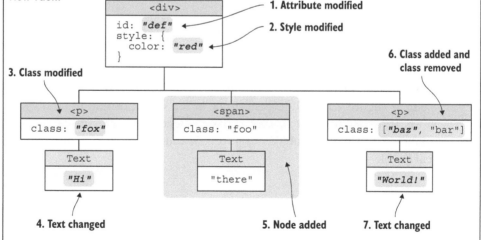

**Figure 7.5   Comparing two virtual DOM trees to find out what changed**

In this figure, the differences are already highlighted, but we'll explore how to find them step by step.

> ### Exercise 7.1
> Being able to translate from a virtual DOM diagram to HTML (and vice versa) is useful. Can you write the HTML that both the old and new virtual trees in figure 7.5 would produce?
>
> Find the solution at http://mng.bz/yZY7.

### STEP 1

You compare the two root `<div>` nodes (figure 7.6) and find that the `id` attribute changed from `"abc"` to `"def"` and the `style` attribute changed from `"color: blue"` to `"color: red"`. These changes, labeled "1. Attribute modified" and "2. Style modified" in figure 7.5, are the first changes you need to apply to the real DOM.

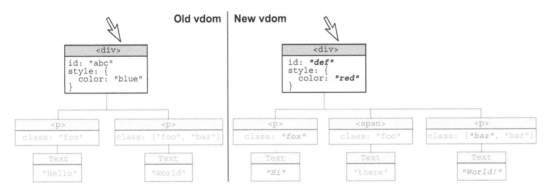

**Figure 7.6   Comparing the root `<div>` nodes**

### STEP 2

You compare the two children of the `<div>` node one by one. The first child is a `<p>` element (figure 7.7), and it seems to be in the same position in both trees; it didn't move. Its `class` attribute, however, has changed from `"foo"` to `"fox"`. This change is labeled "3. Class modified" in figure 7.5, and it's the next change to apply to the real DOM.

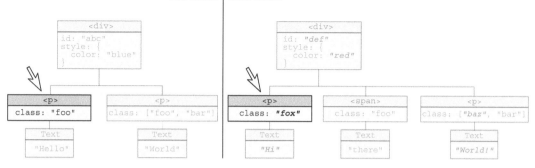

**Figure 7.7** **Comparing the first child of the <div> nodes: A <p> element**

### STEP 3

Remember that you want to iterate the trees in a depth-first manner, so now you compare the children of the <p> element: their text content. The text content has changed from "Hello" to "Hi" (figure 7.8). This change, labeled "4. Text changed" in figure 7.5, is applied to the real DOM next.

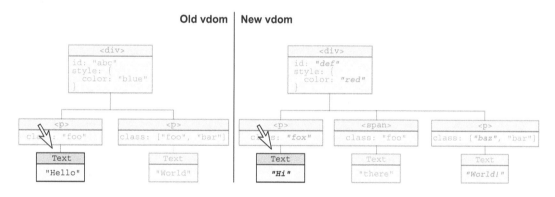

**Figure 7.8** **Comparing the text nodes of the <p> element**

### STEP 4

You find that the second child is a <p> in the old tree, but it's a <span> in the new tree (figure 7.9). By looking at the children of the new <div> node, you quickly realize that the <p> that used to be the second child has moved one position to the right. You conclude that the <span> was added, and it naturally moved the <p> one position to the right. Adding the new <span> node, including its text node, is the next change to apply to the DOM. This change is labeled "5. Node added" in figure 7.5.

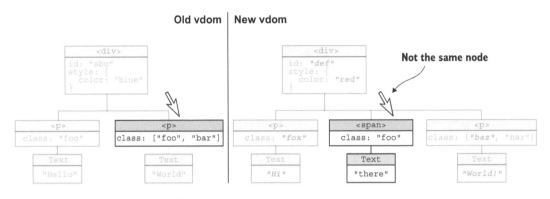

**Figure 7.9   Comparing the second child of the `<div>` nodes: A `<p>` element in the old tree and a `<span>` element in the new tree**

## STEP 5

You look at the `<p>` node that you know moved one position (figure 7.10), and you see that its `class` attribute changed from `["foo", "bar"]` to `["baz", "bar"]`, which means that the class `"foo"` was removed and the class `"baz"` was added. This change is labeled "6. Class added and class removed" in figure 7.5.

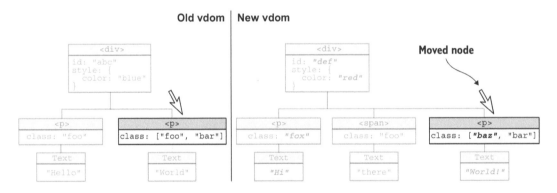

**Figure 7.10   Comparing the `<p>` element that moved one position to the right**

## STEP 6

Last, you check the children of the `<p>` element (figure 7.11), and you find that the text content changed from `"World"` to `"World!"`. This change is labeled "7. Text changed" in figure 7.5.

After comparing the two trees, you found a total of seven changes that need to be applied to the real DOM. The next step is to apply them. Let's see how you do that.

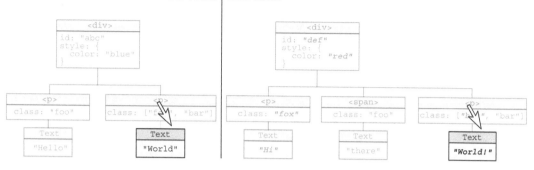

**Figure 7.11  Comparing the text nodes of the <p> element that moved one position to the right**

> **NOTE**  Remember that you'll modify the DOM in chapter 8. But I want you to see how it works here so that you'll have a good high-level understanding of the complete reconciliation process.

### 7.2.2  *Applying the changes*

Let's see how you'd apply these changes in order. Figure 7.12 shows the HTML markup of the old virtual DOM tree.

```
<div id="abc" style="color: blue;">
  <p class="foo">
    Hello
  </p>
  <p class="foo bar">
    World
  </p>
</div>
```

**Figure 7.12  The HTML markup of the old virtual DOM tree**

You'll apply the changes you identified by comparing the two trees in the preceding section. Applying a change means modifying the real DOM to match the new virtual DOM tree. Every change you make will be shown in figures so you can see how the DOM changes with each operation.

#### MODIFYING THE ID AND STYLE ATTRIBUTES OF THE PARENT <DIV> NODE

The first two changes were made to the root <div> node's attributes, as shown in figure 7.13. To apply these changes, you need to update the id and style attributes of the <div> node:

```
div.id = 'def'
div.style.color = 'red'
```

**1. Change ID value.**    **2. Change color value.**

```
<div id="def" style="color: red;">
  <p class="foo">
    Hello
  </p>
  <p class="foo bar">
    World
  </p>
</div>
```

**Figure 7.13  Applying the attribute and style changes to the DOM's <div> node**

#### MODIFYING THE CLASS ATTRIBUTE AND TEXT CONTENT OF THE FIRST <P> NODE

Next are the changes to the first <p> node, as shown in figure 7.14. In this case, you'd need to update the class attribute and the text content of the <p> node:

```
p1.className = 'fox'
p1Text.nodeValue = 'Hi'
```

```
<div id="def" style="color: red;">
  <p class="fox">
    Hi
  </p>
  <p class="foo bar">
    World
  </p>
</div>
```

**3. Change class value.**

**4. Change text content.**

**Figure 7.14  Applying the changes to the first <p> node**

#### ADDING THE NEW <SPAN> NODE

The next change adds the <span> node, as shown in figure 7.15. To add a node (and its children) to the DOM, you can pass the virtual node to the mountDOM() function you wrote earlier, passing the <div> node as the parent node:

```
mountDOM(spanVdom, div)
```

Note that, as it is, the mountDOM() function would append the <span> node to the children array of the <div> node. But you want to specify that the <span> node should be inserted at the second position (index 1) of the children array. You need to modify the mountDOM() function to accept a third argument representing the index where the new node should be inserted:

```
mountDOM(spanVdom, div, 1)
```

You'll modify the mountDOM() function in chapter 8. For now, assume that this function takes an index as the third argument and inserts the new node at that position.

```
<div id="def" style="color: red;">
  <p class="fox">
    Hi
  </p>
  <span class="foo">
    there
  </span>
  <p class="foo bar">
    World
  </p>
</div>
```

5. Add element node.

**Figure 7.15  Adding the new `<span>` node and its text node**

**MODIFYING THE CLASS ATTRIBUTE AND TEXT CONTENT OF THE SECOND `<P>` NODE**

Last, you reach the second `<p>` node. You don't need to move it because when the `<span>` node was added, it naturally moved the second `<p>` node one position to the right. When I say that it was *naturally* moved, I mean that the movement happened as the result of another operation; you don't need to write an explicit move operation. (Keep this example in mind; it'll be important later.) The `class` attribute changed from `["foo", "bar"]` to `["baz", "bar"]`, so you need to change the `classList` property of the `<p>` node:

```
p2.classList.remove('foo')
p2.classList.add('baz')
```

The text content changed from `"World"` to `"World!"`, so you need to update the text node:

```
p2Text.nodeValue = 'World!'
```

You can see these changes in figure 7.16.

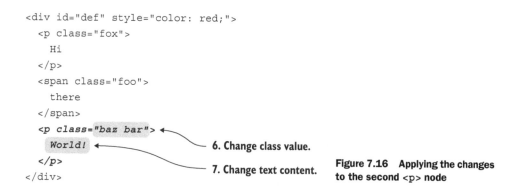

```
<div id="def" style="color: red;">
  <p class="fox">
    Hi
  </p>
  <span class="foo">
    there
  </span>
  <p class="baz bar">
    World!
  </p>
</div>
```

6. Change class value.

7. Change text content.

**Figure 7.16  Applying the changes to the second `<p>` node**

In a nutshell, this discussion shows what the `patchDOM()` function does. To gain better high-level understanding of how the rendering works when the `patchDOM()` function enters the scene, let's start by modifying the `renderApp()` function to call the `patch-DOM()` function instead of destroying and re-creating the DOM every time.

## 7.3   *Changes in the rendering*

To understand the role of the `patchDOM()` function—the implementation of the reconciliation algorithm—it's helpful to see the big picture of how rendering works with it. Figure 7.17 shows the changes in the rendering mechanism, using the `patchDOM()` function. As you can see, the renderer is split into three sections: mounting, patching, and unmounting. Whereas in chapter 6, the same `renderApp()` function was responsible for mounting and updating the DOM, now you'll split it into the two following functions:

- `mount()`—Internally uses `mountDOM()`
- `renderApp()`—Internally uses `patchDOM()`

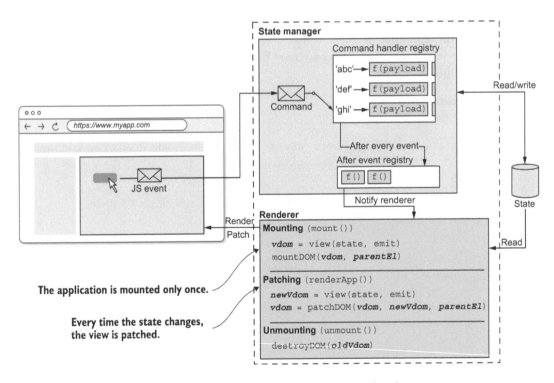

**Figure 7.17   Changes in the rendering mechanism, using the `patchDOM()` function**

You need to modify the code so that the `renderApp()` function doesn't destroy and re-create the DOM anymore, and to do so, you use the `patchDOM()` function. `patchDOM()` takes the last saved virtual DOM (stored in the `vdom` variable inside the application's instance), the new virtual DOM resulting from calling the `view()` function, and the parent element (stored in the `parentEl` instance) of the DOM, where the view was mounted, and figures out the changes that need to be applied to the DOM.

The application's instance `mount()` method doesn't need to use the `renderApp()` function anymore; `renderApp()` is called only when the state changes. `mount()` calls the `view()` function to get the virtual DOM and then calls the `mountDOM()` function to mount the DOM. The user is supposed to call the `mount()` method only once. If they call it more than once, the same application will be mounted multiple times, which is not what you want. You can add a check to prevent this situation by throwing an error if the `vdom` variable isn't `null` (which you'll do in exercise 7.2).

Let's reflect this important change in the code. Open the app.js file, and make the changes shown in the following listing.

**Listing 7.1  Changes in the rendering**

```
import { destroyDOM } from './destroy-dom'
import { Dispatcher } from './dispatcher'
import { mountDOM } from './mount-dom'
import { patchDOM } from './patch-dom'

export function createApp({ state, view, reducers = {} }) {
  let parentEl = null
  let vdom = null

  // --snip-- //

  function renderApp() {
    if (vdom) {
      destroyDOM(vdom)
    }
    const newVdom = view(state, emit)        ◁─── Computes the
    mountDOM(vdom, parentEl)                        new virtual DOM
    vdom = patchDOM(vdom, newVdom, parentEl)  ◁─┐ Patches the DOM
  }                                              │ every time the
                                                 │ state changes
  return {
    mount(_parentEl) {
      parentEl = _parentEl
      renderApp()
      vdom = view(state, emit)
      mountDOM(vdom, parentEl)                 ◁─┐ Mounts the
    },                                           │ DOM only once

    // --snip-- //
  }
}
```

**WARNING**  You're importing the `patchDOM()` from the patch-dom.js file, which you'll write in chapter 8. (Your IDE might complain that the file doesn't exist, but that's okay for now.)

Now that you've changed the rendering flow, let's start thinking about the three functions that you'll use to compare two virtual DOM trees: `objectsDiff()`, `arraysDiff()`, and `arraysDiffSequence()`.

---

**Exercise 7.2**

Implement a check that doesn't allow the user to call the `mount()` method more than once to prevent the same application from being mounted multiple times. If you detect that the application was already mounted, throw an error.

Find the solution at http://mng.bz/M9XE.

---

## 7.4    *Diffing objects*

When comparing two virtual nodes, you need to find the differences between the attributes of the two nodes (the `props` object) to patch the DOM accordingly. You want to know what attributes were added, what attributes were removed, and what attributes changed. We call this process diffing.

To illustrate, figure 7.18 shows the attributes of an `<input>` element. In the figure, you see an old object (the one at the top) and a new object (the one at the bottom). By observing the two objects, you see that the `min` key was added in the new object, the `max` key was removed, and the `disabled` key changed from `false` to `true`.

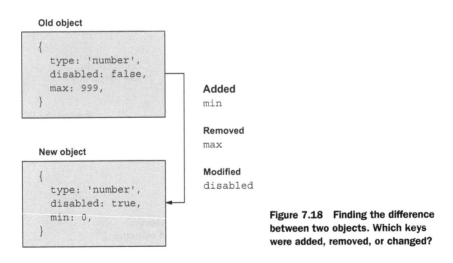

Figure 7.18   **Finding the difference between two objects. Which keys were added, removed, or changed?**

This exercise, which you've done by mere observation, is what the `objectsDiff()` function does. The code you write works similarly to your observation, following these steps:

1   Take a key in the old object. If you don't see it in the new object, you know that the key was removed. Repeat with all keys.

2 Take a key in the new object. If you don't see it in the old object, you know that the key was added. Repeat with all keys.

3 Take a key in the new object. If you see it in the old object and the value associated with the key is different, you know that the value associated with the key changed.

Create a new file inside the utils folder called objects.js, and write the `objectsDiff()` function shown in the following listing.

**Listing 7.2  Finding the difference between two objects (utils/objects.js)**

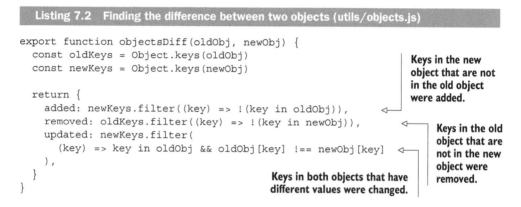

```
export function objectsDiff(oldObj, newObj) {
  const oldKeys = Object.keys(oldObj)
  const newKeys = Object.keys(newObj)

  return {
    added: newKeys.filter((key) => !(key in oldObj)),
    removed: oldKeys.filter((key) => !(key in newObj)),
    updated: newKeys.filter(
      (key) => key in oldObj && oldObj[key] !== newObj[key]
    ),
  }
}
```

Keys in the new object that are not in the old object were added.

Keys in the old object that are not in the new object were removed.

Keys in both objects that have different values were changed.

**NOTE** In the code for the `objectsDiff()` function, I'm iterating the `newKeys` set twice. I could have avoided that part by performing a single iteration in a `for` loop where I saved the added and updated keys. This approach would have been more efficient, but I chose to use two separate iterations—one for the added keys and another for the updated keys—to make the code more readable. As I mention in appendix A, I'm favoring readability and code simplicity over performance. The goal of the code is to show you, the reader, how to build a frontend framework; it isn't being super-performant. But you should feel free to optimize your code if you want.

Fantastic—you've implemented the `objectsDiff()` function. Can you think of a set of unit tests that would help you verify that the function works as expected?

**Exercise 7.3**

Implement a set of test cases to cover all possible scenarios for the `objectsDiff()` function. If you're not familiar with unit testing, try to think of the different cases your function should handle; then execute the function in the browser's console with different inputs to see whether it works as expected.

Find the solution at http://mng.bz/amox.

## 7.5    Diffing arrays

Let's look at the second function that you'll implement, which does a similar job for arrays. Remember that the classes in an element virtual node can be given in the form of an array:

```
h('p', { class: ['foo', 'bar'] }, ['Hello world'])
```

When you compare two virtual nodes, you need to find the differences between the classes of the two nodes (the class array) to patch the DOM accordingly (as you did in the example of figure 7.5, in step 5). In this case, it doesn't matter whether the items in the array are in a different order; you care about only the items that were added or removed. For this purpose, you'll implement the arraysDiff() function next. First, though, consider the example in figure 7.19. The figure shows an old array (the one at the top) and a new array (the one at the bottom). When you compare the two arrays, you see the following:

- A appears in both arrays.
- B and C were removed (appear only in the old array).
- D and E were added (appear only in the new array).

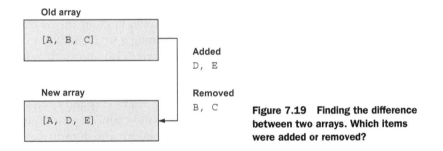

**Figure 7.19    Finding the difference between two arrays. Which items were added or removed?**

Note that in this comparison, items are added or removed but never changed. If an item is changed, you detect it as a removal of the old item and an addition of the new item.

With this example in mind, open the utils/arrays.js file, where you previously implemented the withoutNulls() function, and write the arraysDiff() function as shown in the following listing.

**Listing 7.3    Finding the differences between two arrays (utils/arrays.js)**

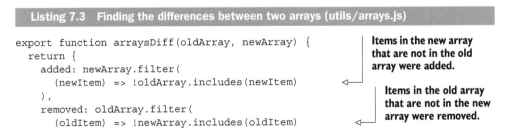

```
export function arraysDiff(oldArray, newArray) {
  return {
    added: newArray.filter(
      (newItem) => !oldArray.includes(newItem)
    ),
    removed: oldArray.filter(
      (oldItem) => !newArray.includes(oldItem)
```

Items in the new array that are not in the old array were added.

Items in the old array that are not in the new array were removed.

```
      ),
    }
  }
}
```

**WARNING**  In the `arraysDiff()` function, you're not specifying the index at which an item was added or removed because to modify the `classList` of an element, you simply add or remove the classes. This approach might be problematic because, as you know, the order of classes in the `classList` matters. A class that comes later in the list can override the styles of a class that comes earlier in the list. You're making this tradeoff to keep the code simple, but bear in mind that a more robust solution is to maintain the order of classes in the `classList`.

With these two items out of the way, you're ready to tackle the beast: the `arrayDiff-Sequence()` function. You might sweat this function a bit, but after you've written it, the rest of the book will feel like a breeze (or something like that). Take a deep breath, and let's move on.

## 7.6 *Diffing arrays as a sequence of operations*

A virtual node has children, and those children can move around from a render to the next one. Child nodes are added and removed all the time as well. When you compare two virtual nodes, you need to find the differences between the children of the two nodes (the `children` array) to patch the DOM accordingly. You want to find a sequence of operations that, when executed on the DOM, transforms the old children array—rendered as HTML elements—into the new children array.

   If you have two arrays and I ask you to come up with a list of `add`, `remove`, and `move` operations that transform the first array into the second one, how would you go about it? You can see an example in figure 7.20. In this figure, the old array is `[A, B, C]`, and the new array is `[C, B, D]`. I was able to find a sequence of three operations that, if applied in order, will transform the old array into the new array.

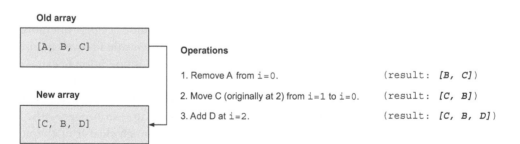

**Figure 7.20**  **Finding a sequence of operations that transforms the original array into the new one**

**NOTE**  Notice that the move operation's `from` index is different from the original index that `C` had in the old array. `C` appeared at `i=2`, but after `A` was removed, it moved to `i=1`. The indices in the operations are always relative to how they find things in the array at the moment of the operation. But you still want to keep track of the original index of the item, and I'll explain why in section 7.6.2.

Many other sequences of operations—an infinite number, in fact—would yield the same result. In other words, the sequence of operations that transforms the old array into the new array isn't unique.

---

**Exercise 7.4**

Can you find a sequence of similar operations that would also transform the old array into the new array?

Find the solution at http://mng.bz/g7oZ.

---

One constraint that you can impose on the sequence is that you want to minimize the number of operations. You could come up with a sequence that starts by moving an item from its position to another one, moves it back to its original position, and repeats that operation a lot of times, but that's not what you want to do—DOM modifications are relatively expensive, so the fewer operations you perform, the better.

### 7.6.1  *Defining the operations you can use*

Let's start by defining the operations you'll use to transform the old array into the new array. The preceding example used three operations: add, remove, and move. Now you need to add a fourth operation: noop (no operation).

You'll use a noop operation when you find an item that's in both arrays, which requires no action to stay where it ends up. Notice that I said "ends up," not "starts." This distinction is important. Some items *move naturally* to their final position because items are added, removed, or moved around them. If you want to go from [A, B] to [B], for example, you simply need to remove A. B falls into place naturally: without any explicit move operation, it goes from i=1 to i=0.

When an item moves naturally, you need to include a noop operation in the sequence. This operation helps you keep track of the items that moved naturally from where they started to where they ended up. You need this operation because patching the DOM is a recursive process: each item in the children array that moved around also needs to be compared for differences. For this operation to be possible, you need to know where each item started and where it ended up—in other words, its initial and final indexes in the array. This topic will become much clearer in chapter 8. The following list shows the operations and the data they need:

- add—{ op: 'add', item: 'D', index: 2 }
- remove—{ op: 'remove', item: 'B', index: 0 }
- move—{ op: 'move', item: 'C', originalIndex: 2, from: 2, index: 0 }
- noop—{ op: 'noop', item: 'A', originalIndex: 0, index: 1 }

As you can see, in all cases the object that describes the operation has an `op` property that indicates the type of operation. The `item` property is the item that's being added, removed, or moved (naturally or forcefully). The `index` property is the index where the item ends up, except in the case of a `remove` operation, where it's the index from which the item was removed. In the `move` and `noop` operations, the `originalIndex` property indicates the index where the item started. Last, in the `move` operation, we also keep track of the `from` property, which is the index from which the item was moved. Note that in the case of a `move` operation, the `from` and `originalIndices` need not be the same. Following the example in figure 7.20, the sequence of operations that transforms the old array into the new array is

```
[
  {op: 'remove', index: 0, item: 'A'}
  {op: 'move', originalIndex: 2, from: 1, index: 0, item: 'C'}
  {op: 'noop', index: 1, originalIndex: 1, item: 'B'}
  {op: 'add', index: 2, item: 'D'}
]
```

> **Exercise 7.5**
>
> Apply the operations in the preceding sequence to the old array (`[A, B, C]`), and check whether you end up with the new array (`[C, B, D]`). You'll likely perform this task manually a couple of times in this chapter to debug the code you'll write.
>
> Find the solution at http://mng.bz/eEMw.

### 7.6.2 *Finding the sequence of operations: The algorithm*

Let's talk about how the algorithm that finds the sequence of operations works. The idea is to iterate over the indices of the new array and, for each step, find a way of transforming the old array so that the items in both arrays are the same at the current index. You focus on one item at a time so that after each step, that item and all the preceding ones are in their final position. The algorithm modifies the old array (a copy of it, to avoid mutating the original one) as it goes, and it keeps track of the operations that transform the old array into the new one.

Going one item at a time and modifying a copy of the old array ensures that every operation is performed over the updated indices of the old array. When the new array is completely iterated over, any excess items in the old array are removed; the new array doesn't have them, so they're not needed. The algorithm is as follows:

1. Iterate over the indices of the new array:
   - Let `i` be the index (`0 ≤ i < newArray.length`).
   - Let `newItem` be the item at `i` in the new array.
   - Let `oldItem` be the item at `i` in the old array (provided that there is one).
2. If `oldItem` doesn't appear in the new array:
   - Add a `remove` operation to the sequence.

- Remove the `oldItem` from the array.
- Start again from step 1 without incrementing `i` (stay at the same index).

**3** If `newItem == oldItem`:
- Add a `noop` operation to the sequence, using the `oldItem` original index (its index at the beginning of the process).
- Start again from step 1, incrementing `i`.

**4** If `newItem != oldItem` and `newItem` can't be found in the old array starting at `i`:
- Add an `add` operation to the sequence.
- Add the `newItem` to the old array at `i`.
- Start again from step 1, incrementing `i`.

**5** If `newItem != oldItem` and `newItem` can be found in the old array starting at `i`:
- Add a `move` operation to the sequence, using the `oldItem` current index and the original index.
- Move the `oldItem` to `i`.
- Start again from step 1, incrementing `i`.

**6** If `i` is greater than the length of `newArray`:
- Add a `remove` operation for each remaining item in `oldArray`.
- Remove all remaining items in `oldArray`.
- Stop the algorithm.

This algorithm isn't straightforward, but it's simpler than it appears at first glance. Figure 7.21 shows a flow chart of the algorithm with the same steps as the preceding list.

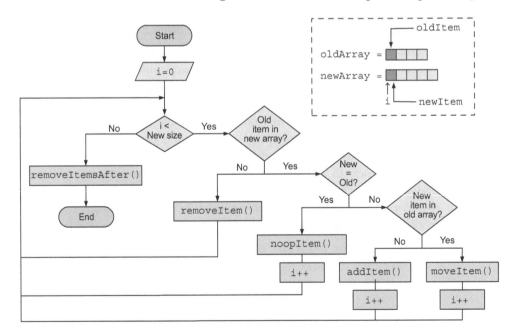

**Figure 7.21   The algorithm's flow chart**

I'll use it in section 7.6.4 when you have to implement the algorithm in code to show where you are in the process. The algorithm is complex, and I want to make sure that you don't get lost.

### 7.6.3 An example by hand

Let's work through an example to see how the algorithm works. Suppose that you have the following arrays:

- `oldArray = [X, A, A, B, C]`
- `newArray = [C, K, A, B]`

Let's apply the algorithm step by step.

#### STEP 1 (I=0)

The x in the old array doesn't appear in the new array, so you want to remove it (figure 7.22).

**Figure 7.22   At** `i=0` **in the old array is** X**, which doesn't appear in the new array; it's a** `remove` **operation.**

After removing the item and adding the `remove` operation to the list of operations, you keep the index at `i=0` because you haven't fulfilled the condition of having the same item in both arrays at that index.

#### STEP 2 (I=0)

You find a c in the new array, but there's an A in the old array at that same index. Let's look for the c in the old array, starting at `i=0`. Oh! There's one at `i=3` (figure 7.23). Note that if there were more than one c in the old array, you'd choose the first one you find.

You add the `move` operation to the sequence of operations and move the c from `i=3` to `i=0` in the old array.

*i=0*

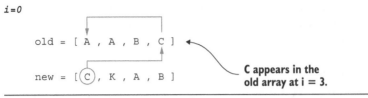

OPERATION: Move C (originally at 4) from i=3 to i=0.

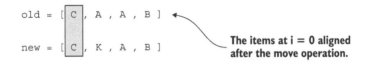

**Figure 7.23**   At i=0, there's a C in the new array. We can move the C in the old array from i=4.

## Step 3 (i=1)

There's a K in the new array but an A in the old array. You look for a K in the old array, starting at i=1. In this case there isn't one, so you need to add it (figure 7.24).

*i=1*

OPERATION: Add K at i=1.

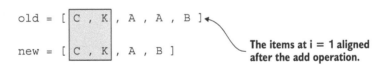

**Figure 7.24**   At i=0 is a K in the new array, but there's no K in the old array. We need an add operation.

You add the K to the old array at i=1 and append the operation to the sequence of operations.

## Step 4 (i=2)

At i=2, both arrays have an A (figure 7.25). Hooray! You add a noop operation in these cases. For that purpose, you need the original index of A in the old array. But that A moved naturally due to the preceding operations:

- It moved one position to the left when the x was removed in step 1.

- It moved one position to the right when the C was moved in step 2, which can-celed the previous move.
- It moved one position to the right when the K was added in step 3.

In total, the A moved one position to the right, so you need to subtract 1 from the cur-rent index of the A in the old array, making the A's original index i=1.

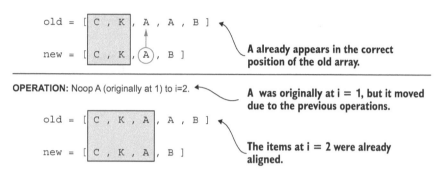

**Figure 7.25  At i=2, both arrays have an A. We add a noop operation, using the original index of the A in the old array.**

You want to keep track of the old array items' original indexes so that you'll have them available when you add noop and move operations. As you can imagine, calculating the original index of an item based on the preceding operations isn't complicated, but it's much better to save it at the beginning of the process.

### STEP 5 (I=3)

At i=3, the new array has a B, but the old array has an A. Look for a B in the old array, starting at i=3. There's one at i=4, so you can move it (figure 7.26).

**Figure 7.26  At i=3, there's a B in the new array. You can move the B in the old array from i=4.**

You append the move operation to the sequence of operations and move the B to i=3 in the old array. At this point, you're done iterating the elements in the new array, and all items from i=0 to i=3 in the old array are aligned with the new array. All you have to do now is remove what's left in the old array because the excess items don't appear in the new array.

### STEP 6

At i=4 in the old array is an extra A that you want to remove (figure 7.27).

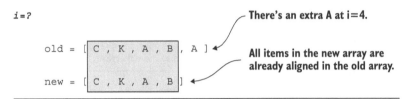

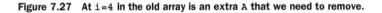

**Figure 7.27    At i=4 in the old array is an extra A that we need to remove.**

If there were more items in the old array, you'd want to remove them as well. All those remove operations would be at index i=4 because as an item is removed, the next one occupies its place at that index.

I hope that the algorithm is clear to you now that you've worked out an example by hand. It's time to implement it in code.

### 7.6.4   *Implementing the algorithm*

Let's start by defining a constant for the operation names. Inside the utils/arrays.js file, add the following constant:

```
export const ARRAY_DIFF_OP = {
  ADD: 'add',
  REMOVE: 'remove',
  MOVE: 'move',
  NOOP: 'noop',
}
```

You want a way to keep track of the old array's original indices so that when you modify a copy of the old array and you apply each operation, you can keep the original indices. A good solution is to create a class—let's call it ArrayWithOriginalIndices—that wraps a copy of the old array and keeps track of the original indices. For whatever item moves inside that array wrapper, the original index also moves.

This wrapper class will search for a given item in the wrapped array (as in step 2 of the preceding example, where you looked for a c somewhere in the array) for which you want a custom comparison function. The items inside the array will be virtual nodes, and you want a function that tells you whether two virtual nodes are equal. (You'll implement this function in chapter 8.)

> **WARNING**  Recall that in JavaScript, two objects are equal if they're the same reference—that is, the same object in memory. Because our virtual nodes are objects, you need to define a custom function to compare them. You can't rely on the default === comparison because if a virtual node is the same as another one but the object is different, the comparison will return false, which is not what you want. You can test that premise as follows:

```
const a = { foo: 'bar' }
const b = { foo: 'bar' }
console.log(a === b) // false
```

In the utils/arrays.js file, add the class in the following listing. You'll add functionality to this class soon.

**Listing 7.4   Keeping track of the original indices (utils/arrays.js)**

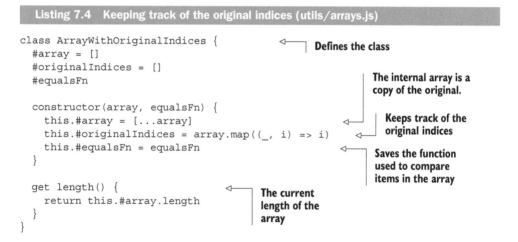

```
class ArrayWithOriginalIndices {          Defines the class
  #array = []
  #originalIndices = []                   The internal array is a
  #equalsFn                               copy of the original.

  constructor(array, equalsFn) {
    this.#array = [...array]              Keeps track of the
    this.#originalIndices = array.map((_, i) => i)   original indices
    this.#equalsFn = equalsFn            Saves the function
  }                                      used to compare
                                         items in the array
  get length() {                The current
    return this.#array.length   length of the
  }                             array
}
```

Let's define the arraysDiffSequence() function with some TODO comments where each case of the algorithm is implemented. Inside the utils/arrays.js file, add the function shown in the following listing.

**Listing 7.5   The arraysDiffSequence() function (utils/arrays.js)**

```
export function arraysDiffSequence(
  oldArray,                    The equalsFn is
  newArray,                    used to compare
  equalsFn = (a, b) => a === b items in the array.
) {
  const sequence = []
```

```
const array = new ArrayWithOriginalIndices(oldArray, equalsFn)

for (let index = 0; index < newArray.length; index++) {
  // TODO: removal case

  // TODO: noop case

  // TODO: addition case

  // TODO: move case
}

  // TODO: remove extra items

  return sequence
}
```

**Iterates the indices of the new array**

**Wraps the old array in an ArrayWithOriginalIndices instance**

**Returns the sequence of operations**

Giving the `equalsFn` parameter a default value using the default equality operator (`===`) will be handy, as you'll test this function (mostly) by passing it arrays of strings in this chapter. Let's start with the remove case.

### THE REMOVE CASE

To find out whether an item was removed, you check whether the item in the old array at the current index doesn't exist in the new array. Figure 7.28 shows this branch of the flow chart.

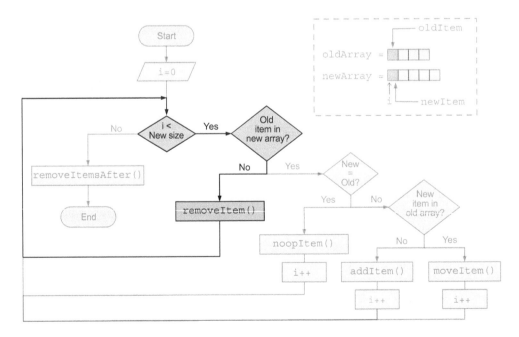

**Figure 7.28   The remove case in the flow chart**

Implement this logic inside a method called `isRemoval()` in the `ArrayWithOriginal-Indices` class, as shown in bold in the following listing.

**Listing 7.6   Detecting whether an operation is a removal (utils/arrays.js)**

```
class ArrayWithOriginalIndices {
  #array = []
  #originalIndices = []
  #equalsFn

  constructor(array, equalsFn) {
    this.#array = [...array]
    this.#originalIndices = array.map((_, i) => i)
    this.#equalsFn = equalsFn
  }

  get length() {
    return this.#array.length
  }

  isRemoval(index, newArray) {
    if (index >= this.length) {                                    If the index is out
      return false                                                 of bounds, there's
    }                                                              nothing to remove.

    const item = this.#array[index]                                Gets the item in
    const indexInNewArray = newArray.findIndex((newItem) =>        the old array at
      this.#equalsFn(item, newItem)                                the given index
    )
                                                                   Tries to find the
    return indexInNewArray === -1                                  same item in
  }                                                                the new array,
}                                                                  returning its
                                                                   index
```

Uses the #equalsFn to compare the items

If the index is -1, the item was removed.

Now let's implement a method to handle the removal of an item and return the operation. You want to reflect the removal operation in both the `#array` and `#original-Indices` properties of the `ArrayWithOriginalIndices` instance. Add the `removeItem()` method to the `ArrayWithOriginalIndices` class, as shown in the following listing.

**Listing 7.7   Removing an item and returning the operation (utils/arrays.js)**

```
class ArrayWithOriginalIndices {
  // --snip-- //

  isRemoval(index, newArray) {
    // --snip-- //
  }

  removeItem(index) {                                              Creates the
    const operation = {                                           operation for
      op: ARRAY_DIFF_OP.REMOVE,                                   the removal
```

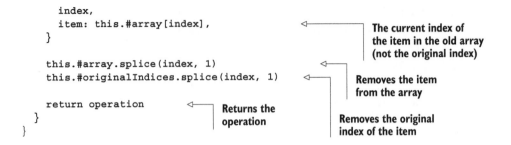

```
          index,
          item: this.#array[index],                        ◁──────   The current index of
        }                                                            the item in the old array
                                                                     (not the original index)
        this.#array.splice(index, 1)               ◁─────
        this.#originalIndices.splice(index, 1)     ◁─────   Removes the item
                                                            from the array
        return operation      ◁──────   Returns the
      }                                  operation          Removes the original
    }                                                       index of the item
```

With these two methods, you can implement the remove case in the `arraysDiff-Sequence()` function. Add the code in bold in the following listing to the `arraysDiff-Sequence()` function.

**Listing 7.8   Implementing the removal case (utils/arrays.js)**

```
export function arraysDiffSequence(
  oldArray,
  newArray,
  equalsFn = (a, b) => a === b
) {
  const sequence = []
  const array = new ArrayWithOriginalIndices(oldArray, equalsFn)

  for (let index = 0; index < newArray.length; index++) {
    if (array.isRemoval(index, newArray)) {        ◁──────   Checks whether the
      sequence.push(array.removeItem(index))       ◁──────   item in the old array
      index--                                      ◁──────   at the current index
      continue                                     ◁──────   was removed
    }
                                                             Removes the item and
    // TODO: noop ecase                                      pushes the operation
                                                             to the sequence
    // TODO: addition case
                                                             Decrements the index to
    // TODO: move case                                       stay at the same index in
  }                                                          the next iteration

  // TODO: remove extra items                                Continues with the loop

  return sequence
}
```

Great! Let's take care of the noop case next.

**THE NOOP CASE**

The noop case happens when, at the current index, both the old and new arrays have the same item. Thus, detecting this case is straightforward. Figure 7.29 highlights the noop case in the flow chart.

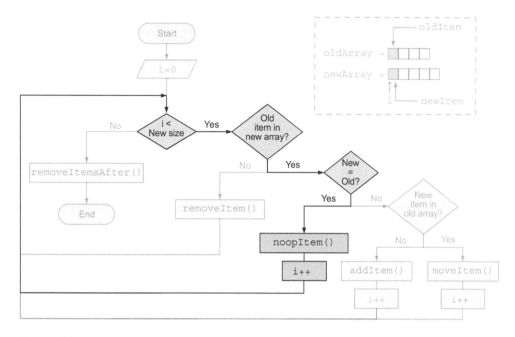

**Figure 7.29   The noop case in the flow chart**

Implement a method called `isNoop()` in the `ArrayWithOriginalIndices` class, as shown in bold in the following listing.

**Listing 7.9   Detecting whether an operation is a `noop` (utils/arrays.js)**

```
class ArrayWithOriginalIndices {
  // --snip-- //

  isNoop(index, newArray) {                If the index is out
    if (index >= this.length) {            of bounds, there
      return false                         can't be a noop.
    }
                                           The item in
    const item = this.#array[index]        the old array
    const newItem = newArray[index]        The item in the new array

    return this.#equalsFn(item, newItem)   Checks whether the
  }                                        items are equal
}
```

When you detect a `noop` at the current index, you need to return the `noop` operation. Here's where the original indices come in handy.

Implement a method called `noopItem()` in the `ArrayWithOriginalIndices` class, as shown in bold in the following listing. Note that you also implement an `original-IndexAt()` method to get the original index of an item in the old array.

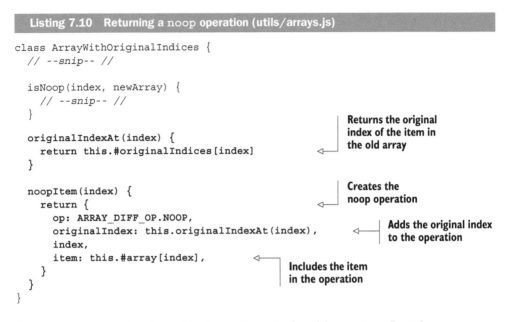

**Listing 7.10   Returning a noop operation (utils/arrays.js)**

```
class ArrayWithOriginalIndices {
  // --snip-- //

  isNoop(index, newArray) {
    // --snip-- //
  }

  originalIndexAt(index) {
    return this.#originalIndices[index]
  }

  noopItem(index) {
    return {
      op: ARRAY_DIFF_OP.NOOP,
      originalIndex: this.originalIndexAt(index),
      index,
      item: this.#array[index],
    }
  }
}
```

Returns the original index of the item in the old array

Creates the noop operation

Adds the original index to the operation

Includes the item in the operation

As you can see, you don't need to do anything to the old array to reflect the noop operation. Things stay the same. With these methods in place, you can implement the noop case in the `arraysDiffSequence()` function. Write the code shown in bold in the following listing inside the `arraysDiffSequence()` function.

**Listing 7.11   Implementing the noop case (utils/arrays.js)**

```
export function arraysDiffSequence(
  oldArray,
  newArray,
  equalsFn = (a, b) => a === b
) {
  const sequence = []
  const array = new ArrayWithOriginalIndices(oldArray, equalsFn)

  for (let index = 0; index < newArray.length; index++) {
    if (array.isRemoval(index, newArray)) {
      sequence.push(array.removeItem(index))
      index--
      continue
    }

    if (array.isNoop(index, newArray)) {
      sequence.push(array.noopItem(index))
      continue
    }

    // TODO: addition case

    // TODO: move case
  }
```

Checks whether the operation is a noop

Pushes the noop operation to the sequence

Continues with the loop

```
    // TODO: remove extra items

  return sequence
}
```

### THE ADDITION CASE

To check whether an item was added in the new array, you need to check whether that item doesn't exist in the old array, starting from the current index. Figure 7.30 shows the addition case in the flow chart.

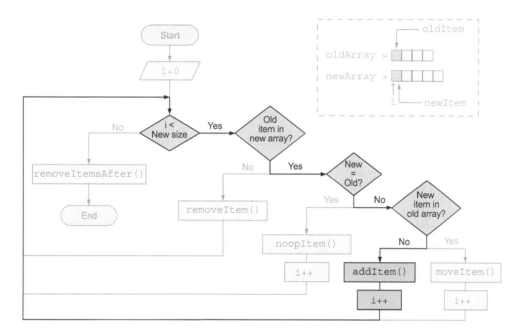

**Figure 7.30   The addition case in the flow chart**

To find the item in the old array starting from a given index, you implement a method called `findIndexFrom()`. When you use that method, the `isAddition()` method is straightforward to implement. Add the code shown in bold font in the following listing to the `ArrayWithOriginalIndices` class.

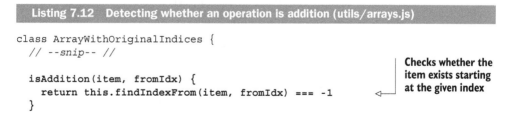

> **Listing 7.12   Detecting whether an operation is addition (utils/arrays.js)**

```
class ArrayWithOriginalIndices {
  // --snip-- //

  isAddition(item, fromIdx) {
    return this.findIndexFrom(item, fromIdx) === -1
  }
```

Checks whether the item exists starting at the given index

```
findIndexFrom(item, fromIndex) {
  for (let i = fromIndex; i < this.length; i++) {
    if (this.#equalsFn(item, this.#array[i])) {
      return i
    }
  }

  return -1
}
```

Starts looking from
the given index

If the item at the index
i equals the given one,
returns i

Returns -1 if the
item wasn't found

Dealing with an addition is as simple as adding the item to the old array and returning the add operation. You have to add an entry to the #originalIndices property, but the added item wasn't present in the original old array, so you can use -1 in this case. Add the addItem() method, shown in bold in the following listing, to the ArrayWith-OriginalIndices class.

> **Listing 7.13   Adding an item and returning an add operation (utils/arrays.js)**

```
class ArrayWithOriginalIndices {
  // --snip-- //

  isAddition(item, fromIdx) {
    return this.findIndexFrom(item, fromIdx) === -1
  }

  findIndexFrom(item, fromIndex) {
    for (let i = fromIndex; i < this.length; i++) {
      if (this.#equalsFn(item, this.#array[i])) {
        return i
      }
    }

    return -1
  }

  addItem(item, index) {
    const operation = {                          Creates the add
      op: ARRAY_DIFF_OP.ADD,                      operation
      index,
      item,
    }
                                                 Adds the new item to
                                                 the old array at the
                                                 given index
    this.#array.splice(index, 0, item)
    this.#originalIndices.splice(index, 0, -1)
                                                 Adds a -1 index to the
                                                 #originalIndices array
    return operation                              at the given index
  }                           Returns the add
}                             operation
```

These two methods make it easy to implement the addition case in the arraysDiff-Sequence() function. Add the code shown in bold in the following listing to the arraysDiffSequence() function.

**Listing 7.14   Implementing the addition case (utils/arrays.js)**

```
export function arraysDiffSequence(
  oldArray,
  newArray,
  equalsFn = (a, b) => a === b
) {
  const sequence = []
  const array = new ArrayWithOriginalIndices(oldArray, equalsFn)

  for (let index = 0; index < newArray.length; index++) {
    if (array.isRemoval(index, newArray)) {
      sequence.push(array.removeItem(index))
      index--
      continue
    }

    if (array.isNoop(index, newArray)) {
      sequence.push(array.noopItem(index))
      continue
    }

    const item = newArray[index]

    if (array.isAddition(item, index)) {
      sequence.push(array.addItem(item, index))
      continue
    }
    // TODO: move case
  }

  // TODO: remove extra items

  return sequence
}
```

Gets the item in the new array at the current index

Checks whether the case is an addition

Continues with the loop

Appends the add operation to the sequence

Let's move to the move case. This one is interesting.

### THE MOVE CASE

The neat thing about the move case is that you don't need to test for it explicitly; if the operation isn't a remove, an add, or a noop, it must be a move. Figure 7.31 highlights this branch of the flow chart.

To move an item, you want to extract it from the array (you can use the splice() method for that purpose) and insert it into the new position (you can use the splice() method again). Keep two things in mind: you also need to move the original index to its new position, and you have to include the original index in the move operation. The importance of saving the original index will become clear in chapter 8. Inside the ArrayWithOriginalIndices class, add the code shown in bold in the following listing to implement the moveItem() method.

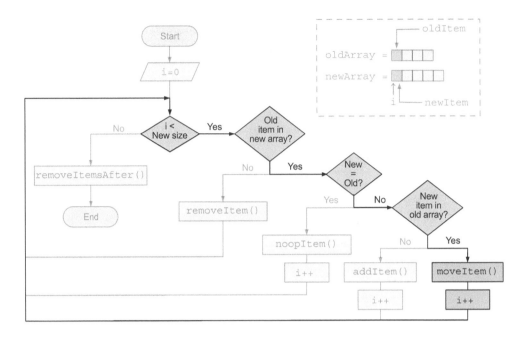

**Figure 7.31   The move case in the flow chart**

Listing 7.15   Detecting whether an operation is addition (utils/arrays.js)

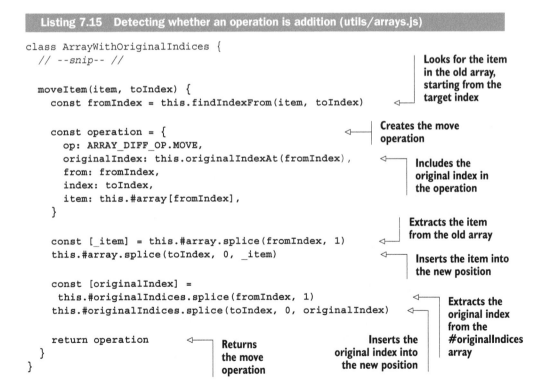

```
class ArrayWithOriginalIndices {
  // --snip-- //

  moveItem(item, toIndex) {
    const fromIndex = this.findIndexFrom(item, toIndex)          ◁— Looks for the item in the old array, starting from the target index

    const operation = {                                          ◁— Creates the move operation
      op: ARRAY_DIFF_OP.MOVE,
      originalIndex: this.originalIndexAt(fromIndex),            ◁— Includes the original index in the operation
      from: fromIndex,
      index: toIndex,
      item: this.#array[fromIndex],
    }

    const [_item] = this.#array.splice(fromIndex, 1)             ◁— Extracts the item from the old array
    this.#array.splice(toIndex, 0, _item)                        ◁— Inserts the item into the new position

    const [originalIndex] =
      this.#originalIndices.splice(fromIndex, 1)                 ◁— Extracts the original index from the #originalIndices array
    this.#originalIndices.splice(toIndex, 0, originalIndex)      ◁— Inserts the original index into the new position

    return operation                                            ◁— Returns the move operation
  }
}
```

Adding the move case to the `arraysDiffSequence()` function is straightforward. Add the line shown in bold in the following listing to the `arraysDiffSequence()` function.

> **Listing 7.16   Adding an item to the old array (utils/arrays.js)**

```
export function arraysDiffSequence(
  oldArray,
  newArray,
  equalsFn = (a, b) => a === b
) {
  const sequence = []
  const array = new ArrayWithOriginalIndices(oldArray, equalsFn)

  for (let index = 0; index < newArray.length; index++) {
    if (array.isRemoval(index, newArray)) {
      sequence.push(array.removeItem(index))
      index--
      continue
    }

    if (array.isNoop(index, newArray)) {
      sequence.push(array.noopItem(index))
      continue
    }

    const item = newArray[index]

    if (array.isAddition(item, index)) {
      sequence.push(array.addItem(item, index))
      continue
    }

    sequence.push(array.moveItem(item, index))
  }

  // TODO: remove extra items

  return sequence
}
```

You're almost there! You need only remove the outstanding items from the old array.

### REMOVING THE OUTSTANDING ITEMS

What happens when you reach the end of the new array and the old array still contains items? You remove them all, of course. Figure 7.32 shows the removal case in the flow chart.

To remove the outstanding items, you want to remove all items past the current index (which is the length of the new array) from the old array. You can use a `while` loop that keeps removing items while the old array is longer than the index. Write the code for the `removeItemsAfter()` method, shown in bold in the following listing.

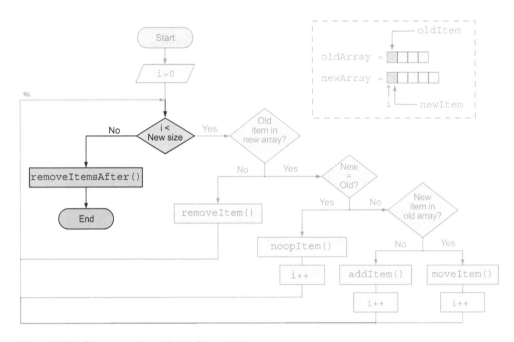

**Figure 7.32   The removal case in the flow chart**

Listing 7.17   Detecting whether an operation is addition (utils/arrays.js)

```
class ArrayWithOriginalIndices {
  // --snip-- //

  removeItemsAfter(index) {
    const operations = []

    while (this.length > index) {
      operations.push(this.removeItem(index))
    }

    return operations
  }
}
```

**Keeps removing items while the old array is longer than the index**

**Adds the removal operation to the array**

**Returns the removal operations**

Finally, add the code shown in bold in the following listing to the arraysDiffSequence()
function to remove the outstanding items. Note that removeItemsFrom() returns not
a single operation, but an array of operations.

Listing 7.18   Removing outstanding items (utils/arrays.js)

```
export function arraysDiffSequence(
  oldArray,
  newArray,
  equalsFn = (a, b) => a === b
) {
```

```
const sequence = []
const array = new ArrayWithOriginalIndices(oldArray, equalsFn)

for (let index = 0; index < newArray.length; index++) {
  if (array.isRemoval(index, newArray)) {
    sequence.push(array.removeItem(index))
    index--
    continue
  }

  if (array.isNoop(index, newArray)) {
    sequence.push(array.noopItem(index))
    continue
  }

  const item = newArray[index]

  if (array.isAddition(item, index)) {
    sequence.push(array.addItem(item, index))
    continue
  }

  sequence.push(array.moveItem(item, index))
}

sequence.push(...array.removeItemsAfter(newArray.length))

return sequence
}
```

Just like that, you have a working implementation of the `arraysDiffSequence()` function! Believe it or not, this algorithm is the hardest one to implement in the whole book. If you're still with me, the rest of the book will be easy to follow.

### Exercise 7.6

Write a function called `applyArraysDiffSequence()` that, given an array and a sequence of operations, applies the operations to the array and returns the resulting array. To test it, pass the following arrays to the `arraysDiffSequence()` function:

- *Old array*—`['A', 'A', 'B', 'C']`
- *New array*— `['C', 'K', 'A', 'B']`

Save the resulting operations in a variable called `sequence`. Then pass the old array and the sequence to the `applyArraysDiffSequence()` function, and check whether the resulting array is the same as the new array.

Find the solution at http://mng.bz/p1JE.

## Summary

- The reconciliation algorithm has two main steps: diffing (finding the differences between two virtual trees) and patching (applying the differences to the real DOM).
- Diffing two virtual trees to find their differences boils down to solving three problems: finding the differences between two objects, finding the differences between two arrays, and finding a sequence of operations that can be applied to an array to transform it into another array.

# The reconciliation
# algorithm: Patching
# the DOM

*8*

**This chapter covers**

- Implementing the `patchDOM()` function
- Using the `objectsDiff()` function to find the differences in attributes and styles
- Using the `arraysDiff()` function to find the differences between CSS classes
- Using the `arraysDiffSequence()` function to find the differences between virtual DOM children
- Using the Document API to patch DOM changes

In chapter 7, you saw how the reconciliation algorithm works in two phases: finding the differences between two virtual Document Object Model (DOM) trees and patching those differences in the real DOM. You implemented the three key functions to find differences between two objects or two arrays: `objectsDiff()`, `arraysDiff()`, and `arraysDiffSequence()`. In this chapter, you'll use these functions to implement the reconciliation algorithm inside the `patchDOM()` function. `patchDOM()` finds the differences between two virtual DOM trees (the one that's currently rendered and the one after the state has changed) and patches the real DOM accordingly.

161

With the `patchDOM()` function, your framework will be able to update the DOM by using a small set of operations instead of replacing the whole DOM tree every time the state changes. Thanks to this function, the new version of your framework—which you'll publish at the end of this chapter—will be much more efficient than the previous version. The best part is that the TODOs application rewrite you did in chapter 6 will still work with the new version of your framework, as its public API doesn't change. You'll need only to update the `import` statement to import the new version of the framework instead of the old one. This time, though, you won't lose the focus from the `<input>` fields every time you type a character because the fields will be updated without being replaced.

We'll end the chapter by looking at a few ways you can use browser developer tools to inspect the DOM and observe how the reconciliation algorithm patches small portions of the DOM.

> **NOTE**   You can find all the listings in this chapter in the listings/ch08 directory of the book's repository (http://mng.bz/XqRv). The code in this chapter can be checked out from the ch8 label (http://mng.bz/yZOB): `$ git switch --detach ch8`.

---

**Code catch-up**

In chapter 7, you modified the `createApp()` so that the returned application's object `renderApp()` method doesn't destroy and re-create the whole DOM; rather, it calls a `patchDOM()` function to patch the changes in the DOM. You'll implement the `patchDOM()` function in this chapter.

Then you wrote the `objectsDiff()` and `arraysDiff()` functions to find the differences between two objects or two arrays, respectively. Last, you implemented the `arraysDiffSequence()` function to find the sequence of operations that transform one array into another. To help this function keep track of the indices of the elements in the original array and the way they change, you wrote the `ArrayWithOriginal-Indices` class.

---

## 8.1   *Mounting the DOM at an index*

To patch the DOM, you compare the two virtual DOM trees by traversing them individually in a depth-first manner and apply the differences you find along the way to the real DOM (as you saw in the opening example of chapter 7). Very often, a new node is added somewhere in the middle of another's node children array. Let's look at an example.

Think of an error message that appears between an `<input>` field and a `<button>` element when the user enters an invalid value in the `<input>` field. Before the error appears, the DOM looks like this:

```
<form>
  <input type="text"/>
```

```
    <button>Validate</button>
</form>
```

Then the user writes some invalid text in the `<input>` field (whatever *invalid* means here) and clicks the validate `<button>`. The error message appears:

```
<form>
  <input type="text"/>
  <p class="error">Invalid text! Try something else</p>
  <button>Validate</button>
</form>
```

As you can see, the error message is inserted between the `<input>` field and the `<button>` element (at position `i=1`) inside the `<form>` element's children, as illustrated in figure 8.1. Your current implementation of the `mountDOM()` function doesn't allow you to insert a node at a given index inside a parent node.

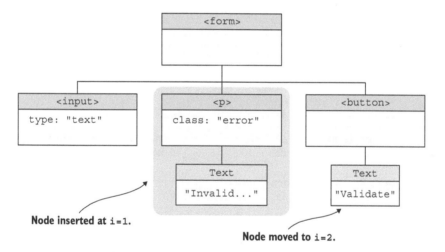

**Figure 8.1   Inserting the node at index `i=1`**

To insert new nodes at arbitrary positions, you need to modify the `mountDOM()` function so that it accepts an index in which to put a node instead of appending it at the end (as the function does at the moment).

### 8.1.1   *The insert() function*

Let's write an `insert()` function inside the mount-dom.js file to insert a node at a given index inside a parent node. Then you can use this function inside the `mountDOM()` function. You also want the function to append nodes at the end without having to figure out what the index would be because that use case is still a common one.

Here's what you can do: if the passed-in `index` is `null` or `undefined`, append the node to the parent node. Then, if the index is defined (neither `null` nor `undefined`), you need to account for the following cases:

- If the index is negative, throw an error because negative indices don't make sense.
- If the index is greater or equal to the number of children, append the node to the parent node.
- Otherwise, you know that the index lies somewhere in the children array, so you insert the node at the given index.

To insert a node at a given index, you can use the `insertBefore()` method (http://mng.bz/M9eW) of the `Node` interface. This method requires two arguments: the new element to insert and the *reference element*, which is the element before which the new element will be inserted. Figure 8.2 illustrates how the `insertBefore()` method would work for the example in figure 8.1.

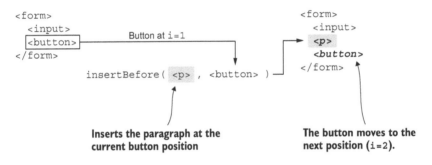

**Figure 8.2   Using the `insertBefore()` method**

---

**Exercise 8.1**

In a blank HTML file, create a `<div>` element with two `<p>` children, as follows:

```
<div>
  <p>One</p>
  <p>Three</p>
</div>
```

Then use the `insertBefore()` method to insert a new `<p>` element between the two existing ones. The new `<p>` element should contain the text `Two`.

Find the solution at http://mng.bz/OP12.

---

Open the mount-dom.js file. Write the `insert()` function inside it, below the `mount-DOM()` function, as shown in the following listing.

**Listing 8.1    The `insert()` function (mount-dom.js)**

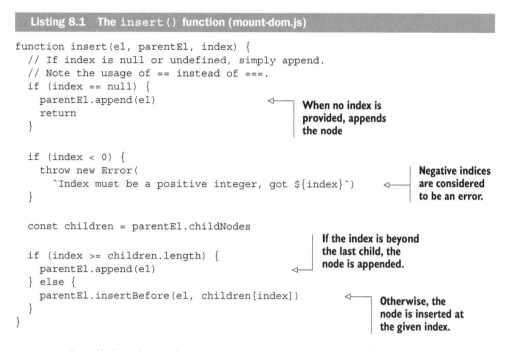

```
function insert(el, parentEl, index) {
  // If index is null or undefined, simply append.
  // Note the usage of == instead of ===.
  if (index == null) {
    parentEl.append(el)
    return
  }

  if (index < 0) {
    throw new Error(
      `Index must be a positive integer, got ${index}`)
  }

  const children = parentEl.childNodes

  if (index >= children.length) {
    parentEl.append(el)
  } else {
    parentEl.insertBefore(el, children[index])
  }
}
```

When no index is provided, appends the node

Negative indices are considered to be an error.

If the index is beyond the last child, the node is appended.

Otherwise, the node is inserted at the given index.

**NOTE**    Recall that depending on how you configured your linter, you might get a complaint about using `==` instead of `===`, which comes from the eqeqeq rule (https://eslint.org/docs/latest/rules/eqeqeq). You can safely ignore this warning. The `==` operator is fine here because you want to check for both `null` and `undefined` values.

With the `insert()` function in place, you can modify the `mountDOM()` function to accept an index as a third parameter (as shown in the following listing) so that you can insert the node at that index. The index should be passed down to the text and element node-creation functions, which will use the `insert()` function to insert the node at the given index.

**Listing 8.2    Adding the `index` as a parameter to the functions (mount-dom.js)**

```
export function mountDOM(vdom, parentEl, index) {
  switch (vdom.type) {
    case DOM_TYPES.TEXT: {
      createTextNode(vdom, parentEl, index)
      break
    }

    case DOM_TYPES.ELEMENT: {
      createElementNode(vdom, parentEl, index)
      break
    }
```

```
    case DOM_TYPES.FRAGMENT: {
      createFragmentNodes(vdom, parentEl, index)
      break
    }

    default: {
      throw new Error(`Can't mount DOM of type: ${vdom.type}`)
    }
  }
}
```

### 8.1.2   Text nodes

Now let's modify the createTextNode(), createElementNode(), and createFragment-Nodes() functions to use the insert() function to insert the node at the given index. To insert a text node at a given index, you modify the createTextNode() function to use the insert() function, as shown in the following listing.

**Listing 8.3   Using** `insert()` **inside** `createTextNode()` **(mount-dom.js)**

```
function createTextNode(vdom, parentEl, index) {
  const { value } = vdom

  const textNode = document.createTextNode(value)
  vdom.el = textNode

  parentEl.append(textNode)
  insert(textNode, parentEl, index)
}
```

### 8.1.3   Element nodes

Let's look at element nodes. In the case of element nodes, the change is exactly the same as for text nodes, as you can see in the following listing.

**Listing 8.4   Using** `insert()` **inside** `createElementNode()` **(mount-dom.js)**

```
function createElementNode(vdom, parentEl, index) {
  const { tag, props, children } = vdom

  const element = document.createElement(tag)
  addProps(element, props, vdom)
  vdom.el = element

  children.forEach((child) => mountDOM(child, element))
  parentEl.append(element)
  insert(element, parentEl, index)
}
```

### 8.1.4 Fragment nodes

The case of fragment nodes is slightly different because you need to insert all the children of the fragment starting at the given index. Each child is inserted at an index that's computed by adding the given index and its own index inside the fragment:

```
children.forEach((child, i) => {
  mountDOM(child, parentEl, index + i)
})
```

Don't forget to account for the case when the passed `index` is `null`, in which case you want to pass `null` to the `insert()` function so that the children are appended at the end of the parent node. Modify the `createFragmentNodes()` function to use the `insert()` function, as shown in the following listing.

> **Listing 8.5  Using `insert()` inside `createElementNode()` (mount-dom.js)**

```
function createFragmentNodes(vdom, parentEl, index) {
  const { children } = vdom
  vdom.el = parentEl

  children.forEach((child) => mountDOM(child, parentEl))
  children.forEach((child, i) =>
    mountDOM(child, parentEl, index ? index + i : null)
  )
}
```

With these changes in place, let's turn our attention to the `patchDOM()` function.

## 8.2  Patching the DOM

In chapter 7, we saw an example of how two virtual DOM trees are compared and the changes are applied to the real DOM. Figure 8.3 (reproduced from chapter 7) shows the two virtual DOM trees in the example and the changes that need to be applied to the real DOM.

We compared the two virtual DOM trees manually, starting with the top-level `<div>` element and then moving to its children in a depth-first manner. Let's turn these steps into an algorithm that you can implement.

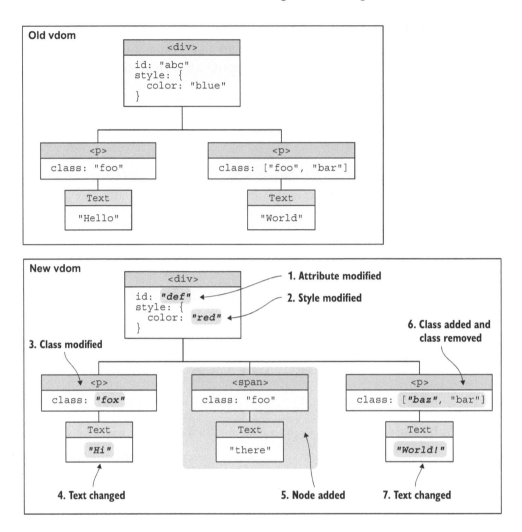

**Figure 8.3   Comparing two virtual DOM trees to find out what changed**

### 8.2.1   The reconciliation algorithm

First, I'll define the algorithm in plain English; then I'll translate it into code. I've already touched on the nature of this algorithm, but it's time for a more formal definition.

> **DEFINITION**   The *reconciliation algorithm* compares two virtual DOM trees, finds the sequence of operations that transforms one into the other, and patches the real DOM by applying those operations to it. The algorithm is recursive, starting at the top-level nodes of both virtual DOM trees. After comparing these nodes, it moves to their children until it reaches the leaves of the trees.

Thanks to the exercise you worked out by hand in chapter 7, you have a fair understanding of what the algorithm does. Now try to put that knowledge into words. Here's the algorithm, step by step:

1 Start at the top-level nodes of both virtual DOM trees.
2 If the nodes are different, destroy the DOM node (and everything that's below it), and replace it with the new node and its subtree.
3 If the nodes are equal:
   a *Text nodes*—Compare and patch their `nodeValue` (the property containing the text).
   b *Element nodes*—Compare and patch their props (attributes, CSS classes and styles, and event listeners).
4 Find the sequence of operations that transforms the first node's children array into the second node's.
5 For each operation, patch the DOM accordingly:
   a *Adding a node.* Mount the new node (and its subtree) at the given index.
   b *Removing a node.* Destroy the node (and its subtree) at the given index.
   c *Moving a node.* Move the node to the new index. Start from step 1, using the moved nodes as the new top-level nodes.
   d *Doing no operation.* Start from step 1, using the current nodes as the new top-level nodes.

**NOTE** The idea of destroying a DOM node and its subtree when it's found to have changed comes from React. Soon, I'll explain why this idea is a good one in practice.

The algorithm doesn't look complicated, but the implementation has a lot of details. The good news is that you implemented the most complex part—the `arraysDiff-Sequence()` function—in chapter 7.

Figure 8.4 shows the algorithm as a flow chart. Keep this figure handy as you read the next section; it'll help you during implementation.

The first thing you should notice is that the algorithm is recursive. When you find two nodes in the children arrays that are the same, you start the algorithm again, this time using those nodes as the top-level nodes. This situation happens in steps 5c and 5d, the cases in which nodes moved—either forcefully or naturally—so you also want to inspect what happened to their subtrees. In figure 8.4, the `move` and `noop` branches after the `patchChildren()` call go back to the top of the algorithm.

The cases in which a child node was added or removed are simple enough: you simply call the `mountDOM()` or `destroyDOM()` function, respectively. If you recall, these functions take care of mounting or destroying the whole subtree, which is why the algorithm isn't recursive in these cases. As you can see in figure 8.4, the `add` and `remove` branches after the `patchChildren()` call don't go back to the top of the algorithm; they end the algorithm.

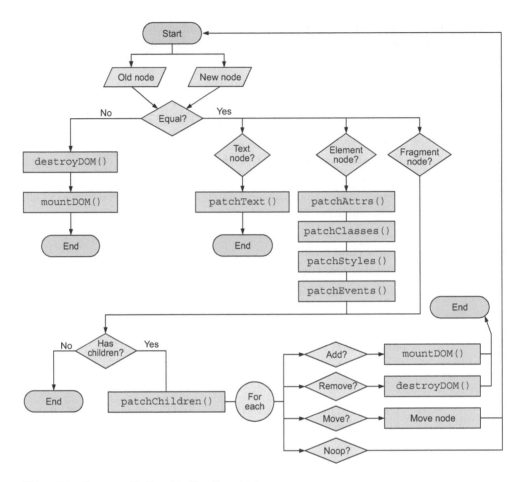

**Figure 8.4   The reconciliation algorithm flow chart**

When you find a fragment node in the children array, instead of keeping it, you want to extract its children. In figure 8.5, the fragment nodes at every level are replaced by their children.

You want to extract the children of a fragment node so that the trees with which the reconciliation algorithm works are as similar as possible to the real DOM. If you recall, fragments aren't part of the DOM; they're simply a way to group nodes. In figure 8.5, the DOM would look like this:

```
<p>
  <span>Once</span>
  <span>upon</span>
  <span>a</span>
  <span>time</span>
</p>
```

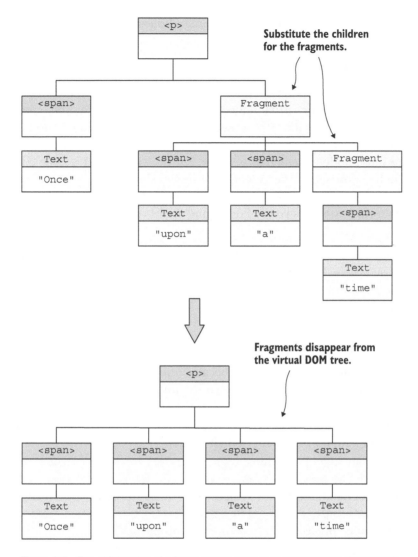

**Figure 8.5  The child nodes of a fragment are extracted and added to the parent's children array.**

As you can see, there's no trace of the fragments in the real DOM. Fragments never make it to the reconciliation algorithm because there are no fragments in the real DOM; fragments are a useful construct to group nodes in the virtual DOM.

The last thing I want you to notice is step 2, where if you find two top-level nodes that are different, you destroy the whole subtree to mount the new one. Two things require some explanation here: what do we mean when we say that two virtual nodes are different, and why do we have to destroy the whole subtree? Doesn't that sound a bit wasteful? I'll discuss node equality first.

### 8.2.2 *Virtual node equality*

You want to know when two virtual nodes are equal so that you can reuse the existing DOM node (as saved in the virtual node's `el` property); if not, that node needs to be destroyed and replaced by a new one. Reusing an existing DOM node and patching its properties is much more efficient than destroying it and mounting a new one, so you want to reuse nodes as much as possible. For two virtual nodes to be equal, first they need to be of the same type. A text node and an element node, for example, can never be equal because you wouldn't be able to reuse the existing DOM node. When you know that the two nodes you're comparing are of the same type, the rules are as follows:

- *Text nodes*—Two text nodes are always equal (even if their `nodeValue` is different).
- *Fragment nodes*—Two fragment nodes are always equal (even if they contain different children).
- *Element nodes*—Two element nodes are equal if their `tagName` properties are equal.

These rules are illustrated in figure 8.6:

- Two text nodes are always equal because their text is something that can be patched, so there's no need to destroy it and mount a new node with a different text.
- Fragment nodes are always equal because they're simply containers for other nodes and have no properties of their own.
- The element node is the most interesting case: for two element nodes to be equal, their tag must be the same. You can't change the tag of a `<div>` to a `<span>` programmatically and expect the browser to render it correctly because a `<div>` and a `<span>` are two different objects (`HTMLDivElement` and `HTMLSpanElement`, to be precise) that have different properties.

> **NOTE** You could change the tag of a `<div>` to a `<span>` in the HTML source by using the browser's developer tools, and that change would work perfectly well. But under the hood, the browser is destroying the old `HTMLDivElement` and creating a new `HTMLSpanElement`. That's exactly what you need to do in your code using the Document API if you compare two element nodes and find the tag changed: destroy the node with the old tag and mount a new one with the new tag.

**Text nodes are always equal.**

**Fragment nodes are always equal.**

**Element nodes are equal if they have the same tag.**

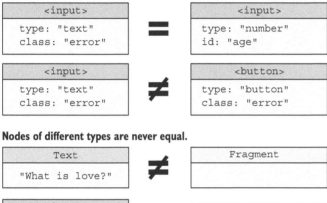

**Nodes of different types are never equal.**

**Figure 8.6  The rules for virtual node equality**

Let's implement a function called `nodesEqual()` to check whether two nodes are equal. If you look at the algorithm's flow chart, the equality check happens at the top, when the old and new nodes enter the algorithm (highlighted in figure 8.7).

To create a function to check whether two nodes are equal, create a new file called nodes-equal.js and write the code in the following listing. The `areNodesEqual()` function applies the aforementioned rules to check whether two nodes are equal.

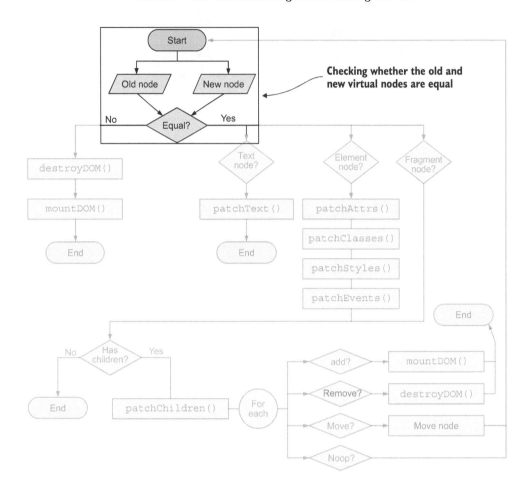

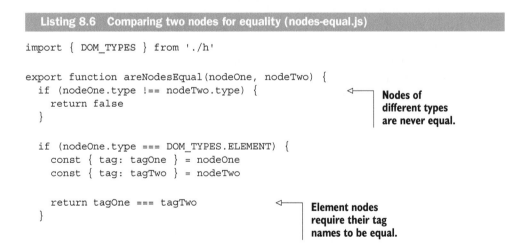

**Figure 8.7   Checking whether the old and new nodes are equal in the algorithm's flow chart**

**Listing 8.6   Comparing two nodes for equality (nodes-equal.js)**

```
import { DOM_TYPES } from './h'

export function areNodesEqual(nodeOne, nodeTwo) {
  if (nodeOne.type !== nodeTwo.type) {
    return false
  }

  if (nodeOne.type === DOM_TYPES.ELEMENT) {
    const { tag: tagOne } = nodeOne
    const { tag: tagTwo } = nodeTwo

    return tagOne === tagTwo
  }
}
```

◁—— **Nodes of different types are never equal.**

◁—— **Element nodes require their tag names to be equal.**

```
        return true
}
```

**Exercise 8.2**

Paste the `areNodesEqual()` function into the browser's console (don't forget to include the `DOM_TYPES` constant) and test it with the following cases:

- Two text nodes with the same text
- Two text nodes with different text
- An element node and a text node
- A `<p>` element node and a `<div>` element node
- Two `<p>` element nodes with different text content

What are the results? Find the solution at http://mng.bz/YRAe.

Now that you have a function to check whether two nodes are equal, you can use it in the algorithm to decide whether to destroy the old node and mount the new one. The second question to answer is why you have to destroy the whole subtree, and I'll answer it in the next section.

### 8.2.3 Subtree change

Destroying the whole subtree and re-creating it when you detect that the node changed sounds like going back to when your framework removed the whole DOM tree and mounted a new one. Isn't that what we're trying to avoid with the reconciliation algorithm? Couldn't you compare their children to check whether at least the subtrees are the same so that you need to re-create only the nodes that are different (figure 8.8)?

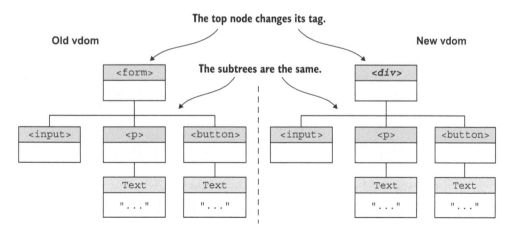

**Figure 8.8** The top node's tag changed, but the subtrees are the same.

In figure 8.8, the top nodes—the ones you're comparing—are different, but their subtrees are the same. You could patch only the top node and leave the subtrees alone. If the children are different, you can patch them with the help of the `arraysDiff-Sequence()` function.

In general, when you detect that a node has changed, it usually means that a new part of the view entered the scene while the old one left. This new part of the view typically has a different subtree below it, one that's unrelated to the old subtree. If you decide to patch the top node and then start comparing the two subtrees, you'd find many differences because the new subtree is different from the old one. You'd end up doing a lot of comparisons and DOM operations that are equivalent to destroying the whole subtree and re-creating it from scratch, only using many more operations.

A more realistic situation than the one shown in figure 8.8 is the one shown in figure 8.9: when a parent node changes, its subtrees are likely to be different. When you go from having a `<form>` to having a `<div>`, you probably can anticipate that something different will be below it. If, however, the parent node changes but the subtree is the same, destroying and re-creating the whole subtree is a price you're willing to pay for the simplicity of the algorithm.

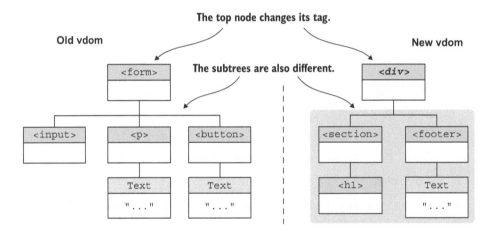

**Figure 8.9  A more realistic case in which the top nodes are different and so are their subtrees**

Now that I've illustrated why it's better to destroy the whole subtree and re-create it when the top virtual nodes being compared are different, let's implement the algorithm, starting by writing the `patchDOM()` function, which is the main entry point of the algorithm. We'll add more cases to the function as we go, but for now, we'll implement only the case in which the top nodes are different—the easiest one to implement.

First, find the index of the old node's element (referenced by the `el` property of the virtual node) in its DOM's parent node (referenced by the `parentEl` property), destroy it, and then mount the new node in the same place. To find this index, you can use the `indexOf()` method of the parent element's list of child nodes (`parentEl.childNodes`), passing it the old node's DOM element. One case to bear in mind, though, is when the index returned by `indexOf()` is `-1`, which means that the old node's DOM element isn't among the parent children. When the old node is a fragment and the `el` property references the parent element, we can't find an element inside itself. In this case, we want to use a `null` index, which means that the new `vdom` will be appended at the end of the parent node's list of child nodes. Figure 8.10 highlights this step in the algorithm's flow chart.

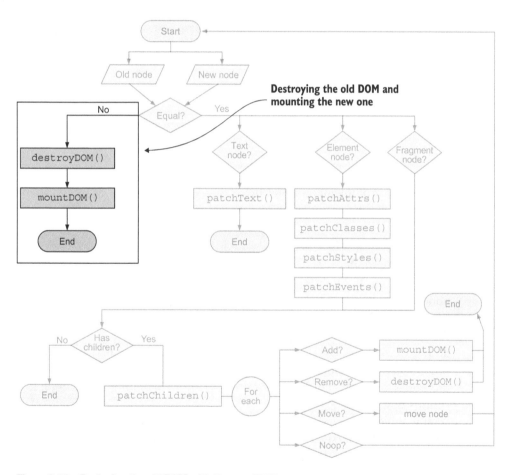

**Figure 8.10  Replacing the old DOM with the new DOM**

Create a new file called patch-dom.js, and write the code in the following listing.

> **Listing 8.7    Patching the DOM when the top nodes are different (patch-dom.js)**

```
import { destroyDOM } from './destroy-dom'
import { mountDOM } from './mount-dom'
import { areNodesEqual } from './nodes-equal'                    Finds the
                                                                 index in the
                                                                 parent node
export function patchDOM(oldVdom, newVdom, parentEl) {           where the old
  if (!areNodesEqual(oldVdom, newVdom)) {                        node is
    const index = findIndexInParent(parentEl, oldVdom.el)   ◁──┘
    destroyDOM(oldVdom)                                     ◁──┐ Destroys the old
    mountDOM(newVdom, parentEl, index)                      ◁─┐│ node and its
                                                             ││ subtree
    return newVdom                                          ││
  }                                                         │  Mounts the new node
}                                                           │  and its subtree

function findIndexInParent(parentEl, el) {
  const index = Array.from(parentEl.childNodes).indexOf(el)
  if (index < 0) {
    return null
  }

  return index
}
```

Great—you've implemented the first case of the algorithm. Let's continue with the case in which the top nodes are text nodes.

### 8.2.4    *Patching text nodes*

Patching text nodes is easy: you set the nodeValue property of the DOM node to the new text when the text is different. If you find that the text content in both virtual nodes is the same, you don't need to do anything.

As you can imagine, the first thing the patchDOM() function does—right after the areNodesEqual() comparison from section 8.2.3—is to check whether the nodes are text nodes. If so, call a function to patch the text node, patchText(), which you need to implement. You can use a switch statement to check the type of the nodes and act accordingly. Figure 8.11 shows patching a text node in the algorithm's flow chart.

If you remember, when you implemented the mountDOM() function, you saved the reference to the DOM element representing the virtual node in the el property of the virtual node. Now, in the patchDOM() function, when the nodes aren't created but simply patched, you need to save this reference from oldVdom to newVdom so that you don't lose it (figure 8.12).

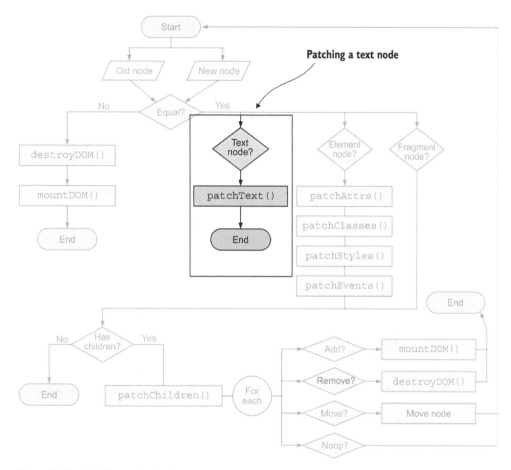

**Figure 8.11    Patching a text node**

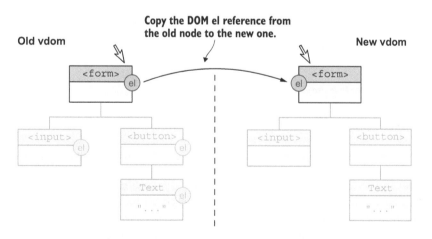

**Figure 8.12    Copying the DOM element reference from the old virtual node to the new one**

Modify the patchDOM() function, adding the code shown in bold in the following listing.

**Listing 8.8   The case of a text node (patch-dom.js)**

```
import { destroyDOM } from './destroy-dom'
import { DOM_TYPES } from './h'
import { mountDOM } from './mount-dom'
import { areNodesEqual } from './nodes-equal'

export function patchDOM(oldVdom, newVdom, parentEl) {
  if (!areNodesEqual(oldVdom, newVdom)) {
    const index = findIndexInParent(parentEl, oldVdom.el)
    destroyDOM(oldVdom)
    mountDOM(newVdom, parentEl, index)

    return newVdom
  }

  newVdom.el = oldVdom.el              ⟵——  Saves the reference
                                              to the DOM element
                                              in the new node
  switch (newVdom.type) {
    case DOM_TYPES.TEXT: {                    Calls the function to
      patchText(oldVdom, newVdom)        ⟵—  patch the text node
      return newVdom             ⟵——
    }                                         Returns the new
  }                                           virtual node

  return newVdom
}
```

Let's write the patchText() function, which compares the texts in the nodeValue property of the old and new virtual nodes. If the texts are different (that is, have changed), set the nodeValue property of the DOM element to the new text. Inside the patch-dom.js file, write the code in the following listing.

**Listing 8.9   Patching a text node (patch-dom.js)**

```
function patchText(oldVdom, newVdom) {
  const el = oldVdom.el
  const { value: oldText } = oldVdom
  const { value: newText } = newVdom

  if (oldText !== newText) {
    el.nodeValue = newText
  }
}
```

Note that in the first line of the function, you're extracting the DOM element from the oldVDom virtual node's el property. You also could have used the newVDom virtual node's reference because before calling this function, patchDOM() has already saved it there. (At this point, oldVdom.el === newVdom.el must be true.)

Let's move on to the case in which the top nodes are element nodes. This case is the most interesting one, as well as the most complex.

### 8.2.5  *Patching element nodes*

Figure 8.13 shows the patching of an element node in the algorithm's flow chart. As you can see, patching an element node requires a few steps—four, to be precise.

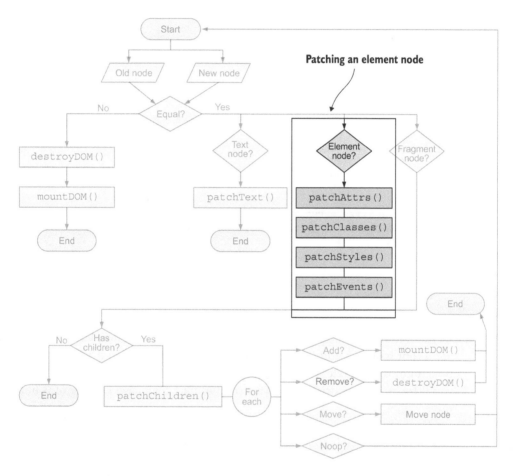

**Figure 8.13  Patching an element node**

Let's start by including the appropriate `switch` case in the `patchDOM()` function. Then I'll explain how to write the `patchElement()` function—the one that does all the work. Add the code in bold to patch-dom.js as shown in the following listing. As you can see, the work of patching element nodes is delegated to the `patchElement()` function.

**Listing 8.10   The case of an element node (patch-dom.js)**

```
import { destroyDOM } from './destroy-dom'
import { DOM_TYPES } from './h'
import { mountDOM } from './mount-dom'
import { areNodesEqual } from './nodes-equal'

export function patchDOM(oldVdom, newVdom, parentEl) {
  if (!areNodesEqual(oldVdom, newVdom)) {
    const index = findIndexInParent(parentEl, oldVdom.el)
    destroyDOM(oldVdom)
    mountDOM(newVdom, parentEl, index)

    return newVdom
  }

  newVdom.el = oldVdom.el

  switch (newVdom.type) {
    case DOM_TYPES.TEXT: {
      patchText(oldVdom, newVdom)
      return newVdom
    }

    case DOM_TYPES.ELEMENT: {
      patchElement(oldVdom, newVdom)
      break
    }
  }

  return newVdom
}
```

Element nodes are more complex than text nodes because they have attributes, styles, and event handlers and because they can have children. You'll take care of patching the children of a node in section 8.2.6, which covers the case of fragment nodes. But you'll focus on the attributes, styles (including CSS classes), and event handlers in this section.

The `patchElement()` function is in charge of extracting the attributes, CSS classes and styles, and event handlers from the old and new virtual nodes and then passing them to the appropriate functions to patch them. You'll write functions to patch attributes, CSS classes and styles, and event handlers separately because they follow different rules:

- `patchAttrs()`—Patches the attributes (such as id, name, value, and so on)
- `patchClasses()`—Patches the CSS class names
- `patchStyles()`—Patches the CSS styles
- `patchEvents()`—Patches the event handlers and returns an object with the current event handlers

The event handlers returned by the `patchEvents()` function should be saved in the `listeners` property of the new virtual node so that you can remove them later. Recall that when you implemented the mountDOM() function, you saved the event handlers in the listeners property of the virtual node.

Inside the patch-dom.js file, write the code for the patchElement() function as shown in the following listing. (You don't need to include the // TODO comments shown in the listing; they're simply reminders of the functions you need to write next.)

Listing 8.11   Patching an element node (patch-dom.js)

```
function patchElement(oldVdom, newVdom) {
  const el = oldVdom.el
  const {
    class: oldClass,
    style: oldStyle,
    on: oldEvents,
    ...oldAttrs
  } = oldVdom.props
  const {
    class: newClass,
    style: newStyle,
    on: newEvents,
    ...newAttrs
  } = newVdom.props
  const { listeners: oldListeners } = oldVdom

  patchAttrs(el, oldAttrs, newAttrs)
  patchClasses(el, oldClass, newClass)
  patchStyles(el, oldStyle, newStyle)
  newVdom.listeners = patchEvents(el, oldListeners, oldEvents, newEvents)
}

// TODO: implement patchAttrs()

// TODO: implement patchClasses()

// TODO: implement patchStyles()

// TODO: implement patchEvents()
```

Now that we've broken the work of patching element nodes into smaller tasks, let's start with the first one: patching attributes.

### PATCHING ATTRIBUTES

The attributes of a virtual node are all the key-value pairs that come inside its props object—except the class, style, and on properties, which have a special meaning. Now, given the two objects containing the attributes of the old and new virtual nodes (oldAttrs and newAttrs, respectively), you need to find out which attributes have been added, removed, or changed. In chapter 7, you wrote a function called objects-Diff() that did exactly that job.

The objectsDiff() function tells you which attributes have been added, removed, or changed. You can get rid of the attributes that have been removed by using the removeAttribute() function, which you wrote in chapter 4 (inside the attributes.js file). The attributes that have been added or changed can be set using the setAttribute() function, which you also wrote earlier.

At the bottom of the patch-dom.js file, write the code for the patchAttrs() function, as shown in the following listing. Don't forget to include the new import statements at the top of the file.

---

**Listing 8.12    Patching the attributes (patch-dom.js)**

```
import {
  removeAttribute,
  setAttribute,
} from './attributes'
import { destroyDOM } from './destroy-dom'
import { DOM_TYPES } from './h'
import { mountDOM } from './mount-dom'
import { areNodesEqual } from './nodes-equal'
import { objectsDiff } from './utils/objects'              Finds out which
                                                           attributes have been
                                                           added, removed, or
// --snip-- //                                             changed

function patchAttrs(el, oldAttrs, newAttrs) {
  const { added, removed, updated } = objectsDiff(oldAttrs, newAttrs)   ◁

  for (const attr of removed) {
    removeAttribute(el, attr)           ◁──┤ Removes the attributes
  }                                         that have been removed

  for (const attr of added.concat(updated)) {
    setAttribute(el, attr, newAttrs[attr])   ◁──┐ Sets the attributes
  }                                              that have been added
}                                                or changed
```

---

**PATCHING CSS CLASSES**

Let's move on to patching CSS classes. The tricky part of patching the CSS classes is that they can come as a string ('foo bar') or as an array of strings (['foo', 'bar']). Here's what you'll do:

- If the CSS classes come in an array, filter the blank or empty strings out and keep them as an array.
- If the CSS classes come as a string, split it on whitespace and filter the blank or empty strings out.

This way, you work with two arrays of strings representing the CSS classes of the old and new virtual DOMs. Then you can use the arraysDiff() function that you implemented in chapter 7 to find out which CSS classes have been added and removed. The DOM element has a classList property (an instance of the DOMTokenList interface) that you can use to add CSS classes to, and remove CSS classes from, the element. Add the new classes by using the classList.add() method, and remove the old ones by using the `classList.remove()` method. The classes that were neither added nor removed don't need to be touched; they can stay as they are.

At the bottom of the patch-dom.js file, write the code for the `patchClasses()` function as shown in the following listing. Again, don't forget to include the new `import` statements at the top of the file. Also, pay attention to a function that you'll need to import: `isNotBlankOrEmptyString()`.

**Listing 8.13  Patching the CSS classes (patch-dom.js)**

```
import {
  removeAttribute,
  setAttribute,
} from './attributes'
import { destroyDOM } from './destroy-dom'
import { DOM_TYPES } from './h'
import { mountDOM } from './mount-dom'
import { areNodesEqual } from './nodes-equal'
import {
  arraysDiff,
} from './utils/arrays'
import { objectsDiff } from './utils/objects'
import { isNotBlankOrEmptyString } from './utils/strings'

// --snip-- //

function patchClasses(el, oldClass, newClass) {
  const oldClasses = toClassList(oldClass)          // Array of old CSS classes
  const newClasses = toClassList(newClass)          // Array of new CSS classes

  const { added, removed } =
    arraysDiff(oldClasses, newClasses)              // Finds out which CSS classes have been added and removed

  if (removed.length > 0) {
    el.classList.remove(...removed)                 // Adds the CSS classes that have been added
  }
  if (added.length > 0) {
    el.classList.add(...added)                      // Removes the CSS classes that have been removed
  }
}

function toClassList(classes = '') {
  return Array.isArray(classes)
    ? classes.filter(isNotBlankOrEmptyString)       // Filters blank and empty strings
    : classes.split(/(\s+)/)
        .filter(isNotBlankOrEmptyString)            // Splits the string on whitespace and filters blank and empty strings
}
```

Now you need to write the `isNotBlankOrEmptyString()` function in the utils/strings.js file. This function takes a string as an argument; it returns `true` if the string is neither blank nor empty and `false` otherwise. Splitting that function is helpful. Use `isNotEmptyString()` to test whether a string is empty. `isNotBlankOrEmptyString()` uses the former function, passing it a trimmed version of the string. Create a new file in the utils directory, name the file strings.js, and write the code for the isNotBlankOrEmpty-String() function as shown in the following listing.

**Listing 8.14   Filtering empty and blank strings (utils/strings.js)**

```
export function isNotEmptyString(str) {
  return str !== ''
}


export function isNotBlankOrEmptyString(str) {
  return isNotEmptyString(str.trim())
}
```

### PATCHING THE STYLE

Patching the style is similar to patching the attributes: you compare the old and new style objects (using the objectsDiff() function), and then you add the new or modified styles and remove the old ones. To set or remove styles, use the setStyle() and removeStyle() functions that you wrote in chapter 4.

Inside the patch-dom.js file, write the code for the patchStyle() function as shown in the following listing. Don't forget to import the removeStyle() and setStyle() functions at the top of the file.

**Listing 8.15   Patching the styles (patch-dom.js)**

```
import {
  removeAttribute,
  setAttribute,
  removeStyle,
  setStyle,
} from './attributes'
import { destroyDOM } from './destroy-dom'
import { DOM_TYPES } from './h'
import { mountDOM } from './mount-dom'
import { areNodesEqual } from './nodes-equal'
import {
  arraysDiff,
} from './utils/arrays'
import { objectsDiff } from './utils/objects'
import { isNotBlankOrEmptyString } from './utils/strings'

// --snip-- //

function patchStyles(el, oldStyle = {}, newStyle = {}) {
  const { added, removed, updated } = objectsDiff(oldStyle, newStyle)

  for (const style of removed) {
    removeStyle(el, style)
  }
```

```
    for (const style of added.concat(updated)) {
      setStyle(el, style, newStyle[style])
    }
}
```

## PATCHING EVENT LISTENERS

Last, let's implement the event-listeners patching. The `patchEvents()` function is a bit different in that it has an extra parameter, `oldListeners` (the second one), which is an object containing the event listeners that are currently attached to the DOM. Let's see why having a reference to the current event listener is necessary.

If you recall, when you implemented the `mountDOM()` function, you wrote a function called `addEventListener()` to attach event listeners to the DOM. Currently, `addEventListener()` uses the function you pass it as the event listener, but remember that I said this situation would change. Indeed, in section 10.2, this function will wrap the event listener you pass it into a new function, and it'll use that new function as an event listener, much like the following example:

```
function addEventListener(eventName, handler, el) {
  // Function that wraps the original handler
  function boundHandler(event) {
    // -- snip -- //

    handler(event)
  }

  el.addEventListener(eventName, boundHandler)

  return boundHandler
}
```

You'll understand soon why you want to do this. For now, know that the functions defined in the virtual DOM to handle events aren't the same as the functions that are attached to the DOM. This situation is why the `patchEvents()` function needs the `oldListeners` object: the function is attached to the DOM. As you know, to remove an event listener from a DOM element, you call its `removeEventListener()` method, passing it the name of the event and the function that you want to remove, so you need the functions that were used to attach the event listeners to the DOM.

The second difference of the `patchEvents()` function compared with the previous ones is that it returns an object containing the event names and handler functions that have been added to the DOM. (The other functions didn't return anything.) You save this object in the `listeners` key of the new virtual DOM node. Later, you use this `listeners` object to remove the event listeners from the DOM when the view is destroyed.

The rest of the job is a matter of using the `objectsDiff()` function to find out which event listeners have been added, modified, or removed and then calling the `addEventListener()` function and the `el.removeEventListener()` method as required. In this case, though, when an event listener has been modified (that is, the event name is the same but the handler function is different), you need to remove the old event listener and then add the new one. Keep this detail in mind.

Pay attention to two important aspects of the code. First, you use the function in `oldListeners[eventName]` to remove the event listener, not the function in `oldEvents[eventName]`. I've already explained the reason, you must write this line of code correctly for your framework to work properly:

```
el.removeEventListener(eventName, oldListeners[eventName])
```

Second, you use your own implementation of the `addEventListener()` function to add the event listeners to the DOM, not the `el.addEventListener()` method of the DOM element. To remove the event listeners, you use the `el.removeEventListener()` method.

Write the code for the `patchEvents()` function as shown in the following listing. Don't forget to import the `addEventListener` function at the top of the file.

**Listing 8.16  Patching the event listeners (patch-dom.js)**

```
import {
  removeAttribute,
  setAttribute,
  removeStyle,
  setStyle,
} from './attributes'
import { destroyDOM } from './destroy-dom'
import { addEventListener } from './events'
import { DOM_TYPES } from './h'
import { mountDOM } from './mount-dom'
import { areNodesEqual } from './nodes-equal'
import {
  arraysDiff,
} from './utils/arrays'
import { objectsDiff } from './utils/objects'
import { isNotBlankOrEmptyString } from './utils/strings'

// --snip-- //

function patchEvents(
  el,
  oldListeners = {},
  oldEvents = {},
  newEvents = {}
) {
  const { removed, added, updated } =           Finds out which
    objectsDiff(oldEvents, newEvents)    ◁┘      event listeners
                                                 changed
```

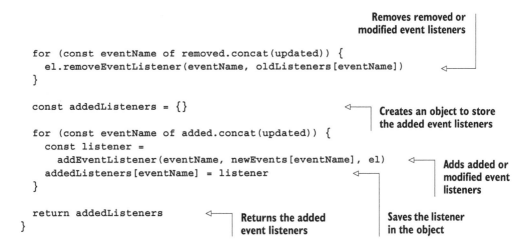

```
for (const eventName of removed.concat(updated)) {
  el.removeEventListener(eventName, oldListeners[eventName])
}

const addedListeners = {}

for (const eventName of added.concat(updated)) {
  const listener =
    addEventListener(eventName, newEvents[eventName], el)
  addedListeners[eventName] = listener
}

return addedListeners
}
```

Removes removed or
modified event listeners

Creates an object to store
the added event listeners

Adds added or
modified event
listeners

Saves the listener
in the object

Returns the added
event listeners

You've implemented the patchElement() function, which patched the DOM element and required four other functions to do so: patchAttrs(), patchClasses(), patch-Styles(), and patchEvents(). Believe it or not, all you have to do now to have a complete implementation of the patchDOM() function is patch the children of a node.

### 8.2.6 Patching child nodes

Both element and fragment nodes can have children, so the patchDOM() function needs to patch the children arrays of both types of nodes. Patching the children means figuring out which children have been added, which ones have been removed, and which ones have been shuffled around. For this purpose, you implemented arraysDiffSequence() in chapter 7.

Figure 8.14 shows the patching of children in the algorithm's flow chart. Remember that in the case of move and noop operations between children, the algorithm calls the patchDOM() function recursively, passing it the old and new children nodes. The add and remove operations terminate the algorithm.

Start by modifying the patchDOM() function to call the patchChildren() function after the switch statement. This function will execute the patchChildren() function for all types of elements except the text nodes, which return early from the patch-DOM() function.

Modify the patchDOM() function by adding the code shown in bold in the following listing. This code imports arraysDiffSequence and ARRAY_DIFF_OP from the utils/arrays.js file and calls the patchChildren() function.

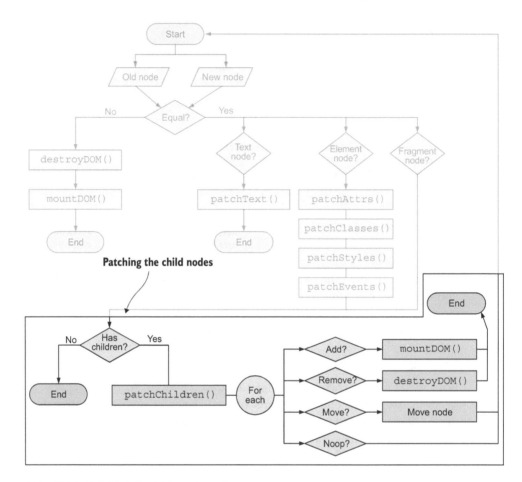

**Figure 8.14    Patching the children of a node**

---

**Listing 8.17    Patching the children of a node (patch-dom.js)**

```
import {
  removeAttribute,
  setAttribute,
  removeStyle,
  setStyle,
} from './attributes'
import { destroyDOM } from './destroy-dom'
import { addEventListener } from './events'
import { DOM_TYPES } from './h'
import { mountDOM } from './mount-dom'
import { areNodesEqual } from './nodes-equal'
import {
  arraysDiff,
  arraysDiffSequence,
```

```
    ARRAY_DIFF_OP,
} from './utils/arrays'
import { objectsDiff } from './utils/objects'
import { isNotBlankOrEmptyString } from './utils/strings'

export function patchDOM(oldVdom, newVdom, parentEl) {
  if (!areNodesEqual(oldVdom, newVdom)) {
    const index = findIndexInParent(parentEl, oldVdom.el)
    destroyDOM(oldVdom)
    mountDOM(newVdom, parentEl, index)

    return newVdom
  }

  newVdom.el = oldVdom.el

  switch (newVdom.type) {
    case DOM_TYPES.TEXT: {
      patchText(oldVdom, newVdom)
      return newVdom
    }

    case DOM_TYPES.ELEMENT: {
      patchElement(oldVdom, newVdom)
      break
    }
  }

  patchChildren(oldVdom, newVdom)

  return newVdom
}

// TODO: implement patchChildren()
```

The `patchChildren()` function extracts the children arrays from the old and new nodes (or uses an empty array in their absence) and then calls the `arraysDiff-Sequence()` function to find the operations that transform the old array into the new one. (Remember that this function requires the `areNodesEqual()` function to compare the nodes in the arrays.) Then, for each operation, it performs the appropriate patching.

First, you need a function—which you can call `extractChildren()`—that extracts the children array from a node in such a way that if it encounters a fragment node, it extracts the children of the fragment node and adds them to the array. This function needs to be recursive so that if a fragment node contains another fragment node, it also extracts the children of the inner fragment node.

Inside the h.js file, where the virtual node-creation functions are defined, write the code for the `extractChildren()` function as shown in the following listing.

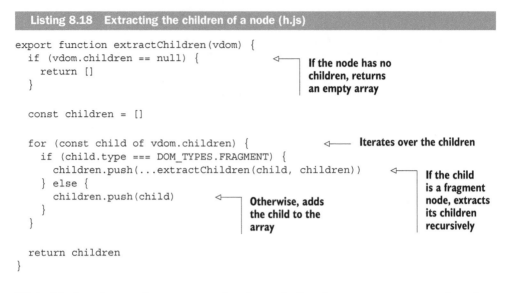

**Listing 8.18    Extracting the children of a node (h.js)**

```
export function extractChildren(vdom) {
  if (vdom.children == null) {          ◄——    If the node has no
    return []                                  children, returns
  }                                            an empty array

  const children = []

  for (const child of vdom.children) {          ◄—— Iterates over the children
    if (child.type === DOM_TYPES.FRAGMENT) {
      children.push(...extractChildren(child, children))    ◄——
    } else {                                                     If the child
      children.push(child)          ◄——  Otherwise, adds        is a fragment
    }                                      the child to the     node, extracts
  }                                        array                its children
                                                                recursively

  return children
}
```

With this function ready, you can write the code for the `patchChildren()` function, shown in the following listing. Don't forget to import the `extractChildren()` function at the top of the file.

**Listing 8.19    Implementing the `patchChildren()` function (patch-dom.js)**

```
import {
  removeAttribute,
  setAttribute,
  removeStyle,
  setStyle,
} from './attributes'
import { destroyDOM } from './destroy-dom'
import { addEventListener } from './events'
import { DOM_TYPES } from './h'
import { mountDOM, extractChildren } from './mount-dom'
import { areNodesEqual } from './nodes-equal'
import {
  arraysDiff,
  arraysDiffSequence,
  ARRAY_DIFF_OP,
} from './utils/arrays'
import { objectsDiff } from './utils/objects'
import { isNotBlankOrEmptyString } from './utils/strings

// --snip-- //
                                           Extracts the old
                                           children array or
function patchChildren(oldVdom, newVdom) {    uses an empty array
  const oldChildren = extractChildren(oldVdom)    ◄——
```

```
const newChildren = extractChildren(newVdom)          Extracts the new children
const parentEl = oldVdom.el                           array or uses an empty array

const diffSeq = arraysDiffSequence(                   Finds the operations to transform
  oldChildren,                                        the old array into the new one
  newChildren,
  areNodesEqual
)
                                                      Iterates over
                                                      the operations
for (const operation of diffSeq) {
  const { originalIndex, index, item } = operation

  switch (operation.op) {                             Switches on the
    case ARRAY_DIFF_OP.ADD: {                         operation type
      // TODO: implement
    }

    case ARRAY_DIFF_OP.REMOVE: {
      // TODO: implement
    }

    case ARRAY_DIFF_OP.MOVE: {
      // TODO: implement
    }

    case ARRAY_DIFF_OP.NOOP: {
      // TODO: implement
    }
  }
}
}
```

All that's left to do is fill in the switch statement with the code for each operation (where the // TODO comments are). This task is simpler than you think. Let's start with the ARRAY_DIFF_OP.ADD operation.

### THE ADD OPERATION

When a new node is added to the children array, it's like mounting a subtree of the DOM at a specific place. Thus, you can simply use the mountDOM() function, passing it the index at which the new node should be inserted. Figure 8.15 shows that when a node addition is detected (an operation of type ARRAY_DIFF_OP.ADD), it's inserted into the DOM.

Write the code shown in bold in the following listing to implement the first case of the switch statement.

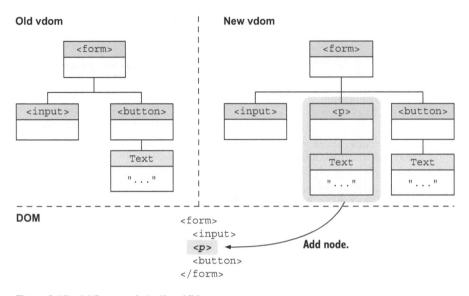

**Figure 8.15   Adding a node to the children array**

**Listing 8.20   Patching the children by adding a node (patch-dom.js)**

```
function patchChildren(oldVdom, newVdom) {
  // --snip-- //

  for (const operation of diffSeq) {
    const { from, index, item } = operation

    switch (operation.op) {
      case ARRAY_DIFF_OP.ADD: {
        mountDOM(item, parentEl, index)
        break
      }

      case ARRAY_DIFF_OP.REMOVE: {
        // TODO: implement
      }

      case ARRAY_DIFF_OP.MOVE: {
        // TODO: implement
      }

      case ARRAY_DIFF_OP.NOOP: {
        // TODO: implement
      }
    }
  }
}
```

### THE REMOVE OPERATION

Next comes the `ARRAY_DIFF_OP.REMOVE` operation. When a node is removed from the children array, you want to unmount it from the DOM. Thanks to the `destroyDOM()` function you wrote in chapter 4, this task is easy. Figure 8.16 illustrates removing a node from the children array (an operation of type `ARRAY_DIFF_OP.REMOVE`) and shows how it's removed from the DOM.

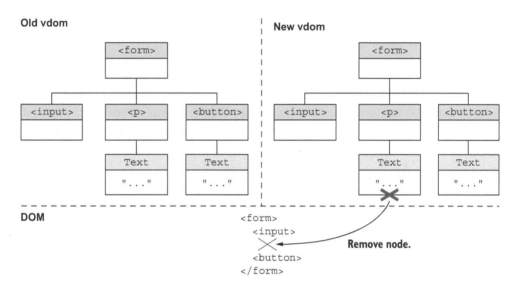

**Figure 8.16   Removing a node from the children array**

Write the code shown in bold in the following listing.

**Listing 8.21   Patching the children by removing a node (patch-dom.js)**

```
function patchChildren(oldVdom, newVdom) {
  // --snip-- //

  for (const operation of diffSeq) {
    const { from, index, item } = operation

    switch (operation.op) {
      case ARRAY_DIFF_OP.ADD: {
        mountDOM(item, parentEl, index)
        break
      }

      case ARRAY_DIFF_OP.REMOVE: {
        destroyDOM(item)
        break
      }
```

```
    case ARRAY_DIFF_OP.MOVE: {
      // TODO: implement
    }

    case ARRAY_DIFF_OP.NOOP: {
      // TODO: implement
    }
    }
  }
}
```

### THE MOVE OPERATION

The ARRAY_DIFF_OP.MOVE operation is a bit more nuanced. When you detect that a node has moved its position in the children array, you have to move it in the DOM as well. To do so, you need to grab the reference to the DOM node and use its insert-Before() method to move it to the new position. The insertBefore() method requires a reference to a DOM node that will be the next sibling of the node you're moving; you need to find the node that's currently at the desired index.

> **NOTE** The browser automatically removes the node from its original position when you move it. You won't end up with the same node in two places.

After moving the node, you want to pass it to the patchDOM() function to patch it. Nodes stay in the DOM from one render to the next, so they may not only have moved around, but also changed in other ways (had a CSS class added to them, for example).

Figure 8.17 shows a node moving its position. Here, when a node moves inside its parent node's children array (an operation of type ARRAY_DIFF_OP.MOVE), the same movement is replicated in the DOM.

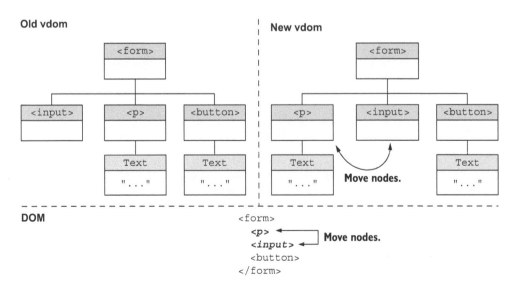

**Figure 8.17   Moving a node inside the children array**

Write the code shown in bold in the following listing.

**Listing 8.22    Patching the children by moving a node (patch-dom.js)**

```
function patchChildren(oldVdom, newVdom) {
  // --snip-- //

  for (const operation of diffSeq) {
    const { from, index, item } = operation

    switch (operation.op) {
      case ARRAY_DIFF_OP.ADD: {
        mountDOM(item, parentEl, index)
        break
      }

      case ARRAY_DIFF_OP.REMOVE: {
        destroyDOM(item)
        break
      }

      case ARRAY_DIFF_OP.MOVE: {
        const oldChild = oldChildren[originalIndex]
        const newChild = newChildren[index]
        const el = oldChild.el
        const elAtTargetIndex = parentEl.childNodes[index]

        parentEl.insertBefore(el, elAtTargetIndex)
        patchDOM(oldChild, newChild, parentEl)

        break
      }

      case ARRAY_DIFF_OP.NOOP: {
        // TODO: implement
      }
    }
  }
}
```

Gets the old virtual node at the original index

Gets the new virtual node at the new index

Gets the DOM element associated with the moved node

Finds the element at the target index inside the parent element

Inserts the moved element before the target element

Recursively patches the moved element

**THE NOOP OPERATION**

The last operation is the ARRAY_DIFF_OP.NOOP operation. If you recall, some of the child nodes may not have moved, or they may have moved because other nodes were added or removed around them (a case that I call natural movements). You don't need to move these nodes explicitly because they fall into their new positions naturally. But you do need to patch them because they may have changed in other ways, as noted earlier. Write the code shown in bold in the following listing.

**Listing 8.23    Patching the children with a noop operation (patch-dom.js)**

```
function patchChildren(oldVdom, newVdom) {
  // --snip-- //
```

```
for (const operation of diffSeq) {
  const { from, index, item } = operation

  switch (operation.op) {
    case ARRAY_DIFF_OP.ADD: {
      mountDOM(item, parentEl, index)
      break
    }

    case ARRAY_DIFF_OP.REMOVE: {
      destroyDOM(item)
      break
    }

    case ARRAY_DIFF_OP.MOVE: {
      const el = oldChildren[from].el
      const elAtTargetIndex = parentEl.childNodes[index]

      parentEl.insertBefore(el, elAtTargetIndex)
      patchDOM(oldChildren[from], newChildren[index], parentEl)

      break
    }

    case ARRAY_DIFF_OP.NOOP: {
      patchDOM(oldChildren[originalIndex], newChildren[index], parentEl)
      break
    }
  }
}
}
```

That's it. You've implemented the reconciliation algorithm. Most remarkably, you've done the implementation from scratch. Next, you'll publish the new, improved version of your framework to see it in action in the TODOs application.

## 8.3    *Publishing the framework's new version*

In chapters 6 and 7, you implemented the patchDOM() function—the reconciliation algorithm. The job took quite a lot of code, but you did it. As a result, your framework can figure out what changed between two virtual DOM trees and patch the real DOM tree accordingly. Now is a good time to publish a new version of your framework that you can use in the TODOs application. First, bump the version of the runtime package by incrementing the version field in the package.json file to 2.0.0:

```
{
  "version": "1.0.0",
  "version": "2.0.0",
}
```

Then run the npm publish command to publish the new version of the package. That's it! Your new and improved version of the framework is available on NPM and unpkg.com.

## 8.4  The TODOs application

It's time to put your improved framework to use. The nice thing is that the public API of your framework hasn't changed, so you can use the TODOs application code from chapter 6.

Clone the examples/ch06/todos directory containing the code of the TODOs app into examples/ch08/todos. You can do this job in your preferred way, but if you're using a UNIX-like operating system, the simplest way is to run the following commands:

```
$ mkdir examples/ch08
$ cp -r examples/ch06/todos examples/ch08/todos
```

Now the only line you need to change is the first line in the index.js file, where you import your framework. Change it to import the new version of the framework from unpkg.com:

```
import { createApp, h, hFragment } from 'https://unpkg.com/<fwk-name>@1'
import { createApp, h, hFragment } from 'https://unpkg.com/<fwk-name>@2'
```

With that simple change, your TODOs application is using the new version of your framework. You can serve the application by running the following command at the root of the project:

```
$ npm run serve:examples
```

Open the application in your browser at http://localhost:8080/ch08/todos/todos .html. Everything should work exactly as it did in chapter 6, but this time, when you type in the input field, its focus is preserved, as the DOM isn't re-created every time you type a character. How can you make sure that your algorithm isn't doing extra work—that it's patching only what changed?

### 8.4.1  Inspecting the DOM tree changes

An interesting way to check whether the reconciliation algorithm is working as expected is to open the browser's developer tools and inspect the DOM tree. (Use the Inspector tab in Mozilla Firefox or the Elements tab in Google Chrome.) This panel in the developer tools shows the DOM tree of the page you're currently viewing, and when a node changes, it's highlighted with a flashing animation.

If you open the TODOs application from chapter 6, where the DOM was re-created every time, and type a character in the input field, you'll see that the entire DOM tree is highlighted (figure 8.18). If you followed the folder-naming conventions in appendix A, your application from chapter 6 should be running at http://localhost :8080/examples/ch06/todos/todos.html.

If you open the TODOs application from this chapter and type a character in the input field, nothing is highlighted because the DOM tree didn't change—only the `value`

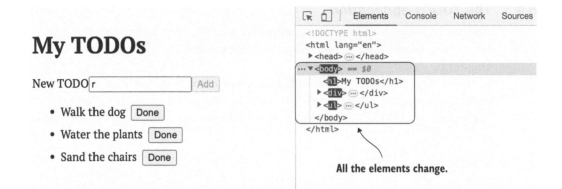

**Figure 8.18   With your previous version of the framework, the entire DOM tree is highlighted when you type a character in the input field.**

property of the input field. But after you type three characters, the `disabled` attribute is removed from the Add `<button>`, and you see this node flashing in the DOM tree (figure 8.19).

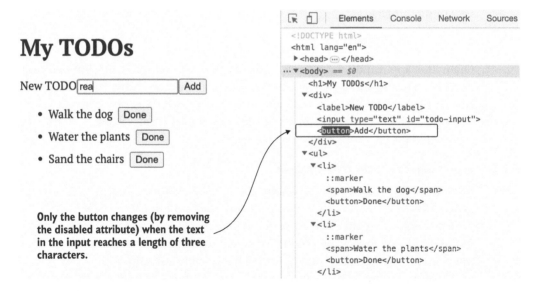

**Figure 8.19   With the new version of your framework, nothing is highlighted when you type a character in the input field until you type three characters, at which point the `disabled` attribute is removed from the Add `<button>`.**

### 8.4.2 Using the paint-flashing tool (Chrome only)

Chrome has a neat feature that allows you to see the areas of the page that are repainted. You can find this feature on the Rendering tab of the developer tools; it's called *paint flashing* (http://mng.bz/amx7). If you select it, green rectangles highlight the parts of the page that the browser repaints. Repeating the experiment by looking at the TODOs application from chapter 6, you see that the entire page is repainted every time you type a character (figure 8.20).

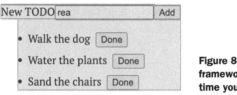

**Figure 8.20    With your previous version of the framework, the entire page is repainted every time you type a character in the input field.**

But if you look at the TODOs application from this chapter, you see that only the input field's text and the field's label are repainted (figure 8.21).

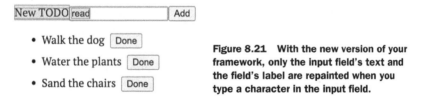

**Figure 8.21    With the new version of your framework, only the input field's text and the field's label are repainted when you type a character in the input field.**

The fact that the New TODO label is repainted is a bit surprising, but it doesn't mean that the framework patched something it shouldn't have. As you saw in the DOM tree, nothing flashes there as you type in the input field. These "paint flashes" are a sign that the rendering engine is doing its job, figuring out the layout of the page and repainting the pixels that might have moved or changed. You have nothing to worry about.

Experiment a bit with the developer tools to understand how your framework patches the DOM. The exercises that follow give you some idea of the experiments you can do.

**Exercise 8.3**

Use the Elements tab in Chrome (or the Inspector tab in Firefox) to inspect the DOM modifications (shown as flashes in the nodes) that occur when you add, modify, or mark a to-do item as completed. Compare what happens in the TODOs application from chapter 6 and the application from this chapter.

Find the solution at http://mng.bz/G96V.

**Exercise 8.4**

Use the Sources tab in Chrome (or the Debugger tab in Firefox) to debug the `patch-DOM()` function (you can set a breakpoint in the first line of the function) as you

- Type a character in the input field.
- Add a new to-do item.
- Mark a to-do item as completed.
- Edit the text of a to-do item.

Find the solution at http://mng.bz/z0Gr.

## Summary

- The reconciliation algorithm compares two virtual DOM trees, finds the sequence of operations that transform one into the other, and patches the real DOM by applying those operations to it. The algorithm is recursive, and it starts at the top-level nodes of both virtual DOM trees. After comparing these nodes, it moves on to their children until it reaches the leaves of the trees.
- To find out whether a DOM node can be reused, compare the corresponding virtual DOM nodes. If the virtual nodes are different types, the DOM node can't be reused. If the virtual nodes are text or fragment nodes, they can be reused. Element nodes can be reused if they have the same tag name.
- When the nodes being compared aren't equal—that is, they can't be reused—the DOM is destroyed and re-created from scratch. This operation makes sense in most cases because if the parent node of a subtree changes, it's likely that the children are different as well.
- You patch text nodes by setting the DOM node's `nodeValue` property to the new node's text.
- You patch element nodes by separately patching their attributes, CSS classes and styles, and event listeners. You use the `objectsDiff()` and `arraysDiff()`

functions to find the differences between the old and new values of these properties; then you apply the changes to the DOM.

- Both fragment and element nodes need to have their children patched. To patch the children of a node, you use the `arraysDiffSequence()` to find the sequence of operations that transform one array of children into the other; then you apply those operations to the DOM.

# *Improving the framework*

The groundwork has been laid, and your framework can successfully render a website based on a virtual DOM representation while keeping it in sync as users interact with it. But let's be honest: having the entire application's state confined to a single object managed by the application isn't the most practical approach. Wouldn't it be more efficient if each component could take charge of its own piece of the state, focusing solely on the view it oversees?

In this final part of the book, you'll delve into the world of stateful components—components that autonomously manage their own state and lifecycles. They are responsible exclusively for the view they oversee and can be combined to create more intricate views. This enhancement empowers the application to bypass the reconciliation algorithm for every change, updating only the components that are affected by the modification.

You'll explore how stateful components can incorporate other components within their view and establish communication among them. You'll also implement a scheduler that enables the asynchronous execution of component lifecycle hooks—a potent feature that a robust framework should offer. Last but not least, you'll master the art of performing thorough unit testing on components defined within your framework, even when they involve asynchronous behavior.

# *Stateful components* 9

**This chapter covers**

- Understanding the anatomy of a stateful component
- Implementing a factory function to define components
- Implementing the first version of a component that manages its own state

Your framework works well; it manipulates the Document Object Model (DOM) so that the developer doesn't need to, and it patches the DOM efficiently thanks to the reconciliation algorithm. But using stateless components (pure functions) forced us to move all the state to the top of the application along with the reducers. This approach isn't ideal for several reasons:

- A component deep down in the hierarchy needs all the components above it to pass the state down to it, even when they don't need it. As the number of levels increases, the number of components that need to pass the state down to their children gets unwieldy.

- As the application grows, the state gets bigger, and the amount of reducers increases as well. Having all these reducers together in a single place can become a bit messy.
- When a component updates the state, all the application is re-rendered, even if the component that updated the state is deep down in the hierarchy. Your reconciliation algorithm traverses the entire application's virtual DOM (vdom) every time the state changes.

To address these problems, you can have your components handle their own state—that is, they can update their internal state and adjust their view accordingly when the state changes. By breaking the state into smaller parts at the component level, you avoid having a massive state object with numerous reducers at the application level. Smaller state objects within components are more focused and simpler to understand. Consequently, when a component's state changes, only that specific component needs to be re-rendered, not the entire application. To create an application with your current framework, you have to pass the `createApp()` function a `state` object, the `reducers` object, and a root component (figure 9.1).

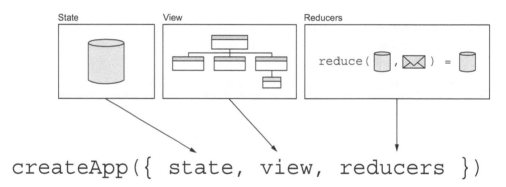

**Figure 9.1  The current framework's application instance requires the global state, reducers, and the root component.**

The plan for the new version of the framework (version 3.0) is to have components that manage their own state and patch only the part of the DOM for which they are responsible. The application will be represented by a hierarchy of components, and the root component—that one at the top of the hierarchy—is passed to the `create-App()` function (figure 9.2). As you'll see in this chapter, components won't use the reducers system of handling the state; we'll go for a simpler approach.

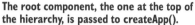

The root component, the one at the top of the hierarchy, is passed to createApp().

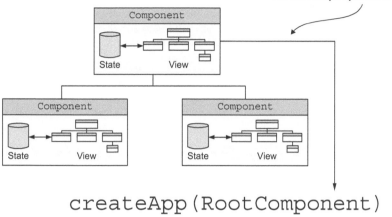

createApp(RootComponent)

**Figure 9.2** The new version of the framework's application instance requires only the root component.

With these changes (which will take four chapters to complete), you're getting closer to the framework's final architecture. You saw that architecture in chapter 1; it's reproduced here in figure 9.3.

Before you start writing the code, let's take a look at the anatomy of the stateful component you'll implement—but only the parts that are relevant to this chapter. You have many ways to implement a stateful component, but you'll go for a simple yet powerful approach. Explaining the parts of a component will help you understand the code you'll write.

> **NOTE** You can find all the listings in this chapter in the listings/ch09 directory of the book's repository (http://mng.bz/eE2Q). The code you write in this chapter is for the framework's version v3.0, which you'll publish in chapter 12. Therefore, the code in this chapter can be checked out from the ch12 label (http://mng.bz/p14z): $ git switch --detach ch12.

### Code catch-up

In chapter 8, you modified the `mountDOM()` function to insert nodes at a specific index in the child list of a parent node. You implemented a function called `insert()` to do the insertion. You modified the `createTextNode()` and `createElement-Node()` functions to receive an index as their third parameter, enabling these functions to use the `insert()` function for appending nodes to the DOM. Then you implemented a function called `areNodesEqual()` to check whether two virtual DOM nodes are equal. This function is used by the `patchDOM()` function, which you implemented next.

**(continued)**

The `patchDOM()` function—depending on the type of the virtual DOM node—called the `patchText()` or `patchElement()` functions to patch the DOM. The `patchElement()` function required you to break the logic into subfunctions: `patchAttrs()`, `patch-Classes()`, `patchStyles()`, and `patchEvents()`.

`patchDOM()` is recursive and calls itself to patch the children of the node it's patching. You implemented the work of patching the children in the `patchChildren()` function.

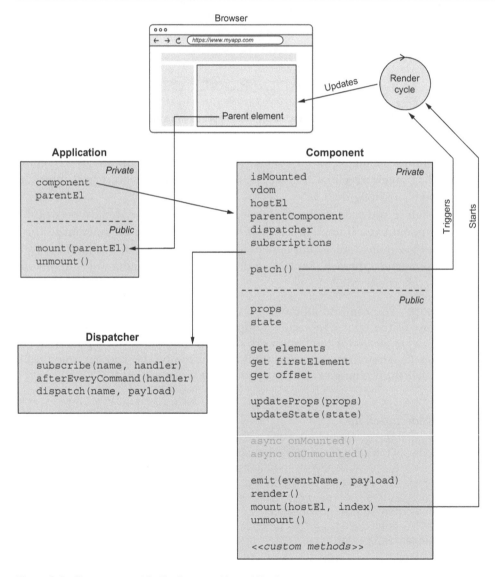

**Figure 9.3   The component in the framework's architecture**

## 9.1   Anatomy of a stateful component

Let's extract the component from figure 9.3 and analyze its anatomy: the properties and methods of a component. Our discussion is based on figure 9.4. A stateful component can't be a pure function anymore because the output of pure functions depends exclusively on their arguments; hence, they can't maintain state. (For a discussion of how React's stateful functional components work, see the nearby sidebar.)

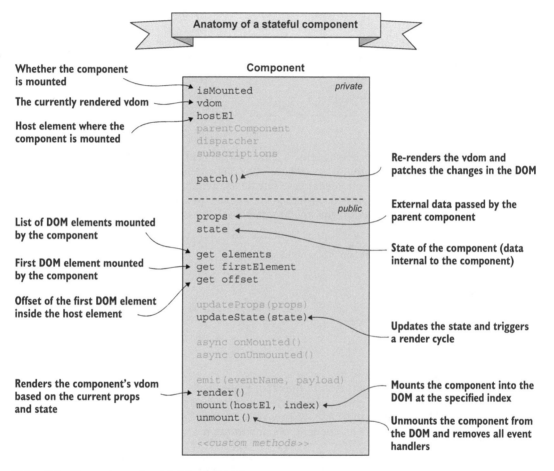

**Figure 9.4   The anatomy of a stateful component**

> **DEFINITION**   A *stateful component* maintains its own state. Stateful components can be instantiated, with each instance having a separate state and lifecycle. A stateful component updates its view when its state changes.

### React's functional stateful components

React once used classes to define components:

```
import { Component } from 'react'

class Greeting extends Component {
  render() {
    return <h1>Hello, {this.props.name}!</h1>
  }
}
```

Those classes can include a state property that can be updated by the setState() method. We'll follow a similar approach. But React now encourages the use of functions (functional components) instead because they're convenient:

```
function Greeting(props) {
  return <h1>Hello, {props.name}!</h1>
}
```

As you can see, the component is the equivalent of implementing the render() method of the class. But, if to have stateful components we need to move away from pure functions, how can React make functional components stateful? The answer is that functional components in React aren't pure functions (which is totally okay!) because to declare state, you need to use the useState() hook:

```
function Counter() {
  const [count, setCount] = useState(0)

  return (
    <div>
      <p>You clicked {count} times</p>
      <button onClick={() => setCount(count + 1)}>Click me!</button>
    </div>
  )
}
```

The useState() hook, used to maintain state inside a functional component, has side effects. In this context, a *side effect* occurs when a function modifies something outside its scope. In this case, useState() is clearly storing the component's state somewhere; thus, the component function where it's used can't be a pure function.

A *pure function* is deterministic: given the same input, it always returns the same output and doesn't have any side effects. But you clearly don't get the same result every time you call the component's function because some state is maintained somewhere, and based on that state, the component returns a different virtual DOM.

When you use the useState() hook, React stores the state of that component inside an array at application level. By keeping track of the position of the state of each component, React can update the state of the component when you call the setState() method and get you the correct value when you ask for it.

You can find the source code for hooks at http://mng.bz/4Ddg, in case you want to take a look. The ReactFiberHooks.js file inside the react-reconciler package (http://mng.bz/OPOE) is also worth looking at. The `mountState<S>()` function implements the functionality behind the `useState()` hook.

Let me finish this discussion by saying that what React has achieved with functional components and hooks is simply brilliant—the fruit of talented engineers working on designing a better way to build user interfaces. Kudos to them!

Here are the four main characteristics of the component system that you'll implement:

- The view of a component depends on its props and state. Every time one of these changes, the view needs to be patched.
- Components can have other components as children as part of their view's virtual DOM.
- A component can pass data to its children, and the child components receive this data as props.
- A component can communicate with its parent component by emitting events to which the parent component can listen.

We'll focus on the first point in this chapter and leave the communication between components for chapter 10. Let's take a look at figure 9.4 and briefly discuss the properties and methods of a stateful component that you'll implement in this chapter.

The figure isn't exhaustive, but it covers the most important properties and methods of a component. Some of the components are grayed out here; you'll implement them in the following chapters.

## 9.1.1 *The properties of a stateful component*

The public properties of a stateful component (simply called *component* from now on) are

- `props`—The data that the component receives from its parent component
- `state`—The data that the component maintains internally

Even though these properties are public, they shouldn't be modified directly. Why not? If they're modified directly, the component won't know that they have changed, so it won't update its view. You'll use the `updateState()` method to update the state of a component and `updateProps()` for the props; we'll discuss these methods in section 9.1.2 and chapter 10, respectively. Apart from updating the state and props, the methods trigger the re-rendering of the component. A component also has three interesting get-only properties:

- `elements`—A list of the DOM elements mounted by the component. When the top node of the view of a component is a fragment, this list consists of the DOM elements mounted by the component's children. If the component has a single root node, the list has a single element.

- `firstElement`—The first element of the `elements` list.
- `offset`—The offset of the `firstElement` inside the component's host element in the DOM. You need this offset to patch the component's DOM correctly, as you'll see in section 9.3.3.

The component also has three private properties:

- `isMounted`—A Boolean that indicates whether the component is mounted
- `vdom`—The virtual DOM of the component that's currently rendered in the DOM
- `hostEl`—The element in the DOM where the component is mounted

### 9.1.2   *The methods of a stateful component*

Let's take a look at the methods of a component. A component has two methods that you'll use to mount and unmount it:

- `mount()`—Mounts the component in the DOM
- `unmount()`—Unmounts the component from the DOM and unsubscribes all the subscriptions

To update the state that the component maintains internally, use `updateState()`, which also triggers the re-rendering of the component. This method should be called inside the component whenever the state of the component changes.

As you'll see in this chapter and the following chapters, the state of a component can be the props of its children components; a component can pass its internal state to its children components as props. When new props are passed to a component, the component should re-render its view. To that end, the component uses two methods:

- `render()`—Returns the virtual DOM of the component, based on the current props and state of the component.
- `patch()`—Patches the DOM of the component with the new virtual DOM. This private method is called as part of updating the state or props of the component, but it isn't meant to be called from outside the component.

The best way to understand how this component system works is to implement it, so let's get started. We'll start simply and add features as we go. Warm up your code editor and stretch your fingers, because you'll write a lot of code in this chapter!

## 9.2   *Components as classes*

Start by creating a new file inside the src/ folder called component.js. We'll write all the code in this section in this file. Now think about how you can define a component. You want to be able to instantiate components, and each component instance should have its own state. Therefore, you can use classes to define the component like so (you don't need to write this code yet; you'll do that below):

```
class Component {}
```

Now you can instantiate the component (new Component()), but it doesn't do anything . . . yet. You want components to be able to render their view, and for that purpose, they need a render() method:

```
class Component {
  render() {
    // return the virtual DOM of the component
  }
}
```

But here comes the first complication. Each component that the user defines is different; each render() method returns a different virtual DOM. In the TODOs app you wrote in chapter 8, for example, the CreateTodo() and TodoList() components return different virtual DOMs (which makes sense, right?). So how do you define the render() method of the Component class when you don't know what the virtual DOM of the component will be beforehand? The solution is to define the defineComponent() function, which takes an object containing a render() function that creates the virtual DOM of that specific component and returns the component class:

```
export function defineComponent({ render }) {
  class Component {
    render() {
      return render()
    }
  }

  return Component
}
```

The defineComponent() function returns a class, so you can have as many component classes as you want simply by defining how each component renders its view:

```
const CreateTodo = defineComponent({
  render() {
    // return the virtual DOM of the component
  }
})

const TodoList = defineComponent({
  render() {
    // return the virtual DOM of the component
  }
})
```

In a sense, `defineComponent()` is a factory function that, given a `render()` function, creates a component class that uses that function to render its view. The returned component class can be instantiated as many times as you want, and all of its instances render the same view (figure 9.5). When we add state to the component instance, each component might render a different—although similar—view because as you know, the view of a component depends on its state.

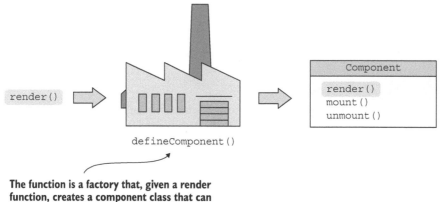

The function is a factory that, given a render function, creates a component class that can be instantiated and renders the same view.

**Figure 9.5**  The `defineComponent()` factory function creates component classes.

The component also needs `mount()` and `unmount()` methods so that their view can be added to the DOM and removed from it, so let's add those methods to the `Component` class. Complete the `Component` class with the code in the following listing.

**Listing 9.1  Basic component methods (component.js)**

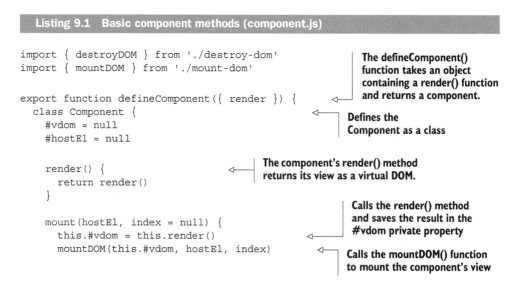

```
import { destroyDOM } from './destroy-dom'
import { mountDOM } from './mount-dom'

export function defineComponent({ render }) {
  class Component {
    #vdom = null
    #hostEl = null

    render() {
      return render()
    }

    mount(hostEl, index = null) {
      this.#vdom = this.render()
      mountDOM(this.#vdom, hostEl, index)
```

The defineComponent() function takes an object containing a render() function and returns a component.

Defines the Component as a class

The component's render() method returns its view as a virtual DOM.

Calls the render() method and saves the result in the #vdom private property

Calls the mountDOM() function to mount the component's view

```
      this.#hostEl = hostEl
    }

    unmount() {
      destroyDOM(this.#vdom)            ◄─┐  Calls the destroyDOM()
                                            function to unmount the
      this.#vdom = null                     component's view
      this.#hostEl = null
    }
  }
                              ┌  Returns the
  return Component            └  Component class
}                        ◄─
```

Great! But you could mount the same instance of a component multiple times, as follows

```
const component = new MyComponent()
component.mount(document.body)
component.mount(document.body) // Same component mounted twice!
```

or unmount it before it is mounted:

```
const component = new MyComponent()
component.unmount() // Unmounting a component that's not mounted!
```

To prevent these situations, you need to keep track of the mounting state of the component. Add an `#isMounted` private property to the `Component` class and throw an error if you detect the aforementioned situations. Write the code shown in bold in the following listing.

**Listing 9.2  Checking whether the component is already mounted (component.js)**

```
export function defineComponent({ render }) {
  class Component {
    #isMounted = false            ◄─┐  The #isMounted private
    #vdom = null                       property keeps track of
    #hostEl = null                     the component's state.

    render() {
      return render()
    }
                                               ┌  A component can't
    mount(hostEl, index = null) {              │  be mounted more
      if (this.#isMounted) {          ◄────────┘  than once.
        throw new Error('Component is already mounted')
      }

      this.#vdom = this.render()
      mountDOM(this.#vdom, hostEl, index)        ┌  When the component
                                                 │  is mounted, sets the
      this.#hostEl = hostEl                      │  #isMounted property
      this.#isMounted = true          ◄──────────┘  to true
    }
```

```
    unmount() {
      if (!this.#isMounted) {
        throw new Error('Component is not mounted')
      }

      destroyDOM(this.#vdom)

      this.#vdom = null
      this.#hostEl = null
      this.#isMounted = false
    }
  }

  return Component
}
```

A component can't be unmounted if it's not mounted.

When the component is unmounted, sets the #isMounted property to false

This code is a great start, but where's the state of the component? So far, the `Component` class doesn't have any state or external props, so the `render()` method always returns the same virtual DOM (unless it depends on global data defined outside the component, which it shouldn't). Let's add the state and props to the component.

---

**Exercise 9.1**

Using the `defineComponent()` function and the code it depends on (the `mountDOM()` and `destroyDOM()` functions), create a component that renders the following HTML:

```
<h1>Important news!</h1>
<p>I made myself coffee.</p>
<button>Say congrats</button>
```

The button should print the following message in the console when clicked: `Good for you!` Mount the component inside the web page of your choice (such as your local newspaper's website). Click the button, and check whether the message is printed in the console. Last, unmount the component from the DOM, and verify that the component's HTML is removed from the page.

Find the solution at http://mng.bz/0lrm.

---

## 9.3    *Components with state*

The components that the `defineComponent()` function creates are static; they always render the same virtual DOM. You haven't implemented the state of the component yet, so the `render()` method inside your component can't return different virtual DOMs. What you want to do is pass `defineComponent()`, a function that returns the initial state of the component (figure 9.6).

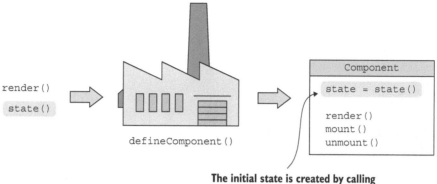

The initial state is created by calling
the passed-in state function.

**Figure 9.6**   The `defineComponent()` **factory function uses the** `state()` **function to create
the initial state of the component.**

Inside the component's constructor, you can call the `state()` function to create the
initial state of the component and save it in the `state` property (you don't need to
write this code yet; you'll do that below):

```
class Component {
  constructor() {
    this.state = state()
  }
}
```

Here's how you'd define the `state()` function that returns the initial state for a component that keeps track of the number of times a button is clicked:

```
const Counter = defineComponent({
  state() {
    return { count: 0 }
  },
  render() { ... }
})
```

You may want to be able to set the initial state of a component's instance when you
instantiate it. Maybe you don't want all instances of a component to have the same initial state. Consider the `Counter` component in the preceding example. By default, the
count starts at `0`, but you may want to start the count of a specific instance at `10`. To sat-
isfy this need, you can pass the `state()` function the props passed to the component's
constructor so that the initial state can be based on the props:

```
class Component {
  constructor(props = {}) {
    this.state = state(props)
  }
}
```

In the counter example, you could do something like this:

```
const Counter = defineComponent({
  state(props) {
    return { count: props.initialCount ?? 0 }
  },
  render() { ... }
})

const props = { initialCount: 10 }
const counter = new Counter(props)
```

Add the code shown in bold in the following listing to implement the component's initial state and props.

Listing 9.3 **Adding the `state()` method (component.js)**

```
export function defineComponent({ render, state }) {        ◁─┐  defineComponent() takes
  class Component {                                              an object with a state()
    #isMounted = false                                          function to create the
    #vdom = null                                                initial state.
    #hostEl = null

    constructor(props = {}) {
      this.props = props                                  ◁────  The component can be
      this.state = state ? state(props) : {}              ◁──    instantiated with an object
    }                                                            containing the props.

    render() {
      return render()                                            The state() function
    }                                                            returns the initial state
                                                                 of the component based
    mount(hostEl, index = null) {                                on the props.
      // --snip-- //
    }

    unmount() {
      // --snip-- //
    }
  }

  return Component
}
```

Now the component has both state and props. You've used the props to initialize the state of the component, but now you'll leave the props aside and focus on the state. I'll come back to props in chapter 10. In section 9.3.1, you'll implement the `update-State()` function to update the state of the component and patch the DOM with the new view.

### 9.3.1   Updating the state and patching the DOM

The state of the component evolves as the user interacts with it. Thus, you want to implement a function that updates the state of the component by merging the passed state with the current state. The code looks something like this:

```
this.state = { ...this.state, ...newState }
```

This way, those pieces of the state that aren't updated are preserved.

After the state has been updated, the DOM needs to be patched with the new virtual DOM. Patching the DOM should be handled by a different method, `#patch()`, in the component. This process involves two steps:

1  Call the component's `render()` method to get the new virtual DOM based on the new state.
2  Call the `patchDOM()` function to patch the DOM with the old and new virtual DOM trees. Save the result of the `patchDOM()` function in the `#vdom` property of the component.

A caveat: the component can't be patched if it's not mounted. Keep this fact in mind when implementing the `#patch()` method. Write the code shown in bold in the following listing to implement the `updateState()` and `#patch()` methods.

**Listing 9.4   Update the state and the component's DOM (component.js)**

```
import { destroyDOM } from './destroy-dom'
import { mountDOM } from './mount-dom'
import { patchDOM } from './patch-dom'

export function defineComponent({ render, state }) {
  class Component {
    #isMounted = false
    #vdom = null
    #hostEl = null

    constructor(props = {}) {
      this.props = props
      this.state = state ? state(props) : {}
    }

    updateState(state) {                             ◁── Merges the new state
      this.state = { ...this.state, ...state }            with the current state
      this.#patch()                                ◁─┐ Calls the #patch()
    }                                                 │ method to reflect the
                                                      │ changes in the DOM
    render() {
      return render()
    }

    mount(hostEl, index = null) {
      // --snip-- //
    }
```

```
    unmount() {
      // --snip-- //
    }

    #patch() {
      if (!this.#isMounted) {                          If the component is not
        throw new Error('Component is not mounted')     mounted, the DOM
      }                                                 can't be patched.

      const vdom = this.render()                       Calls the render() method
      this.#vdom = patchDOM(this.#vdom, vdom, this.#hostEl)   to get the new virtual DOM
    }
  }
                                                    Calls the patchDOM() function to
  return Component                                  patch the DOM and saves the result
}                                                         in the #vdom property
```

Great! Now you have a component whose state can be updated, and the DOM is patched with the new virtual DOM. You can access the `state` property inside the `render()` method to render the virtual DOM based on the state of the component. Also, the `updateState()` method can be called from within the component's `render()` method as part of the event handlers. Let's go back to the counter example. If next to the counter label, you have a button to increment the counter, you could do something like this:

```
const Counter = defineComponent({
  state() {
    return { count: 0 }
  },

  render() {
    return hFragment([                               Accesses the state
      h('p', {}, [`Count: ${this.state.count}`]),     of the component
      h(
        'button',
        {
          on: {                                      Updates the state of
            click() {                                   the component
              this.updateState({ count: this.state.count + 1 })
            },
          },
        },
        ['Increment'],
      ),
    ])
  },
})
```

But if you tried this code right now, however—and I encourage you to do so—you'd get the following error:

```
Uncaught TypeError: Cannot read properties of undefined (reading 'count')
```

Can you guess why? Here's the problem: the `this` keyword inside the `render()` function that's called inside the `render()` method isn't bound to the component; rather, it's bound to the `Window` object. (In strict mode, it would be `undefined`.) This happens because the `render()` function passed to the `defineComponent()` function isn't a method of the class, in which case the `this` keyword would be bound to the component.

> **NOTE**  You can read more about the `this` keyword in the MDN web docs at http://mng.bz/QPGe. You need to understand the rules that dictate how `this` is bound in JavaScript so that you can follow the code in this book. I highly recommend that you also read the "This works" chapter of the *Objects and Classes* book from the *You Don't Know JavaScript* series, by Kyle Simpson. You can read this chapter in Simpson's GitHub account at http://mng.bz/XN8M. This chapter contains everything you might need to know about the `this` keyword, which you'll use in this chapter and the following chapters of the book. Trust me when I say that the chapter is worth your time.

To fix this problem, you need to use explicit binding to bind the `this` keyword inside the `render()` function to the component. The fix is simple, as shown in the following listing. Modify your code so that it matches the code in the listing.

**Listing 9.5   Binding the `call()` function to the component (component.js)**

```
export function defineComponent({ render, state }) {
  class Component {
    // --snip-- //

    render() {
      return render()
      return render.call(this)
    }

    // --snip-- //
  }

  return Component
}
```

## 9.3.2   Result

Let's quickly review the code you've written so far. You've created a `define-Component()` function that takes an object with a `render()` function to create a component. The `render()` function returns a virtual DOM based on the state of the component. The component's state can be updated with the `updateState()` function, which merges the new state with the current state and patches the DOM with the new virtual DOM. If you followed along, your component.js file should look like the following listing.

**Listing 9.6  The** `defineComponent()` **function so far (component.js)**

```
import { destroyDOM } from './destroy-dom'
import { mountDOM } from './mount-dom'
import { patchDOM } from './patch-dom'

export function defineComponent({ render, state }) {
  class Component {
    #isMounted = false
    #vdom = null
    #hostEl = null

    constructor(props = {}) {
      this.props = props
      this.state = state ? state(props) : {}
    }

    updateState(state) {
      this.state = { ...this.state, ...state }
      this.#patch()
    }

    render() {
      return render.call(this)
    }

    mount(hostEl, index = null) {
      if (this.#isMounted) {
        throw new Error('Component is already mounted')
      }

      this.#vdom = this.render()
      mountDOM(this.#vdom, hostEl, index)

      this.#hostEl = hostEl
      this.#isMounted = true
    }

    unmount() {
      if (!this.#isMounted) {
        throw new Error('Component is not mounted')
      }

      destroyDOM(this.#vdom)

      this.#vdom = null
      this.#hostEl = null
      this.#isMounted = false
    }

    #patch() {
      if (!this.#isMounted) {
        throw new Error('Component is not mounted')
      }
```

```
        const vdom = this.render()
        this.#vdom = patchDOM(this.#vdom, vdom, this.#hostEl)
    }
  }

  return Component
}
```

Now let's discuss an interesting implication of patching the DOM owned by a component when those DOM elements are inserted into an element in which other elements are present. If you don't take this subtle detail into account, you'll patch the component's DOM incorrectly. First, why don't you try to solve the following challenge?

---

**Exercise 9.2: Challenge**

Using the `defineComponent()` function and the code it depends on (the `mountDOM()` and `destroyDOM()` functions), create a component called `FlyingButton`, which renders a `<button>` element absolutely positioned at a random position inside the browser's viewport. The button's label should be `Move`. When the button is clicked, the button should move to a random position inside the viewport. Bear in mind that the position of the button should be random but never be outside the viewport—at least, not entirely.

You can mount the button in the `<body>` element or in any other element you want (it's absolutely positioned, so it shouldn't affect the layout of the page) inside your favorite website.

Find the solution at http://mng.bz/K944.

---

### 9.3.3   *The component's offset*

Suppose that you have a component whose HTML is mounted in the same `<div>` as a `<p>` element. In this configuration, we say that the `<div>` is the component's *host element*—the one that contains the component's HTML. The view of this component consists of a fragment containing a `<p>` element and a `<span>` element (figure 9.7).

Here's the thing that's important to notice: because the component's view is made of a fragment, all its elements are siblings of the `<p>` element that's outside the component's view. Now suppose that the component, after a change in its state, decides that it wants to swap the `<p>` element with the `<span>` element. Figure 9.8 shows the result.

After the state is changed, the `updateState()` method calls the `#patch()` method, which in turn calls the `patchDOM()` function, passing it its virtual DOM. Recall that this virtual DOM is a fragment containing a `<p>` element and a `<span>` element, but not the first `<p>` element with the text A; that element is outside the component's view. `patchDOM()` in turn asks `arraysDiffSequence()` to find the sequence of operations that transforms the current DOM into the new virtual DOM.

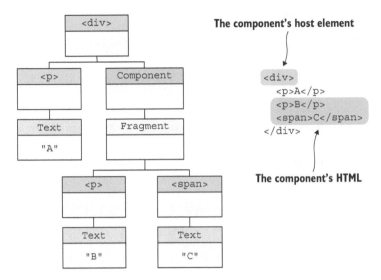

**Figure 9.7    A `<div>` element containing a `<p>` element and a component**

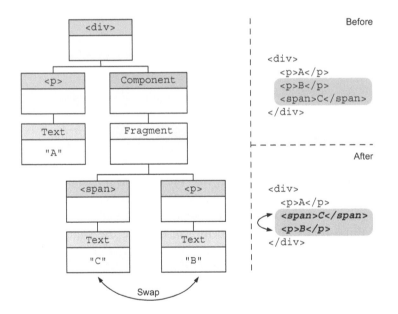

**Figure 9.8    Swap the `<p>` element with the `<span>` element inside the component.**

Your robust and well-implemented `arraysDiffSequence()` function returns the following sequence of operations:

**1** Move the `<span>` element from `i=1` to `i=0`.

**2** Noop the `<p>` element from `i=0` to `i=1`.

Then the function applies the sequence of operations to the DOM. Figure 9.9 shows the result of applying the first operation to the DOM. Before you look at the figure, can you guess what the result will be? Is it what you expected? Is it correct?

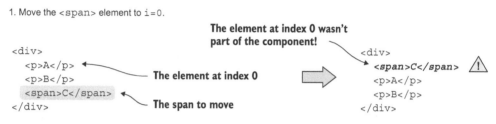

**Figure 9.9** Move the `<span>` element from `i=1` to `i=0`.

That's wrong! The problem is that the `arraysDiffSequence()` calculates the indices of the operations relative to the lists of nodes it receives as arguments, which are the nodes inside the component's fragment. This list of nodes doesn't include all the elements below the parent `<div>` element; it's missing the first `<p>` element that's outside the component's view. This situation arises from having components whose vdom is a fragment because its elements are inserted into a node that's outside the component—a host element that might contain other elements external to the component. When the component's view has a single root element, this problem doesn't occur (why this is I'll leave as an exercise for you; the answer is at the end of the chapter).

The indices of the move operations are relative to the fragment; they don't account for the elements outside the component's fragment. Something similar happens when a node is added in the component's view if the component's view is a fragment. The index where the node is to be added is relative to the fragment items, not accounting for the elements outside the fragment.

How do we go about fixing this problem? It's time to introduce the concept of a component's *offset*.

> **DEFINITION** The *offset* of a component is the number of elements that precede the component's first element in the parent element when the former's view top node is a fragment. In other words, it's the index of the component's first element in the parent element.

If you can compute the offset of a component, you can correct the indices of the move and add operations returned by `arraysDiffSequence()`. The offset for the example component is 1 because the first element of the component is the second element in the parent element (figure 9.10).

The component's host element

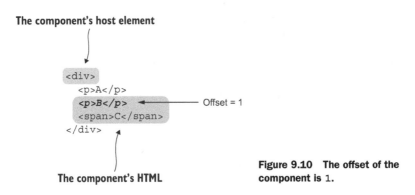

Offset = 1

**Figure 9.10   The offset of the component is 1.**

The component's HTML

If we correct the index of the operations by adding the offset, the operations will be relative to the parent element, not to the fragment. Figure 9.11 shows the correct application of the move operation.

1. Move the `<span>` element to $i=0+offset$.

**Figure 9.11   Move the `<span>` element from `i=2` to `i=1` (corrected).**

Let's implement a getter for the component's offset. Just below the component's constructor, write the code shown in bold in the following listing.

**Listing 9.7   Getting the component's first element offset  (component.js)**

```
import { destroyDOM } from './destroy-dom'
import { DOM_TYPES, extractChildren } from './h'
import { mountDOM } from './mount-dom'
import { patchDOM } from './patch-dom'

export function defineComponent({ render, state }) {
  class Component {
    #isMounted = false
    #vdom = null
    #hostEl = null

    constructor(props = {}) {
      this.props = props
      this.state = state ? state(props) : {}
    }
```

```
  get elements() {
    if (this.#vdom == null) {           ◄──  If the vdom is
      return []                               null, returns an
    }                                         empty array            If the vdom top node
                                                                     is a fragment, returns
    if (this.#vdom.type === DOM_TYPES.FRAGMENT) {      ◄──           the elements inside
      return extractChildren(this.#vdom).map((child) => child.el)    the fragment
    }
                                        If the vdom top
    return [this.#vdom.el]         ◄──  node is a single node,
  }                                     returns its element

  get firstElement() {
    return this.elements[0]        ◄──  The component's
  }                                     first element             The component's
                                                                  first element offset
  get offset() {                                                  inside the parent
    if (this.#vdom.type === DOM_TYPES.FRAGMENT) {      ◄──        element
      return Array.from(this.#hostEl.children).indexOf(this.firstElement)
    }

    return 0                 ◄──┐  When the component's view
  }                             │  isn't a fragment, the offset is 0.

  updateState(state) {
    this.state = { ...this.state, ...state }
    this.#patch()
  }

  // --snip-- //
  }

  return Component
}
```

Now that you can ask a component about its offset, you can correct the indices of the operations returned by arraysDiffSequence(). In section 9.3.4, you'll refactor the patchDOM() function to include the offset.

### 9.3.4   Patching the DOM using the component's offset

To use the component's offset in the patchDOM() function, you need to pass the component instance to the function. The following listing shows how.

> **Listing 9.8   Passing the component instance to the patchDOM() function (component.js)**

```
export function defineComponent({ render, state }) {
  class Component {
    // --snip-- //

    #patch() {
      if (!this.#isMounted) {
        throw new Error('Component is not mounted')
      }
```

```
        const vdom = this.render()
        this.#vdom = patchDOM(this.#vdom, vdom, this.#hostEl, this)     ◄─────┐
      }
    }                                                          Passes the
                                                          component instance to
    return Component                                       the patchDOM() function
}
```

Now you want to include the host component as an argument of the patchDOM()
function and pass it to the patchChildren() function. That component will have a
default value of null. In the patch-dom.js file, write the code shown in bold in the
following listing.

**Listing 9.9   Passing a host component to the patchDOM() function (patch-dom.js)**

```
export function patchDOM(                                  Passes the host
  oldVdom, newVdom, parentEl, hostComponent = null     ◄─┤ component instance to
) {                                                        the patchDOM() function
  if (!areNodesEqual(oldVdom, newVdom)) {
    const index = findIndexInParent(parentEl, oldVdom.el)
    destroyDOM(oldVdom)
    mountDOM(newVdom, parentEl, index)

    return newVdom
  }

  newVdom.el = oldVdom.el

  switch (newVdom.type) {
    case DOM_TYPES.TEXT: {
      patchText(oldVdom, newVdom)
      return newVdom
    }

    case DOM_TYPES.ELEMENT: {
      patchElement(oldVdom, newVdom)
      break                                          Passes the
    }                                                component instance
  }                                                  to the patchChildren()
                                                     function
  patchChildren(oldVdom, newVdom, hostComponent)  ◄─┘

  return newVdom
}
```

Now comes the important part: you need to use the component's offset to correct the
indices of the operations returned by arraysDiffSequence(), but only if a host component is passed. Otherwise, you can assume that the component's offset is 0, which means
that you're dealing with a root component—one that doesn't have a parent component.
Thus, the component can't have an offset. Only the operations that reference elements
in the DOM by their index need to be corrected. If you recall, only the move and add

operations refer to DOM nodes by their index. Thus, neither the remove nor the noop operation needs to be corrected, but you still have to modify both operations to pass the `hostComponent` argument back to the `patchDOM()` function.

You saw a graphical example of the move operation in figure 9.8. Figure 9.12 shows a graphical example of the add operation. As you can see, the index of the add operation is relative to the fragment, not to the parent element, so you need to correct it by adding the component's offset. Include the code shown in bold in listing 9.10.

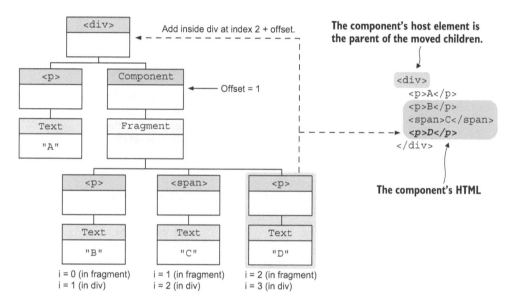

**Figure 9.12  Adding a node to the component's view with an offset**

Listing 9.10  **Patching the children using the offset (patch-dom.js)**

```
function patchChildren(oldVdom, newVdom, hostComponent) {
  const oldChildren = extractChildren(oldVdom)
  const newChildren = extractChildren(newVdom)
  const parentEl = oldVdom.el

  const diffSeq = arraysDiffSequence(
    oldChildren,
    newChildren,
    areNodesEqual
  )

  for (const operation of diffSeq) {
    const { from, index, item } = operation
    const offset = hostComponent?.offset ?? 0

    switch (operation.op) {
      case ARRAY_DIFF_OP.ADD: {
```

Adds the host component as an argument to the patchChildren() function

Gets the host component's offset, if there is one; offset is zero otherwise

```
        mountDOM(item, parentEl, index + offset, hostComponent)
        break
    }
```

When a node is added, takes account of the host component's offset

```
    case ARRAY_DIFF_OP.REMOVE: {
      destroyDOM(item)
      break
    }
```

When a node is moved, uses the offset to find the correct position in the DOM

```
    case ARRAY_DIFF_OP.MOVE: {
      const el = oldChildren[from].el
      const elAtTargetIndex = parentEl.childNodes[index + offset]

      parentEl.insertBefore(el, elAtTargetIndex)
      patchDOM(
        oldChildren[from],
        newChildren[index],
        parentEl,
        hostComponent
      )

      break
    }
```

Passes the host component back to the patchDOM() function

```
    case ARRAY_DIFF_OP.NOOP: {
      patchDOM(
        oldChildren[from],
        newChildren[index],
        parentEl,
        hostComponent
      )
      break
    }
  }
 }
}
}
```

Passes the host component to the patchChildren() function

With this nuance out of the way, we can focus on the component's methods.

---

**Exercise 9.3**

Can you explain why the problem of the component's offset doesn't arise when the component's view is a single root element?

Find the solution at http://mng.bz/9QNa.

---

## Summary

- A stateful component can be modeled as a class that can be instantiated.
- Each instance of a component has its own state and lifecycle, and it manages its own DOM subtree.
- To allow users to create component classes with custom states, render functions, and other methods, you can use a factory function.

- The state of a component is created at instantiation time, and you can update it by calling the `updateState()` method.
- When the `updateState()` method is called, the component patches its view.
- The `render()` function and event handlers of a component need to be explicitly bound to the component instance so that `this` refers to the component instance inside them.

# Component methods

**This chapter covers**

- Implementing component methods to handle events
- Binding a method's context to the component
- Passing the host component reference to mount and patch functions

What happens when you're handling an event in a component that requires a couple of lines of code? One-liners, like this one, look fine inside the virtual Document Object Model (DOM) definition:

```
render() {
  const { count } = this.state

  return hFragment([
    h(
      'button',
      { on: { click: () => this.updateState({ count: count - 1 }) }}
      ['Decrement']
    ),
    h('span', {}, [count]),
    h(
```

Handles the click event by decrementing the count

```
    'button',
    { on: { click: () => this.updateState({ count: count + 1 }) }}
    ['Increment']
  )
])
}
```

Handles the click
event by incrementing
the count

But what happens when you want to do more than you can fit in a single line? Well, you could fit the code inside the virtual DOM (vdom) definition, but then the code will be harder to read. Look at the following example list, in which clicking a button loads more items from the server:

```
render() {
  const { items, offset, isLoading } = this.state

  return hFragment([
    h(
      'ul',
      {},
      items.map((item) => h('li', {}, [item])),
    ),
    isLoading
      ? h('p', {}, ['Loading...'])
      : h(
          'button',
          {
            on: {
              click: async () => {
                const { items, offset } = this.state
                this.updateState({ isLoading: true })

                const newItems = await fetchItems(offset)

                this.updateState({
                  items: [...items, ...newItems],
                  isLoading: false,
                  offset: offset + newItems.length,
                })
              },
            },
          },
          ['Load more'],
        ),
  ])
}
```

The event handler spans
multiple lines, making the
code harder to read.

This code doesn't look as nice as the preceding example. Instead, we want to move the event-handler code to a method of the component and reference the method as the handler for the event. This approach results in much cleaner code:

```
render() {
  const { items, offset, isLoading } = this.state
```

```
    return hFragment([
      h(
        'ul',
        {},
        items.map((item) => h('li', {}, [item])),
      ),
      isLoading
        ? h('p', {}, ['Loading...'])
        : h(
            'button',
            {
              on: { click: this.loadMore },
            },
            ['Load more'],
          ),
    ])
}
```

> Now the event handler is a reference to the loadMore() method.

So a `loadMore()` method inside the component would handle the event. You need a way to add custom methods to the component. How do you go about it? You can pass the `defineComponent()` function together with the `render()` and `state()` functions, which are other arbitrary methods. In the preceding example, you'd define the component as follows:

```
const InfiniteList = defineComponent(
  state() { ... },
  render() { ... },
  async loadMore() {
    const { items, offset } = this.state
    this.updateState({ isLoading: true })

    const newItems = await fetchItems(offset)

    this.updateState({
      items: [...items, ...newItems],
      isLoading: false,
      offset: offset + newItems.length,
    })
  },
)
```

> The loadMore() method is defined as part of the component.

The objective of this chapter is to modify the `defineComponent()` function so that it can receive custom methods to handle events. The changes are straightforward, but the methods won't be bound to the component's context correctly when they're used as event handlers. As you'll see soon, you need to explicitly bind the event handlers to the component's context. This topic will take up most of the chapter.

> **NOTE**  You can find all the listings in this chapter in the listings/ch10 directory of the book's repository (http://mng.bz/YREA). The code you write in this chapter is for the framework's version v3.0, which you'll publish in chapter 12.

Therefore, the code in this chapter can be checked out from the ch12 label (http://mng.bz/G9QO): `$ git switch --detach ch12`.

---

**Code catch-up**

In chapter 9, you wrote the `defineComponent()` function, which receives the `render()` and `state()` functions as arguments and returns a `Component` class. You implemented the following methods in the `Component` class:

- `render()`—Renders the component's virtual DOM
- `mount()`—Mounts the component's view into the DOM
- `unmount()`—Unmounts the component from the DOM
- `#patch()`—Patches the component's view in the DOM
- `updateState()`—Updates the component's state and patches the view in the DOM

You also modified the `patchChildren()` function to receive one more argument: the host component (the component that owns the children). You needed this component to calculate the offset of the children so that the operations that require moving nodes in the DOM could be performed correctly. For the `patchChildren()` function to receive the host component, you also had to modify the `patchDOM()` function, adding the `hostComponent` argument to it.

---

## 10.1  Component methods

We need to update our analogy from chapter 9, in which `defineComponent()` was a component factory. This factory, in addition to the `render()` and `state()` functions, can receive other methods that will be added to the component's prototype (figure 10.1).

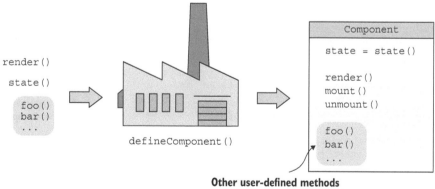

**Figure 10.1  Using `defineComponent()` to define a component with custom methods**

To add custom methods to the component, you can use JavaScript's prototypal inheritance (http://mng.bz/MBem). Classes in JavaScript are syntactic sugar for prototypes, and extending a prototype to include a new method is as simple as

```
class Component {}

Component.prototype.loadMore = function () { ... }
```

But you want to prevent the user from redefining a method that already exists in the component, such as `updateState()` or `mount()`. Overriding these methods would break the component. First, you want to use the `hasOwnProperty()` method to check whether the method already exists in the component's prototype. Unfortunately, this method isn't safe to use (a malicious user could use it to do some harm), and ESLint will complain about it. Fortunately for us, the same ESLint rule that complains about `hasOwnProperty()` also provides a suggestion for a safe implementation of it.

> **NOTE** If you want to understand better why using an object's `hasOwnProperty()` method is unsafe, see http://mng.bz/yQOE. You may also want to learn more about JavaScript's prototypal inheritance. If so, I recommend that you take some time to read http://mng.bz/MBem.

Inside the utils/objects.js file, add the `hasOwnProperty()` function as shown in the following listing.

**Listing 10.1   A safe implementation of `hasOwnProperty()` (utils/objects.js)**

```
export function hasOwnProperty(obj, prop) {
  return Object.prototype.hasOwnProperty.call(obj, prop)
}
```

Now go back to the component.js file. Write the code shown in bold in the following listing to add custom methods to the component.

**Listing 10.2   Adding custom methods to the component (component.js)**

```
import { destroyDOM } from './destroy-dom'
import { DOM_TYPES, extractChildren } from './h'
import { mountDOM } from './mount-dom'
import { patchDOM } from './patch-dom'
import { hasOwnProperty } from './utils/objects'          Destructures the rest
                                                          of the methods passed
                                                          to defineComponent()
export function defineComponent({ render, state, ...methods }) {   ◁─┘
  class Component {
    // --snip-- //                    Iterates over the      Ensures that the
  }                                   method names           component doesn't
                                                             already have a method
  for (const methodName in methods) {              ◁─┘      with the same name
    if (hasOwnProperty(Component, methodName)) {   ◁─┘
      throw new Error(
        `Method "${methodName}()" already exists in the component.`
```

```
      )
    }

    Component.prototype[methodName] = methods[methodName]    ⊲─┐  Adds the
  }                                                              method to the
                                                                 component's
  return Component                                               prototype
}
```

This code is great, but the `InfiniteList` component from the preceding example won't work now:

```
const InfiniteList = defineComponent(
  state() { ... },

  render() {
    const { items, offset, isLoading } = this.state

    return hFragment([
      h(
        'ul',
        {},
        items.map((item) => h('li', {}, [item])),
      ),
      isLoading
        ? h('p', {}, ['Loading...'])
        : h(
            'button',
            {
              on: { click: this.loadMore }
            },
            ['Load more'],
          ),
    ])
  },

  async loadMore() { ... },
)
```

We get an error because `this` is bound to the `<button>` element that's emitting the click event, not to the component. Hence, `this.loadMore()` is undefined because buttons in the DOM don't include a `loadMore()` method; if they did, you wouldn't see any error, but your `loadMore()` method would never be called. The culprit is the line in bold:

```
h(
  'button',
  {
    // Fails, because 'this' is bound to the <button> element
    on: { click: this.loadMore },
  },
  ['Load more'],
)
```

When you add an event handler by using the `addEventHandler()` method, the `this` keyword of the function is bound to the element that emitted the event—in the preceding example, the `<button>` element. You don't want the `this` keyword to be bound to the element; you want it to be bound to the component so that the methods inside it can be resolved correctly, as shown in figure 10.2.

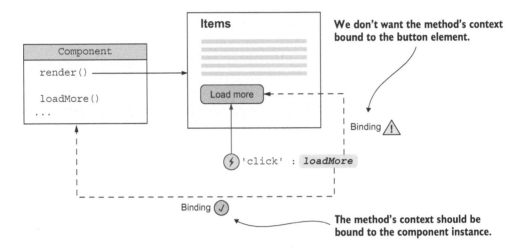

**Figure 10.2  Binding of the `loadMore()` method's `this` keyword**

You can get around this problem quickly by wrapping the event handler in an arrow function:

```
h(
  'button',
  {
    // Works by wrapping the event handler in an arrow function
    on: { click: () => this.loadMore() },
  },
  ['Load more'],
)
```

> **NOTE**  Arrow functions can't have their own `this` keyword, so the `this` keyword inside the arrow function is inherited from the containing function. Arrow functions are *lexically scoped*, which means that the `this` keyword is bound to the value of `this` in the enclosing (function or global) scope.

In our case, this function is the `render()` function, and the `this` keyword is bound to the component, which is why you had to do `render.call(this)` inside the component's render method. Arrow functions use lexical scoping (http://mng.bz/0lN6), so the `addEventListener()` method can't bind the `this` keyword to the element that emitted the event.

We don't want to force the user to wrap the event handler in an arrow function, however. We want them to be able to reference a method from the component and have it work. For that purpose, we need to explicitly bind the event handler to the component so that the `this` keyword is bound to the component.

## 10.2 *Binding event handlers to the component*

Open the events.js file. You need to make some modifications to the `addEvent-Listener()` function. You want to pass the host component reference to the function, which can be `null` in case the event handler isn't bound to a component. If the `host-Component` argument isn't `null`, you want to bind the event handler to the component by using the `.apply()` method. This method is similar to `.call()`, but you can pass it an array of arguments instead of passing arguments one by one. When the `host-Component` is `null`, you want to call the event handler as is:

```
hostComponent
  ? handler.apply(hostComponent)
  : handler()
```

Keep in mind that an event handler can receive arguments, so you need to pass those arguments to the event handler when you call it. You can wrap the code from the preceding code snippet in a new handler function that passes its arguments to the original handler function:

```
function boundHandler() {
  hostComponent
    ? handler.apply(hostComponent, arguments)
    : handler(...arguments)
}
```

> **NOTE** If you're not familiar with the `arguments` object, you can read more about it at http://mng.bz/a1xY. In a nutshell, `arguments` is an arraylike object that contains the arguments passed to a function. Bear in mind that inside an arrow function, the `arguments` object isn't available.

Now that the plan is clear, modify your code inside the events.js file as shown in the following listing.

---
Listing 10.3 **Event handlers bound to the component (events.js)**

```
export function addEventListeners(
  listeners = {},
  el,
  hostComponent = null        ◁── Adds the host
) {                                component argument
  const addedListeners = {}        to the function

  Object.entries(listeners).forEach(([eventName, handler]) => {
    const listener = addEventListener(
```

```
    eventName,
    handler,
    el,
    hostComponent
  )
  addedListeners[eventName] = listener
})

return addedListeners
}

export function addEventListener(
  eventName,
  handler,
  el,
  hostComponent = null
) {
  el.addEventListener(eventName, handler)
  return handler
  function boundHandler() {
    hostComponent
      ? handler.apply(hostComponent, arguments)
      : handler(...arguments)
  }

  el.addEventListener(eventName, boundHandler)

  return boundHandler
}
```

**Passes the host component to the addEventListener() function** (points to `hostComponent`)

**Adds the host component argument to the function** (points to `hostComponent = null`)

**If a host component exists, binds it to the event handler context...** (points to `handler.apply(hostComponent, arguments)`)

**...otherwise, calls the event handler** (points to `handler(...arguments)`)

**Adds the bound event listener to the element** (points to `el.addEventListener(eventName, boundHandler)`)

Now that your event handlers are properly bound to the component—in case there is one—you need to modify the mountDOM() and patchDOM() functions so that they pass the host component to the addEventListener() function.

## 10.3   *Mounting the DOM with a host component*

Open the mount-dom.js file to modify the mountDOM() function. Add the code shown in bold in the following listing so that the host component can be passed as an argument.

> **Listing 10.4   Passing the host component to the mountDOM() function (mount-dom.js)**

```
export function mountDOM(
  vdom,
  parentEl,
  index,
  hostComponent = null
) {
  switch (vdom.type) {
    case DOM_TYPES.TEXT: {
      createTextNode(vdom, parentEl, index)
      break
    }
```

**Adds the host component as an argument to the function** (points to `hostComponent = null`)

```
case DOM_TYPES.ELEMENT: {
  createElementNode(vdom, parentEl, index, hostComponent)       ◄──────┐
  break                                                                │
}                                   Passes the host component to the   │
                                       createElementNode() function    │
case DOM_TYPES.FRAGMENT: {
  createFragmentNodes(vdom, parentEl, index, hostComponent)     ◄──────┐
  break                                                                │
}                                   Passes the host component to the   │
                                      createFragmentNodes() function   │
default: {
  throw new Error(`Can't mount DOM of type: ${vdom.type}`)
}
}
}
}
```

You passed the `hostElement` reference down to the `createElementNode()` and `create-FragmentNodes()` functions. Now modify them to accept that argument. First, add the `hostComponent` argument to the `createElementNode()` function, as shown in the following listing. From there, you can pass the `hostComponent` argument to the `addProps()` function and back to the `mountDOM()` function.

**Listing 10.5   Passing the host component (mount-dom.js)**

```
function createElementNode(vdom, parentEl, index, hostComponent) {    ◄──────┐
  const { tag, props, children } = vdom                                      │
                                               Adds the host component as an  │
                                                 argument to the function     │
  const element = document.createElement(tag)
  addProps(element, props, vdom, hostComponent)          ◄──┐
  vdom.el = element                                         │ Passes the host
                                                            │ component to the
                                                            │ addProps() function
  children.forEach((child) =>
    mountDOM(child, element, null, hostComponent)          ◄──┐
  )                                                            │ Passes a null index and
  insert(element, parentEl, index)                            │ the host component to the
}                                                             │ mountDOM() function
```

Now modify the `addProps()` function so that the passed-in `hostComponent` argument is passed to the `addEventListeners()` function, as shown in the following listing. This change is the most important one in this section because it's where you pass the host component to the `addEventListener()` function you modified earlier.

**Listing 10.6   Passing the host component (mount-dom.js)**

```
function addProps(el, props, vdom, hostComponent) {    ◄──┐ Adds the host component
  const { on: events, ...attrs } = props                  │ as an argument to the
                                                           │ function

  vdom.listeners = addEventListeners(events, el, hostComponent)    ◄──────┐
  setAttributes(el, attrs)                                                 │
}                                        Passes the host component to the  │
                                           addEventListeners() function    │
```

Last, modify the `createFragmentNodes()` function so that the `hostComponent` argument is passed back to the `mountDOM()` function, as shown in the following listing.

**Listing 10.7  Passing the host component (mount-dom.js)**

```
function createFragmentNodes(
  vdom,
  parentEl,
  index,
  hostComponent                    Adds the host component
                                   as an argument to the
) {                                function
  const { children } = vdom
  vdom.el = parentEl

  children.forEach((child) =>
    mountDOM(
      child,
      parentEl,                    Passes the host
      index ? index + i : null,    component to the
      hostComponent                mountDOM() function
    )
  )
}
```

Great! Let's end the chapter by modifying the `patchDOM()` function so that the host component is passed and can be used to patch event handlers.

## 10.4  Patching the DOM with a host component

If you recall, you modified the `patchDOM()` function in chapter 9 so that it passes the host component to the `patchChildren()` function. You made this change so you could pass it to the `patchChildren()` function, taking the component's offset into account. Open the patch-dom.js file again, and this time, pass the `hostComponent` reference to the `mountDOM()` function (the case when the DOM is re-created) and to the `patchElement()` function, as shown in the following listing.

**Listing 10.8  Passing the host component (patch-dom.js)**

```
export function patchDOM(
  oldVdom,
  newVdom,
  parentEl,
  hostComponent = null
) {
  if (!areNodesEqual(oldVdom, newVdom)) {
    const index = findIndexInParent(parentEl, oldVdom.el)
    destroyDOM(oldVdom)
    mountDOM(newVdom, parentEl, index, hostComponent)    Passes the host
                                                         component to
    return newVdom                                       the mountDOM()
  }                                                      function
```

```
  newVdom.el = oldVdom.el

  switch (newVdom.type) {
    case DOM_TYPES.TEXT: {
      patchText(oldVdom, newVdom)
      return newVdom
    }

    case DOM_TYPES.ELEMENT: {
      patchElement(oldVdom, newVdom, hostComponent)
      break
    }
  }

  patchChildren(oldVdom, newVdom, hostComponent)

  return newVdom
}
```

> Passes the host
> component to the
> patchElement()
> function

Let's modify the `patchElement()` function so that it receives the `hostComponent` argument, as shown in the following listing. You also want to pass it down to the `patch-Events()` function, which you'll modify next.

**Listing 10.9  Passing the host component (patch-dom.js)**

```
function patchElement(oldVdom, newVdom, hostComponent) {
  const el = oldVdom.el
  const {
    class: oldClass,
    style: oldStyle,
    on: oldEvents,
    ...oldAttrs
  } = oldVdom.props
  const {
    class: newClass,
    style: newStyle,
    on: newEvents,
    ...newAttrs
  } = newVdom.props
  const { listeners: oldListeners } = oldVdom

  patchAttrs(el, oldAttrs, newAttrs)
  patchClasses(el, oldClass, newClass)
  patchStyles(el, oldStyle, newStyle)
  newVdom.listeners = patchEvents(
    el,
    oldListeners,
    oldEvents,
    newEvents,
    hostComponent
  )
}
```

> Adds the host
> component as an
> argument to the
> function

> Passes the host
> component to the
> patchEvents() function

Now add the `hostComponent` argument to the `patchEvents()` function, as shown in the following listing. When an event handler is added or updated, the `addEvent-Listener()` is called, so remember to pass the `hostComponent` argument to it.

**Listing 10.10   Passing the host component (patch-dom.js)**

```
function patchEvents(
  el,
  oldListeners = {},
  oldEvents = {},              ◁——  Adds the host
  newEvents = {},                    component as an
  hostComponent                      argument to the function
) {
  const { removed, added, updated } = objectsDiff(oldEvents, newEvents)

  for (const eventName of removed.concat(updated)) {
    el.removeEventListener(eventName, oldListeners[eventName])
  }
  const addedListeners = {}

  for (const eventName of added.concat(updated)) {
    const listener = addEventListener(
      eventName,
      newEvents[eventName],       Passes the host component
      el,                         to the addEventListener()
      hostComponent          ◁——  function
    )
    addedListeners[eventName] = listener
  }

  return addedListeners
}
```

Finally, go back to the component.js file. Modify the `mount()` function so that it passes the `hostComponent` argument to the `mountDOM()` function, as shown in the following listing.

**Listing 10.11   Component's `mount()` passing `this` reference (component.js)**

```
export function defineComponent({ render, state, ...methods }) {
  class Component {
    // --snip-- //

    mount(hostEl, index = null) {
      if (this.#isMounted) {
        throw new Error('Component is already mounted')
      }
                                            Passes the component
                                            reference to the
      this.#vdom = this.render()            mountDOM() function
      mountDOM(this.#vdom, hostEl, index, this)   ◁——
```

```
      this.#hostEl = hostEl
      this.#isMounted = true
    }

    // --snip-- //
  }

  // --snip-- //

  return Component
}
```

You're done! Before we close the chapter, let's review what should result when the `defineComponent()` function returns a `Component` class. Then I'll give you a challenge exercise to test your knowledge.

Your component.js file should look like the following listing. Make sure that you got all the details right before moving on to chapter 11. Can you explain what each property and method of the `Component` class does?

**Listing 10.12  Result of the `defineComponent()` function (component.js)**

```
import { destroyDOM } from './destroy-dom'
import { DOM_TYPES, extractChildren } from './h'
import { mountDOM } from './mount-dom'
import { patchDOM } from './patch-dom'
import { hasOwnProperty } from './utils/objects'

export function defineComponent({ render, state, ...methods }) {
  class Component {
    #isMounted = false
    #vdom = null
    #hostEl = null

    constructor(props = {}) {
      this.props = props
      this.state = state ? state(props) : {}
    }

    get elements() {
      if (this.#vdom == null) {
        return []
      }

      if (this.#vdom.type === DOM_TYPES.FRAGMENT) {
        return extractChildren(this.#vdom).map((child) => child.el)
      }

      return [this.#vdom.el]
    }

    get firstElement() {
      return this.elements[0]
    }
```

HT 734 3075

```
  get offset() {
    if (this.#vdom.type === DOM_TYPES.FRAGMENT) {
      return Array.from(this.#hostEl.children).indexOf(this.firstElement)
    }

    return 0
  }

  updateState(state) {
    this.state = { ...this.state, ...state }
    this.#patch()
  }

  render() {
    return render.call(this)
  }

  mount(hostEl, index = null) {
    if (this.#isMounted) {
      throw new Error('Component is already mounted')
    }

    this.#vdom = this.render()
    mountDOM(this.#vdom, hostEl, index, this)

    this.#hostEl = hostEl
    this.#isMounted = true
  }

  unmount() {
    if (!this.#isMounted) {
      throw new Error('Component is not mounted')
    }

    destroyDOM(this.#vdom)

    this.#vdom = null
    this.#hostEl = null
    this.#isMounted = false
  }

  #patch() {
    if (!this.#isMounted) {
      throw new Error('Component is not mounted')
    }

    const vdom = this.render()
    this.#vdom = patchDOM(this.#vdom, vdom, this.#hostEl, this)
  }
}

for (const methodName in methods) {
  if (hasOwnProperty(Component, methodName)) {
    throw new Error(
      `Method "${methodName}()" already exists in the component.`
```

```
    )
  }

  Component.prototype[methodName] = methods[methodName]
}

return Component
}
```

Now it's time for the challenge exercise!

---

**Exercise 10.1: Challenge**

A free API returns random cocktails. Try it in your browser to see what it returns:

`GET https://www.thecocktaildb.com/api/json/v1/1/random.php`

For this challenge exercise, I want you to write the code for a component that fetches a random cocktail and displays it. When the component is mounted, it should show HTML similar to the following:

```
<h1>Random cocktail</h1>
<button>Get a cocktail</button>
```

When the button is clicked, the component should fetch a random cocktail and display it. You should display a `Loading . . .` message while the cocktail is being fetched and maybe add an artificial timeout of 1 or 2 seconds for the message to have time to be displayed. When the cocktail is fetched, display its name (`strDrink` field), image (`strDrinkThumb` field), and preparation instructions (`strInstructions` field). Include a button to load another cocktail:

```
<h1>Cocktail name</h1>
<p>Preparation instructions</p>
<img src="cocktail-image-url" />
<button>Get another cocktail</button>
```

Copy and paste the code for your component (and the framework code that's needed for it to work) into the console of your browser, and mount it inside a website of your choice.

Find the solution at http://mng.bz/j1By.

---

## Summary

- Methods are convenient for handling events in components. When the handling logic has more than a couple of lines, it's cleaner to define a method for it.
- Methods can be used as event handlers in the `on` object of the `h()` function. They can be referenced as `this.methodName` in the `on` object.
- Functions added as event handlers have to be explicitly bound to the component instance so that `this` inside the function refers to the component.

# Subcomponents: Communication via props and events

## This chapter covers

- Adding a new virtual DOM type to represent components
- Implementing subcomponents
- Passing data from a parent component to its children using props
- Communicating among components by using events

What's the value of a component if it can't include other components? The `Component` class that you implemented in chapters 9 and 10 can't return other components from its `render()` method; it can return only fragments, elements, or text nodes. But, as you can imagine, building a complex application by using a single component that renders the entire view isn't very practical.

In this chapter, you learn how to add *subcomponents* (components inside other components) to your framework and how to communicate among them by using props and events. A parent component can pass data to its children by using props, and children can communicate with their parents by emitting events, as illustrated in figure 11.1.

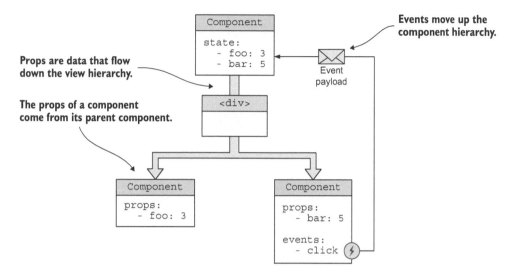

**Figure 11.1  Props flow down; events flow up.**

Let's briefly review the "Anatomy of a stateful component" diagram from chapter 9 and the annotated properties and methods you'll implement in this chapter (figure 11.2).

In this chapter, you'll add the following private properties to the Component class:

- parentComponent—A reference to the component that contains the current component. This property is null for the top-level component.
- dispatcher—An instance of the Dispatcher class used to emit events and subscribe handlers to them.
- subscriptions—An array of subscriptions of event handlers to events emitted by the component. These subscriptions need to be unsubscribed when the component is unmounted.

You'll also implement two important methods:

- updateProps()—This method is called when the component receives new props; it updates the component's props property and triggers a re-render. I'll show you an optional optimization that you can implement to avoid re-rendering the component if the new props are the same as the current ones.
- emit()—This method is used to emit events from the component.

When you finish this chapter, you'll have a fully functional component prototype that handles its own state and lifecycle and that can include other components. That work is an enormous step forward in the development of your framework, so let's get started!

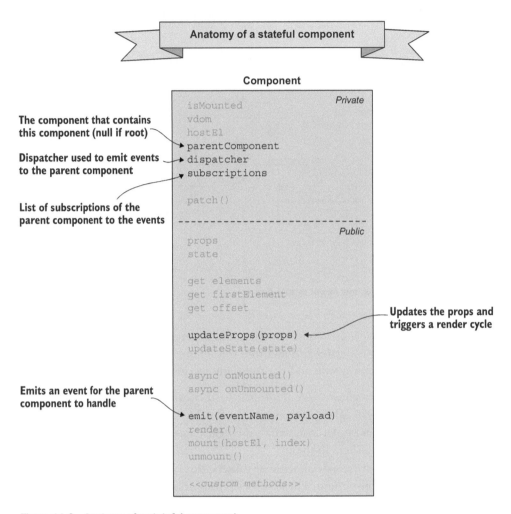

**Anatomy of a stateful component**

Component

The component that contains
this component (null if root)

Dispatcher used to emit events
to the parent component

List of subscriptions of the
parent component to the events

```
                                          Private
isMounted
vdom
hostEl
parentComponent
dispatcher
subscriptions

patch()
- - - - - - - - - - - - - - - - - - - -
                                          Public
props
state

get elements
get firstElement
get offset

updateProps(props)
updateState(state)

async onMounted()
async onUnmounted()

emit(eventName, payload)
render()
mount(hostEl, index)
unmount()

<<custom methods>>
```

Updates the props and
triggers a render cycle

Emits an event for the parent
component to handle

**Figure 11.2   Anatomy of a stateful component**

**NOTE**  You can find all the listings in this chapter in the listings/ch11 directory of the book's repository (http://mng.bz/4Jqj). The code you'll write in this chapter is for the framework's version v3.0, which you'll publish in chapter 12. Therefore, the code in this chapter can be checked out from the ch12 label (http://mng.bz/X1wa): `$ git switch --detach ch12`.

**Code catch-up**

In chapter 10, you modified the `defineComponent()` function to include custom methods in the component's prototype. You had to modify the `addEventListeners()` function so that if the element to which the listener is to be attached has a host component, the listener is bound to it. This change required you to modify the `mountDOM()`,

> `createElementNode()`, and `createFragmentNodes()` functions. You also modified the `patchDOM()`, `patchElement()`, and `patchEvents()` functions in all cases to add the host component argument that needs to be passed around so that the `add-EventListeners()` function can access it.

## 11.1 Adding components as a new virtual DOM type

The reason why your component—as implemented in the preceding two chapters—can't return other components is that you currently have no way to include components in the virtual DOM tree. Ideally, you'd want to use the `h()` function to create component nodes, like this:

```
const FooComponent = defineComponent({ ... })
const BarComponent = defineComponent({ ... })

const ParentComponent = defineComponent({
  render() {
    return hFragment([
      h(FooComponent),
      h(BarComponent),
    ])
  }
})
```

The `render()` method of the `ParentComponent` returns a fragment with two component nodes: `FooComponent` and `BarComponent`. The virtual DOM tree could look something like the following example:

```
{
  type: 'fragment',
  children: [
    { type: 'component', tag: FooComponent, props: {}, children: [] },
    { type: 'component', tag: BarComponent, props: {}, children: [] },
  ]
}
```

Notice that the `type` property of the component nodes is `'component'` and that the `tag` property contains the component prototype instead of a string with the HTML tag name. But the `h()` function doesn't know how to mount component nodes—at least not yet, so let's see how to do it.

To add components inside a virtual DOM tree, you need to add a new virtual DOM type to the `DOM_TYPES` constant to represent those components. Then you need to teach the `h()` function how to differentiate between element nodes and component nodes. One way is to check whether the `tag` argument is a string, in which case you know that the node must be an element node. In JavaScript, the `typeof` operator returns `'function'` for classes, as you can check yourself in the console:

```
class Component {}
typeof Component // 'function'
```

You could use this operator to check whether the `tag` argument is a component, but I chose to check whether the `tag` argument is a string. Both approaches work the same way.

Open the h.js file, and add the COMPONENT constant to the DOM_TYPES object. Then add the condition to check whether the `tag` argument is a string, as the code shown in bold in the following listing.

Listing 11.1   Adding components as a new virtual DOM type (h.js)

```
export const DOM_TYPES = {
  TEXT: 'text',
  ELEMENT: 'element',
  FRAGMENT: 'fragment',
  COMPONENT: 'component',
}

export function h(tag, props = {}, children = []) {
  const type =
    typeof tag === 'string' ? DOM_TYPES.ELEMENT : DOM_TYPES.COMPONENT

  return {
    tag,
    props,
    type,
    children: mapTextNodes(withoutNulls(children)),
    type: DOM_TYPES.ELEMENT,
  }
}
```

Now that virtual node trees can include component nodes, you want to update the `Component` class's `elements` getter to return the elements of a component node.

### 11.1.1   Updating the elements getter

You'll recall that in chapter 9, we discussed the `elements` getter, which retrieves the top-level HTML elements of the virtual node tree representing the component's view. You used this getter to calculate the `offset` property of the component. This offset was crucial for accurately updating the component's DOM when the top-level node was a fragment.

You need to modify the case when the top-level node is a fragment to account for the subcomponents that might be inside the fragment. In this case, you call the `elements` getter recursively, as illustrated in figure 11.3. Look at the figure from bottom to top. Each component in the hierarchy assembles an array of its view's first-level elements, and if it finds a component, it calls the `elements` getter—hence, the recursion. As you can see, the topmost component has a fragment at the root of its view, so it looks inside it to find the first-level elements. First, it finds a component that has two

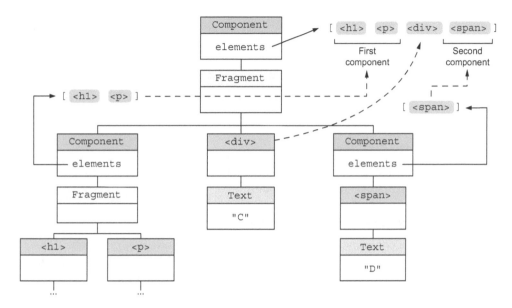

**Figure 11.3   Calling the `elements` getter recursively to get the parent component's elements**

elements in its first level (inside the fragment): an `<h1>` and a `<p>` element. Then it finds a `<div>` element, which is the second element in the fragment. Finally, it finds another component, which has a single `<p>` element in its first level.

The component's `elements` getter returns an array, not a single element, so you want to use the `flatMap()` method to flatten the array of arrays. In the component.js file, make the changes shown in bold in the following listing.

---

**Listing 11.2   Extracting the elements of a component (component.js)**

```
export function defineComponent({ render, state, ...methods }) {
  class Component {
    // --snip-- //

    get elements() {
      if (this.#vdom == null) {
        return []
      }

      if (this.#vdom.type === DOM_TYPES.FRAGMENT) {
        return extractChildren(this.#vdom).map((child) => child.el)
        return extractChildren(this.#vdom).flatMap((child) => {
          if (child.type === DOM_TYPES.COMPONENT) {
            return child.component.elements
          }

          return [child.el]
        })
      }
```

Annotations:
- *Flat-maps the arrays* → `return extractChildren(this.#vdom).flatMap((child) => {`
- *Checks whether the node is a component* → `if (child.type === DOM_TYPES.COMPONENT) {`
- *Calls the elements getter recursively* → `return child.component.elements`
- *Otherwise, returns the node's element inside an array* → `return [child.el]`

```
      return [this.#vdom.el]
  }

  // --snip-- //
  }

  // --snip-- //

  return Component
}
```

With this small but necessary change out of the way, let's focus on mounting, destroying, and patching component nodes.

### 11.1.2  *Mounting component virtual nodes*

To mount component nodes, first you need to include the DOM_TYPES.COMPONENT case in the mountDOM() function's switch statement. The boldface code in the following listing shows how. Make this change in the mount-dom.js file.

---
**Listing 11.3   Mounting component virtual nodes (mount-dom.js)**

```
export function mountDOM(vdom, parentEl, index, hostComponent = null) {
  switch (vdom.type) {
    case DOM_TYPES.TEXT: {
      createTextNode(vdom, parentEl, index)
      break
    }

    case DOM_TYPES.ELEMENT: {
      createElementNode(vdom, parentEl, index, hostComponent)
      break
    }

    case DOM_TYPES.FRAGMENT: {
      createFragmentNodes(vdom, parentEl, hostComponent)
      break
    }                                                            ◁── Checks whether
                                                                      the node is a
    case DOM_TYPES.COMPONENT: {                             ◁──       component
      createComponentNode(vdom, parentEl, index, hostComponent)   ◁──
      break
    }                                                                 Mounts the
                                                                      component node
    default: {
      throw new Error(`Can't mount DOM of type: ${vdom.type}`)
    }
  }
}
```

The job of mounting the component is delegated to a function called createComponent-Node(), which you need to implement next. Let's see what this function needs to do.

First, you want to extract the component's instance from the virtual node's `tag` key and instantiate it, using code similar to the following:

```
const vnode = {
  type: 'component',
  tag: FooComponent,
  props: {},
}

const Component = vnode.tag
const component = new Component()
```

In chapter 9, you learned that you can instantiate a component class by passing it a `props` object. These `props` objects contain data received from the parent component. The virtual node you defined also includes a `props` object. Initially, you used this object to pass attributes and event handlers to element nodes; you can use it to pass props and event handlers to component nodes as well.

Let's explore an example that demonstrates how to achieve this goal. Suppose that you've defined a component called `Greetings` that receives a `name` prop and renders a paragraph with a greeting message:

```
const Greetings = defineComponent({
  render() {
    const { name } = this.props

    return h('p', {}, [`Hello, ${name}!`])
  }
})
```

To instantiate this component including the `name` prop, you can do something like the following:

```
const vnode = {
  type: 'component',
  tag: Greetings,
  props: { name: 'Jenny' },
}

const Component = vnode.tag
const component = new Component(vnode.props)
```

Next, you want to mount the component. To do so, call the component instance's `mount()` method, which renders its view via the `render()` method and passes the resulting virtual DOM tree to the `mountDOM()` function. Whenever another component is found in the virtual DOM tree, the process is repeated. Figure 11.4 illustrates this cycle.

Keep in mind one very important thing when you mount component nodes: you want to keep the instance of the component in the virtual node. Components have state—state that changes as the user interacts with its view. You want to keep this state

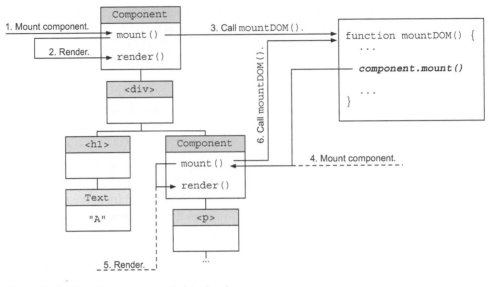

**Figure 11.4  Mounting a component virtual node**

"alive" throughout the application's lifecycle. If the component is instantiated every time the DOM is patched, the state is lost. This internal state is the key difference between your new stateful components and the previous version, which were pure functions without internal state. By saving the component instance in the virtual node, you can access it inside the patchDOM() function and, thus, don't need to instantiate it again. Figure 11.5 shows how the component instance is saved in the virtual node.

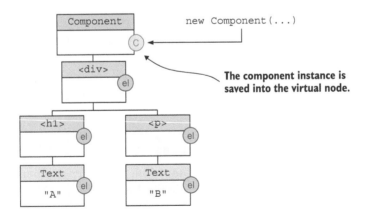

**Figure 11.5  A reference to the component instance is saved in the virtual node.**

Following the preceding example, after you instantiate and mount the component, you save the instance in the virtual node inside a property called `component`, as follows:

```
const Component = vnode.tag
const component = new Component(vnode.props)

component.mount(parentEl)
vdom.component = component
```

Don't forget to keep a reference to the component's DOM element in the virtual node's `el` property (figure 11.6).

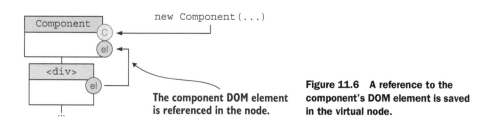

The component DOM element is referenced in the node.

**Figure 11.6   A reference to the component's DOM element is saved in the virtual node.**

But wait! Again, you'll recall from chapter 9 that if a component's view is a fragment, it doesn't have one single HTML element as its root, but an array of elements. What do you do in this case?

The use case for the `el` reference is the reconciliation algorithm. In the case of a component, the `el` reference's sole use is to serve as a reference node to insert elements before the component. To move a node to a different position, use the `insert-Before()` method, which requires a reference node after the location where the node will be inserted. To insert an element before a component, you should make sure that the `el` property points to the component's first element (figure 11.7).

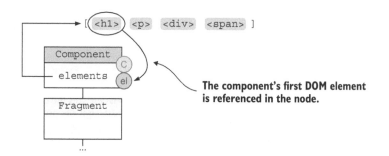

The component's first DOM element is referenced in the node.

**Figure 11.7   The `el` property points to the component's first element.**

By keeping the `el` reference of a component node pointing to the first element, you can move DOM nodes before the component, as shown in figure 11.8. In this case, the view of the component is made of a fragment containing an `<h1>` and a `<p>` element. A `<div>` outside the component is moved before the component, for which purpose the component's first element—the `<h1>` element—is used as the reference node.

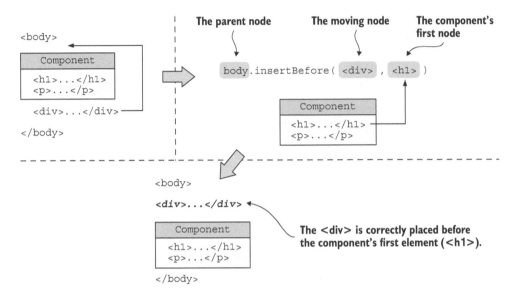

Figure 11.8  **Moving a component to a different position in the DOM tree**

You're ready to implement the `createComponentNode()` function. Inside the mount-dom.js file, add the code in the following listing.

**Listing 11.4   Mounting a component node (mount-dom.js)**

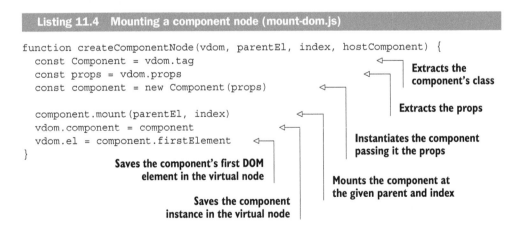

**NOTE**  You passed the `hostComponent` as the fourth argument to the `create-ComponentNode()` function, but you haven't used it yet; you'll use it in section

11.2 to implement the event listeners. I thought it would be convenient to have the function in place before you get to that point.

Hooray! Now you can mount component nodes, which means that you can have subcomponents inside your components. These child components can be rendered only once—when the component is mounted (because your patching algorithm doesn't handle components at the moment)—but this is a good start. In section 11.1.3, you find out how to destroy component nodes.

---

### Exercise 11.1

Write a component called `List` that renders a list of items inside a `<ul>` element. These items are passed to the component as a prop called `items`, which is an array of strings. Each item should be rendered using another component called `ListItem`, which renders a `<li>` element with the item's text.

The result of mounting the component as follows

```
const items = ['foo', 'bar', 'baz']
const list = new List({ items })
list.mount(document.body)
```

should be the following HTML:

```
<ul>
   <li>foo</li>
   <li>bar</li>
   <li>baz</li>
</ul>
```

Look at the answer in the following link if you get stuck. You must understand how to define subcomponents as you move forward in this chapter.

Find the solution at http://mng.bz/W1rx.

---

### 11.1.3 Destroying component virtual nodes

Once again, destroying is always easier than creating. Destroying a component is as simple as calling its `unmount()` method. You implemented the `unmount()` method in chapter 9, and, if you recall, that method calls the `destroyDOM()` by passing it the component's virtual DOM tree. If the component has subcomponents, the `destroyDOM()` method is called recursively (figure 11.9).

Because you saved the component instance in the virtual node, now you can access it inside the `destroyDOM()` function, which is a straightforward addition to the `destroyDOM()` method. Open the destroy-dom.js file, and add the code shown in bold in the following listing.

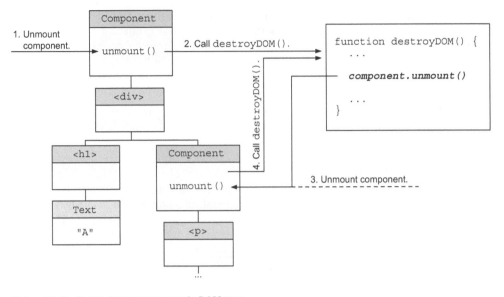

**Figure 11.9    Destroying a component's DOM tree**

**Listing 11.5    Destroying the component (destroy-dom.js)**

```
export function destroyDOM(vdom) {
  const { type } = vdom

  switch (type) {
    case DOM_TYPES.TEXT: {
      removeTextNode(vdom)
      break
    }

    case DOM_TYPES.ELEMENT: {
      removeElementNode(vdom)
      break
    }

    case DOM_TYPES.FRAGMENT: {
      removeFragmentNodes(vdom)
      break
    }

    case DOM_TYPES.COMPONENT: {
      vdom.component.unmount()        ◁──  Calls the node's
      break                                component instance
    }                                       unmount() method

    default: {
      throw new Error(`Can't destroy DOM of type: ${type}`)
    }
  }
```

```
        delete vdom.el
}
```

### 11.1.4 Patching component virtual nodes

Now let's look at how you can patch component nodes. When the state of a component changes or when it receives new props, this component patches its view and instructs its subcomponents to do the same. The view of a component can change only if its state changes or its props change. So when the state changes or the props of a component change, the component patches its view and passes the new props to its subcomponents. The subcomponents state doesn't change, but their props might. Figure 11.10 illustrates how a component whose state changes notifies its subcomponents to patch their views.

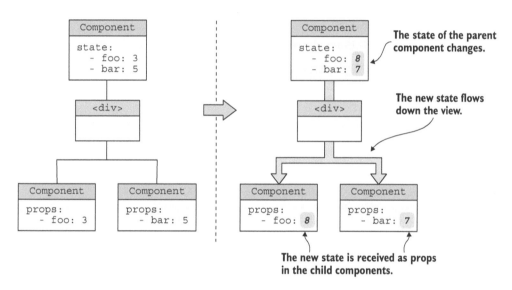

**Figure 11.10  The state of a component changes, and its subcomponents receive new props.**

Then, to patch the subcomponents inside the virtual DOM tree of a component, you need to extract the new props passed to them and call their `updateProps()` method, which internally calls the `patch()` method of the component. Let's implement the `updateProps()` method in the `Component` class to update the props of the component and re-render it. Add the boldface code in the following listing to the component.js file.

**Listing 11.6  Updating the props of a component (component.js)**

```
export function defineComponent({ render, state, ...methods }) {
  class Component {
    // --snip-- //
```

```
    updateProps(props) {
      this.props = { ...this.props, ...props }        ◁───   Merges the new
      this.#patch()                              ◁─┐          props with the
    }                                              │          old ones
                                                   │
    updateState(state) {                           │       Re-renders the
      this.state = { ...this.state, ...state }     │       component
      this.#patch()                              ──┘
    }

    // --snip-- //
  }

  // --snip-- //
}
```

Now add the code to patch component nodes (shown in bold in the following listing) to the patch-dom.js file. You add a `case` inside the `switch` statement that checks what type of node you're patching.

**Listing 11.7   Adding the component case to the `patchDOM()` function (patch-dom.js)**

```
export function patchDOM(
  oldVdom,
  newVdom,
  parentEl,
  hostComponent = null,
) {
  if (!areNodesEqual(oldVdom, newVdom)) {
    const index = findIndexInParent(parentEl, oldVdom.el)
    destroyDOM(oldVdom)
    mountDOM(newVdom, parentEl, index, hostComponent)

    return newVdom
  }

  newVdom.el = oldVdom.el

  switch (newVdom.type) {
    case DOM_TYPES.TEXT: {
      patchText(oldVdom, newVdom)
      return newVdom
    }

    case DOM_TYPES.ELEMENT: {
      patchElement(oldVdom, newVdom, hostComponent)
      break
    }
                                                    ┌──  Calls the method
    case DOM_TYPES.COMPONENT: {                     │    that patches the
      patchComponent(oldVdom, newVdom)        ◁─────┘    component
      break
    }
  }
```

```
    patchChildren(oldVdom, newVdom, hostComponent)

    return newVdom
}

// TODO: implement patchComponent()
```

Next, you implement the `patchComponent()` function. This function is in charge of extracting the new props from the virtual node and calling the component's `update-Props()` method. The function should also save the component instance in the new virtual node so that it can be accessed later. Because components can change their top-level element between renders, you want to save the component's first DOM element in the node's `el` property. Write the code in the following listing inside the patch-dom.js file.

Listing 11.8 Patching a component node (patch-dom.js)

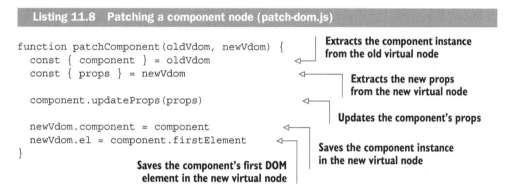

And just like that, you can use child components inside your components and patch them when the state of the parent component changes. If you're interested in optimizing the patching of components, avoiding unnecessary re-renders, you can read section 11.1.5, which is optional. Otherwise, jump to section 11.2, which discusses how child components can communicate with their parent components via events.

### 11.1.5 A rendering optimization (optional)

You may have realized that you have a good opportunity here to optimize the patching of components. Can you guess what it is? Exactly: you can check whether the props of the component have changed and re-render only if they have. By comparing the old and new prop objects, you can avoid patching the component—and all its subcomponents—if its props haven't changed, as shown in figure 11.11.

This approach may eliminate the need to check entire (and potentially long) branches of the virtual DOM tree. But this benefit comes at a cost: you need to compare the old and new props objects, which can be expensive if the objects are large.

As it turns out, comparing objects in JavaScript isn't as straightforward as comparing primitive values. The `===` operator returns `true` only if both objects are the same object (reference equality). When the `render()` function of a component is called, it

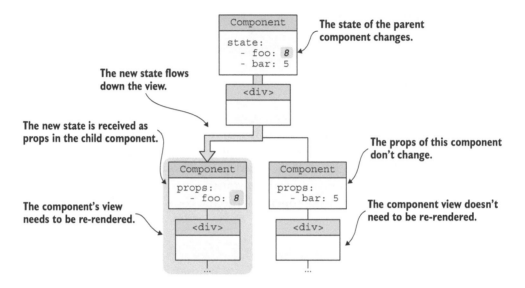

**Figure 11.11   The state of a component changes, but not all the props of its child components change.**

produces a fresh virtual DOM object, which means that the old and new `props` objects will never be the same object.

This situation isn't a big deal because the community has satisfied this need by creating libraries that handle deep-object comparison. One such library is `fast-deep-equal` (https://www.npmjs.com/package/fast-deep-equal), which is small and does exactly what we need.

This optimization is optional, so feel free to skip this section if you're not interested in it. First, you need to add the `fast-deep-equal` library to your runtime package as follows (making sure that you're in the packages/runtime folder):

```
npm install fast-deep-equal
```

Then you need to import the library into the component.js file and use it to compare the old and new `props` objects inside the component's `updateProps()` method:

```
import equal from 'fast-deep-equal'

// --snip-- //


export function defineComponent({ render, state, ...methods }) {
  class Component {
    // --snip-- //

    updateProps(props) {
      #this.props = { ...this.props, ...props }
      const newProps = { ...this.props, ...props }
```

> Creates a new props object by merging the old and new props

```
    if (equal(this.props, newProps)) {          Compares the old and new
      return                                     props objects; returns if
    }                                            they're equal

    this.props = newProps          Updates the
    this.#patch()                  component's props
  }

  // --snip-- //
  }
}
```

With this simple change, your components will be patched only if their props have changed. But to bundle the code in the `fast-deep-equal` library, you need to install two extra rollup plugins:

- `@rollup/plugin-commonjs` (http://mng.bz/y8Bd)—Transforms the `fast-deep-equal` library code from CommonJS to ES syntax, allowing Rollup to bundle the library code.
- `@rollup/plugin-node-resolve` (http://mng.bz/MZRB)—Resolves the `fast-deep-equal` library, which is a third-party module, and includes it in the bundle. By default, Rollup resolves only modules that are part of your project. This plugin allows you to resolve third-party modules and include them in the bundle.

Install the libraries in the packages/runtime folder as `dev` dependencies:

```
$ npm install --save-dev @rollup/plugin-commonjs @rollup/plugin-node-resolve
```

Now you need to edit the rollup configuration file, packages/runtime/rollup.config.js, to add the plugins to the `plugins` array:

```
import commonjs from '@rollup/plugin-commonjs'
import { nodeResolve } from '@rollup/plugin-node-resolve'
import cleanup from 'rollup-plugin-cleanup'
import filesize from 'rollup-plugin-filesize'

export default {
  input: 'src/index.js',
  plugins: [commonjs(), nodeResolve(), cleanup()],
  output: [
    {
      file: 'dist/fe-fwk.js',
      format: 'esm',
      plugins: [filesize()],
    },
  ],
}
```

Run the `npm run build` script to make sure that your configuration is correct and the output JavaScript file is generated correctly. If you open the bundled JavaScript file for

your framework, inside the dist folder, you should see the `fast-deep-equal` library
code included in the bundle. Look for a function called `fastDeepEqual()`:

```
var fastDeepEqual = function equal(a, b) {
  if (a === b) return true;
  if (a && b && typeof a == 'object' && typeof b == 'object') {
    if (a.constructor !== b.constructor) return false;
    // --snip-- //
  }
  // --snip-- //
}
```

With this small change, you've added a useful optimization to your framework.

## 11.2   Events

A component can pass information to its child components via props, which is how a
parent component communicates with its children. But how can a child component
communicate with its parent? It communicates via events that the parent component
can listen to, as shown in figure 11.12.

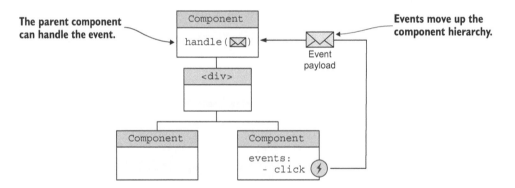

**Figure 11.12   A child component communicates with its parent via events.**

The parent component defines the event-handler function and registers it to listen to
events emitted by the child component. The events emitted by a child component
aren't DOM events; they're custom events identified by a name and containing a payload. The child component that receives the event-handler function from the parent
component needs to save that function in a registry, where it can be called when the
event is emitted. (If this process reminds you a lot of your `Dispatcher` class, you're
headed in the right direction.)

## Events vs. callbacks

If you've used React, you're probably used to passing callbacks from parent to child components:

```
function MyButton({ onClick }) {
  return <button onClick={onClick}>Click me</button>
}
```

Then the parent component defines a function that will be called when the button is clicked and passes it to the child component:

```
function App() {
  function handleClick() {
    console.log('Ooh la la!')
  }

  return <MyButton onClick={handleClick} />
}
```

In other frameworks, such as Vue, you emit an event from the child component instead and never receive the callback function from the parent component:

```
<template>
  <button @click="$emit('click')">Click me</button>
</template>
```

The `$emit()` method, which is similar to what you'll implement in this section, emits a custom (non-DOM) event. Then the parent component listens to that event:

```
<script setup>
  import MyButton from './MyButton.vue'

  function handleClick() {
    console.log('Ooh la la!')
  }
</script>

<template>
  <MyButton @click="handleClick" />
</template>
```

Although these two approaches seem to be different, you'll see as you implement this feature that they've very similar. The difference is mostly syntactical, related to how a framework decides to expose the feature to the developer.

In the case of React, using JSX (which is a more convenient way of defining the virtual DOM tree for your view), you operate at the virtual DOM level. Thus, you must explicitly pass the event-handler function from the parent to the child component.

*(continued)*

In the case of Vue, you work with a template. It feels natural to add event handlers inside the template of a component to handle the events that its child components emit. But under the hood, Vue compiles your template into a render function that operates at the virtual DOM level, where the event handler is passed to the child component as a prop—the same thing that happens in React.

A parent component listening to an event from a child component fits well with the way you've implemented the virtual DOM in your framework. If you recall from chapter 3, to add an event listener function to an element node, you include it inside the on object of the props parameter of the h() function:

```
h(
  'button',
  { on: { click: () => console.log('Ooh la la!') } },
  ['Click me']
)
```

You can make your components emit events. These events won't be instances of the Event interface (http://mng.bz/aENm), which represents events arising from the user's interaction with the DOM; they'll be simple JavaScript objects with the desired payload. The key idea is that you can add event listeners to your components by using exactly the same syntax that you use to add event listeners to DOM elements. Here's an example:

```
h(
  MyFancyButton,
  { on: { btnClicked: () => console.log('Much fancy, too cool, wow!') } },
  ['Click me']
)
```

Next, you'll see how to implement this feature in your Component prototype.

### 11.2.1 Saving the event handlers inside the component

You want to save those event listeners passed by the parent component inside the component that emits the event (the subcomponent or child component). Suppose that you have a MyFancyButton component emitting a custom event called btnClicked, and its parent component renders it like so:

```
h(
  MyFancyButton,
  {
    on: {
      btnClicked: () => { ... }
    }
  },
```

```
    ['Click me']
)
```

You want to save the passed-in `btnClicked` event handler inside the `MyFancyButton` component. The component can accept that event-handler object as a parameter in its constructor and save it in a private property called `#eventHandlers`.

Then, when the child component (`MyFancyButton`) emits an event, it can look up the event handler in the `#eventHandlers` object and call it. Do you recall the `Dispatcher` class that you implemented in chapter 5? It's the perfect fit for this task—registering handlers for events and calling them when the event is emitted. You used `Dispatcher` to dispatch and handle commands, but you can use it to dispatch and handle events as well. (Remember that the difference between commands and events is mostly in the nomenclature: events represent something that happened in the past, whereas commands represent something that should happen in the future.)

You need to take one important subtlety into account, though: when a parent component declares an event handler attached to a child component, it expects the event handler to be called with the parent component as the `this` value. A common use case is when the event handler modifies the state of the parent component:

```
const ParentComponent = defineComponent({
  state() {
    return { counter: 0 }
  },

  render() {
    const { counter } = this.state

    return hFragment([
      h('p', {}, [The count is: ${counter}]),
      h(
        MyFancyButton,
        {
          on: {
            btnClicked: () => {
              this.updateState({ counter: counter + 1 })   ◁──┐  Inside the handler,
            },                                                 │  this should be
          },                                                  │  ParentComponent.
        },
        ['Increment']
      )
    ])
  }
})
```

You want to explicitly bind the `this` value of the event handler to the parent component, not the child component executing the event handler (figure 11.13). This point is very important, so keep it in mind: the `this` value of the event handler should be the parent component, not the child component calling the event handler.

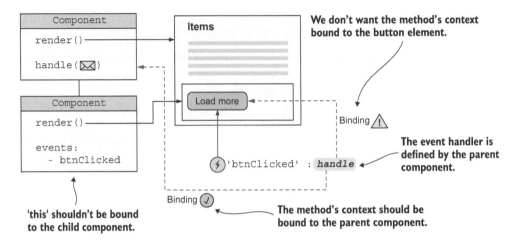

**Figure 11.13**  The this value of the event handler should be the parent component.

Let's add the #eventHandlers property to the Component prototype. We'll also pass the reference to the parent component to the constructor so that we can use it to explicitly bind the event handler's context. Inside the component.js file, add the code shown in bold in the following listing.

**Listing 11.9  Passing event handlers to a component (component.js)**

```
export function defineComponent({ render, state, ...methods }) {
  class Component {
    #isMounted = false
    #vdom = null
    #hostEl = null
    #eventHandlers = null          ◁─ Declares the eventHandlers
    #parentComponent = null             private property

    constructor(                        ◁─ Declares the parentComponent
      props = {},                          private property
      eventHandlers = {},
      parentComponent = null,
    ) {
      this.props = props
      this.state = state ? state(props) : {}
      this.#eventHandlers = eventHandlers      ◁─ Saves the passed-in
      this.#parentComponent = parentComponent       event handlers

    }                                        ◁─ Saves the passed-in
                                                parent component
    // --snip-- //                              reference
  }

  // --snip-- //

  return Component
}
```

Before you implement the wiring of the event handlers, you want to go back to the mount-dom.js and patch-dom.js files, and pass the event handlers and the parent component reference to the component constructor.

### 11.2.2 Extracting the props and events for a component

As you probably remember from destructuring the props and events for an element node (refer to the mount-dom.js file inside the `addProps()` function), separating the props from the events is as simple as this:

```
const { on: events, ...props } = vdom.props
```

You could simply add that same line to the `createComponentNode()` function (in the mount-dom.js file) and the `patchComponent()` function (in the patch-dom.js file) functions. But you'll add some extra logic to the props and events extraction in chapter 12 when you learn about keyed lists. (You want to remove the `key` prop, but let's not get ahead of ourselves.) To avoid duplicating the same logic in two places, I prefer to create a separate file inside the utils/ directory, call it props.js, and write a function that extracts the props and events for a component. In that utils/props.js file, add the `extractPropsAndEvents()` function shown in the following listing.

> **Listing 11.10** Extracting the props and events for a component (utils/props.js)

```
export function extractPropsAndEvents(vdom) {
  const { on: events = {}, ...props } = vdom.props

  return { props, events }
}
```

Now open the mount-dom.js file, import the `extractPropsAndEvents()` function, and use it inside the `createComponentNode()` function to extract the props and events. Then you want to pass the props, event handlers, and parent component to the component constructor. The parent component is the fourth `hostComponent` parameter passed to the `createComponentNode()` function. You added this parameter in listing 11.4 but didn't use it then. Implement these changes as shown in bold in the following listing.

> **Listing 11.11** Extracting the props and events (mount-dom.js)

```
import { extractPropsAndEvents } from './utils/props'

// --snip-- //

function createComponentNode(vdom, parentEl, index, hostComponent) {
  const Component = vdom.tag
  const props = vdom.props
  const component = new Component(props)
  const { props, events } = extractPropsAndEvents(vdom)   ◁── Extracts the
                                                               props and events
```

```
const component = new Component(props, events, hostComponent)       ◄─────────┐

component.mount(parentEl, index)
vdom.component = component                        Passes the props, event handlers,
vdom.el = component.firstElement                   and parent component to the
}                                                     component constructor
```

Similarly, open the patch-dom.js file, import the `extractPropsAndEvents()` function, and use it inside the `patchComponent()` function, as shown in the following listing. In this case, you pass only the props; we're expecting that the event handlers won't change between patches.

> **Listing 11.12   Extracting the props and events (patch-dom.js)**

```
import { extractPropsAndEvents } from './utils/props'

// --snip--

function patchComponent(oldVdom, newVdom) {
  const { component } = oldVdom
  const { props } = newVdom
  const { props } = extractPropsAndEvents(newVdom)

  component.updateProps(props)

  newVdom.component = component
  newVdom.el = component.firstElement
}
```

With this little detour out of the way, you can go back to the component.js file and implement the logic to wire the event handlers.

> **NOTE**   After the child component is mounted, we don't allow the parent component to change the event handlers or register new ones. This design decision is deliberate because it simplifies the implementation of the component patching logic. A few good use cases for event handlers to change between renders might exist, but they're not very common. You can try to implement this logic as an exercise.

### 11.2.3  *Wiring the event handlers*

When the component is mounted, you want to iterate over the `#eventHandlers` object and register the event handlers in the component. How can you register event handlers in a component? You use the `Dispatcher` class you implemented in chapter 5. Each component instance has its own dispatcher where it can register event handlers and emit the events.

You want to save the functions that the `subscribe()` method returns so you can call them later to unsubscribe the event handlers when the component is unmounted. (If you recall, the `subscribe()` method returns a function that, when called, unsubscribes the event handler.)

Inside the `Component` class, write a private method called `#wireEventHandler()` that takes the event name and the event handler as parameters and subscribes the event handler to the component's dispatcher. Don't forget to bind the event handler's context to the parent component instance—the component that's defining the event handler. Then, for convenience, a second method called `#wireEventHandlers()` (in plural) can do the work of iterating over the `#eventHandlers` object and call the `#wireEventHandler()` method for each event handler, saving the unsubscribe functions in a `#subscriptions` private property.

In your component.js file, add the code shown in bold in the following listing. Don't forget to import the `Dispatcher` class from the dispatcher.js file.

---

**Listing 11.13   Wiring the event handlers from the parent component (component.js)**

```
import equal from 'fast-deep-equal'
import { destroyDOM } from './destroy-dom'
import { Dispatcher } from './dispatcher'
import { DOM_TYPES, extractChildren } from './h'
import { mountDOM } from './mount-dom'
import { patchDOM } from './patch-dom'
import { hasOwnProperty } from './utils/objects'

export function defineComponent({ render, state, ...methods }) {
  class Component {
    #isMounted = false
    #vdom = null
    #hostEl = null
    #eventHandlers = null
    #parentComponent = null
    #dispatcher = new Dispatcher()           ◁  Creates a new dispatcher
    #subscriptions = []                       ◁  Creates an array for the unsubscribe functions

    // --snip-- //

    #wireEventHandlers() {
      this.#subscriptions = Object.entries(this.#eventHandlers).map(   ◁
        ([eventName, handler]) =>
          this.#wireEventHandler(eventName, handler)          Iterates over the event handler's object
      )
    }

    #wireEventHandler(eventName, handler) {
      return this.#dispatcher.subscribe(eventName, (payload) => {
        if (this.#parentComponent) {
          handler.call(this.#parentComponent, payload)    ◁  If there is a parent component, binds the event handler's context to it and calls it
        } else {
          handler(payload)                   ◁  If no parent component exists, calls the event handler with no context
        }
      })
    }

    // --snip-- //
  }
```

```
// --snip-- //

  return Component
}
```

Now you can call the `#wireEventHandlers()` method from the `mount()` method. You also want to unsubscribe the event handlers when the component is unmounted. Add the changes shown in bold in the following listing.

**Listing 11.14   Wiring the event handlers (component.js)**

```
export function defineComponent({ render, state, ...methods }) {
  class Component {
    // --snip-- //

    mount(hostEl, index = null) {
      if (this.#isMounted) {
        throw new Error('Component is already mounted')
      }

      this.#vdom = this.render()                         ┐  Wires the event
      mountDOM(this.#vdom, hostEl, index, this)          │  handlers when the
      this.#wireEventHandlers()              ◄───────────┘  component is mounted

      this.#isMounted = true
      this.#hostEl = hostEl
    }

    unmount() {
      if (!this.#isMounted) {                               Unsubscribes the
        throw new Error('Component is not mounted')       event handlers when
      }                                                     the component is
      destroyDOM(this.#vdom)                                   unmounted
      this.#subscriptions.forEach((unsubscribe) => unsubscribe())  ◄──┘

      this.#vdom = null
      this.#isMounted = false
      this.#hostEl = null
      this.#subscriptions = []       ◄──┐  Clears the
    }                                    │  subscriptions
    // --snip-- //                       │  array
  }

  // --snip-- //

  return Component
}
```

Now you can subscribe event handlers passed from the parent component in a child component, but you want a way of emitting these events from your component. As you can guess, that's as easy as calling the dispatcher's `emit()` method. Section 11.2.4 shows how.

> **Exercise 11.2**
>
> Can you explain why you need to bind the event handler's context to the parent component instance when you subscribe the event handler?
>
> Find the solution at http://mng.bz/84W2.

### 11.2.4 *Emitting events*

You can emit events from the component by calling the `emit()` method on the component's dispatcher:

```
const MyFancyButton = defineComponent({
  render() {
    return h(
      'button',
      {
        on: { click: () => this.#dispatcher.dispatch('click') }
      },
      ['Click me!']
    )
  }
})
```

But that code is a bit verbose. You want the users of your framework to use an API that's as simple as possible. Something like the following would be ideal:

```
const MyFancyButton = defineComponent({
  render() {
    return h(
      'button',
      {
        on: { click: () => this.emit('click') }
      },
      ['Click me!']
    )
  }
})
```

You can achieve that goal easily by adding an `emit()` method to the `Component` class. Add the code shown in bold in the following listing to your component.js file.

**Listing 11.15  Emitting events from the component (component.js)**

```
export function defineComponent({ render, state, ...methods }) {
  class Component {
    // --snip-- //
```

```
    emit(eventName, payload) {
      this.#dispatcher.dispatch(eventName, payload)
    }
  }

  // --snip-- //

  return Component
}
```

With this last change, your `Component` class is complete. In chapter 12, you'll refactor the `createApp()` function to return an application instance made of stateful components. Then you'll look into an interesting problem: what happens when stateful components move around the DOM? Does the reconciliation algorithm know how to handle it? After solving that problem, you'll publish the new version of your framework.

---

**Exercise 11.3**

Write the code for a component called `SearchField` that renders an input field and emits a `search` event when the user types in the field. You want to debounce the event by 500 milliseconds. (Assume that you have a `debounce()` function that takes a function and a delay as parameters and returns a debounced version of the function.)

Find the solution at http://mng.bz/E9Vl.

---

## Summary

- A parent component can pass data to a child component by passing it as props.
- A child component can pass data to a parent component by emitting events to which the parent component can subscribe.
- The child component saves the registered event handlers in a `#eventHandlers` object and subscribes them to its dispatcher when the component is mounted.
- When the state of a component changes or its props change, the component re-renders its view. In this process, when a subcomponent appears in the view tree, the parent component passes the subcomponent's props to it and tells it to re-render its view.

# Keyed lists

**This chapter covers**

- Working with keyed lists of components
- Working with keyed lists of elements
- Updating the application instance
- Publishing the new version of the framework

Components have internal state. This state is hidden from the outside world—not reflected in the virtual DOM tree that represents the view—and thus can't be used to compare two component virtual DOM nodes. But to patch the view correctly, you must make sure that when you have a list of components, the reconciliation algorithm can distinguish among them.

Let's look at an example. Suppose that you have a `Counter` component with a `count` state property, which can be initialized with a different value for each component instance:

```
const Counter = defineComponent({
  state(props) {
    return { count: props.initialCount }
  },
```

279

```
  render() {
    return h('p', {}, [`Count: ${this.state.count}`])
  },
})
```

Then you render a list of three `Counter` components, each of which has a different value for the `count` state:

```
h('div', {}, [
  h(Counter, { initialCount: 0 }),
  h(Counter, { initialCount: 1 }),
  h(Counter, { initialCount: 2 }),
])
```

Note that the value of each `count` state property isn't reflected in the virtual DOM tree. That information is part of the component's state, stored inside the `Counter` component instances. The rendered HTML would look like the following:

```
<div>
  <p>Count: 0</p>
  <p>Count: 1</p>
  <p>Count: 2</p>
</div>
```

What happens if the `Counter` component in the middle of the list is removed? The new virtual DOM tree would look like this:

```
h('div', {}, [
  h(Counter, { initialCount: 0 }),
  h(Counter, { initialCount: 2 }),
])
```

But the reconciliation algorithm you wrote can't know which `Counter` component was removed, as illustrated in figure 12.1. The reconciliation algorithm doesn't know how to distinguish among the components at all; all components look the same to it.

By comparing the two virtual DOM trees, the `arraysDiffSequence()` function would wrongly conclude that the last `Counter` component was removed. The resulting HTML would (incorrectly) be

```
<div>
  <p>Count: 0</p>
  <p>Count: 1</p>
</div>
```

when it should have been

```
<div>
  <p>Count: 0</p>
  <p>Count: 2</p>
</div>
```

**Old vdom**   **New vdom**

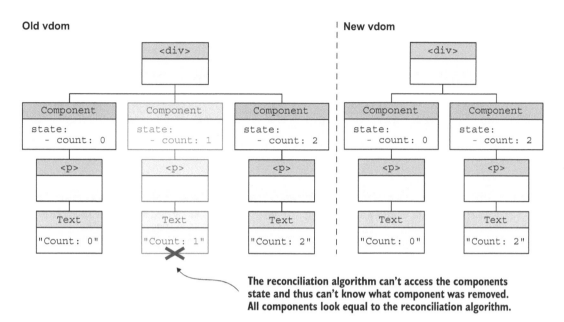

The reconciliation algorithm can't access the components state and thus can't know what component was removed. All components look equal to the reconciliation algorithm.

**Figure 12.1  All components look the same to the reconciliation algorithm.**

You might think that the solution is as straightforward as making the `areNodes-Equal()` compare the internal state and props of the components to determine whether they're equal; a component is fully characterized by its internal data. Unfortunately, this solution isn't possible. Before reading the next paragraph, try to think why.

This solution isn't possible because the `areNodesEqual()` function receives one node from the old virtual DOM tree, which contains a reference to the component instance, and another node from the new virtual DOM tree, which doesn't. Without access to the instantiated component in the new virtual DOM, you can't access its internal state and props, as shown in figure 12.2.

Your `areNodesEqual()` function would receive the following old and new nodes:

```
const oldNode = {
  type: 'component',
  tag: Counter,
  props: {},
  component: <instance of Counter>,
}

const newNode = {
  type: 'component',
  tag: Counter,
  props: {},
}
```

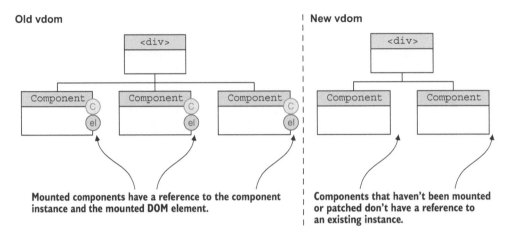

**Figure 12.2   The new virtual DOM tree doesn't contain a reference to the component instance.**

It's obvious that you can't access the count property of the component instance from the newNode object; thus, you can't use it to compare whether the two nodes are equal. Clearly, you need another solution.

The goal of this chapter is to explore the solution to this problem. As you might have guessed from the title of the chapter, that solution is the key attribute that the developer can provide to each component. The chapter also explores some poor practices that you should avoid when using the key attribute. Finally, you'll publish a new version of the framework, version 3.0, that supports stateful components.

> **NOTE** You can find all the listings in this chapter in the listings/ch12/ directory of the book's repository (http://mng.bz/gvrv). The code in this chapter can be checked out from the ch12 label (http://mng.bz/eowV):
> ```
> $ git switch --detach ch12.
> ```

### Code catch-up

In chapter 11, you added the component as a new type of virtual DOM node and extended the h() function to support it. You modified the mountDOM() function to include a case for the component type, handled by the createComponentNode() function. You also modified the destroyDOM() function to include a case for the component, in this case simply calling the component's unmount() method.

Then you worked on adapting the patchDOM() function to support the component type. For that purpose, you had to include a new method in the Component class: updateProps(). This method is called inside the patchComponent() function, which you wrote to handle the component case in the patchDOM() function.

You implemented a mechanism for components to handle events emitted by their child components, which involved adding two new private properties to the Component class: #eventHandlers and #parentComponent. Then you wrote a function called extractPropsAndEvents() to extract the props and events from the props object of a virtual DOM node and used it inside the createComponentNode() and patch-Component() functions. A component subscribes to the events by using the #wire-EventHandlers() private method, which you call inside mount(). You managed these subscriptions by using an instance of the Dispatcher class, saved inside the component as the #dispatcher private property.

Last, you wrote a new method, emit(), used to emit events from a component to its parent component.

## 12.1 The key attribute

If your framework has no way of comparing two component nodes in virtual DOM trees to determine whether they are the same, how can you solve the reconciliation problem? In this case, you let the developer provide a unique identifier for each component: a key attribute. Following the Counter example from the introduction, the developer would provide a key attribute to each component as follows:

```
h('div', {}, [
  h(Counter, { key: 'counter-0', initialCount: 0 }),
  h(Counter, { key: 'counter-1', initialCount: 1 }),
  h(Counter, { key: 'counter-2', initialCount: 2 }),
])
```

So when the Counter component in the middle of the list is removed, the new virtual DOM tree would look like this:

```
h('div', {}, [
  h(Counter, { key: 'counter-0', initialCount: 0 }),
  h(Counter, { key: 'counter-2', initialCount: 2 }),
])
```

Now the reconciliation algorithm is able to compare the key attribute of the Counter components to determine which one was removed. The only drawback is that you rely on the developer to provide a unique key attribute for each component. When each item in the list that produces the components doesn't have a unique identifier, developers resort to using the index of the item in the list as the key attribute. I've taken this approach myself, but this approach is a bad idea, as you'll see in section 12.3.1. Your framework won't be resilient in these cases; all the responsibility is on the developer.

Let's start by including the component case in the areNodesEqual() function. Your framework currently doesn't know how to compare component nodes (as of now, it deems all component pairs to be different), so this step is a good place to start. You want this function to know at least when two components are instances of the same component prototype. When the function is passed two component nodes that are instances of a different prototype, it should return `false`; if they are instances of the same prototype, it should return `true`, for now.

### 12.1.1  *Component nodes equality*

How can you compare two component virtual DOM nodes to determine whether they're equal? First, you need to check whether their `type` properties are equal to `DOM_TYPES.COMPONENT`; then you want to know whether they are the same component prototype. In JavaScript, a prototype (or class definition) is, unsurprisingly, always equal to itself, so you can compare the `tag` properties of the two nodes. You can test this fact yourself in the browser console:

```
class Component {}

Component === Component // true
```

Open the nodes-equal.js file, and add the code shown in bold in the following listing to include the component case in the `areNodesEqual()` function.

Listing 12.1   **Comparing two component nodes for equality (nodes-equal.js)**

```
export function areNodesEqual(nodeOne, nodeTwo) {
  if (nodeOne.type !== nodeTwo.type) {
    return false
  }

  if (nodeOne.type === DOM_TYPES.ELEMENT) {
    const { tag: tagOne } = nodeOne
    const { tag: tagTwo } = nodeTwo

    return tagOne === tagTwo
  }

  if (nodeOne.type === DOM_TYPES.COMPONENT) {        ◁—  Checks whether the
    const { tag: componentOne } = nodeOne                type is component
    const { tag: componentTwo } = nodeTwo          ◁—  Extracts the first node's
                                                        component prototype
    return componentOne === componentTwo         ◁—  Extracts the second
  }                                                    node's component
  return true                                          prototype
}
                        Compares the two
                        component prototypes
```

This section is a great start. Next, let's support the `key` attribute in the `areNodesEqual()` function.

### 12.1.2 Using the key attribute

You want developers to include a key attribute in a component node when it's part of a dynamic list of components in which the nodes might be reordered, added, or removed. As we saw in the initial example, the key attribute is passed as a prop to the component, so you need to extract it from the props object.

You want to extract the key attribute from both nodes' props objects and compare them. If the key values aren't provided, they'll be undefined, so you can still use the === operator to compare them. As you know, despite all JavaScript equality wilderness, undefined is equal to itself. (Yay!) Add the code shown in bold in the following listing.

Listing 12.2  Using the key attribute to compare component nodes (nodes-equal.js)

```
export function areNodesEqual(nodeOne, nodeTwo) {
  if (nodeOne.type !== nodeTwo.type) {
    return false
  }

  if (nodeOne.type === DOM_TYPES.ELEMENT) {
    const { tag: tagOne } = nodeOne
    const { tag: tagTwo } = nodeTwo

    return tagOne === tagTwo
  }

  if (nodeOne.type === DOM_TYPES.COMPONENT) {
    const {
      tag: componentOne,
      props: { key: keyOne },          // Extracts the first node's key prop
    } = nodeOne
    const {
      tag: componentTwo,
      props: { key: keyTwo },          // Extracts the second node's key prop
    } = nodeTwo

    return componentOne === componentTwo && keyOne === keyTwo   // Compares the two key props
  }

  return true
}
```

With that small change, your framework supports the key attribute to compare component nodes. How easy was that? But wait—you need to make one more important change. When the developer provides a key attribute to a component, you don't want to pass it to the component as a prop. You want to remove it from the props object before passing the props to the component; otherwise, the component will receive a key prop that it doesn't know what to do with.

### 12.1.3  *Removing the key attribute from the props object*

In chapter 11, you implemented a function called extractPropsAndEvents(); its job was to separate the props from the events in the props object of a virtual DOM node. I told you that although this function was a single line of code, it made sense to extract it into a separate function because you'd need to modify it later.

"Later" is now. Open the utils/props.js file, and add the code shown in bold in the following listing to remove the key attribute from the props object before passing it to the component.

> **Listing 12.3   Removing the key from the props object (utils/props.js)**

```
export function extractPropsAndEvents(vdom) {
  const { on: events = {}, ...props } = vdom.props
  delete props.key                                     ◁─┐  Removes the key
                                                          │  attribute from the
  return { props, events }                               │  props object
}
```

You may wonder whether removing the key attribute from the props object in the virtual DOM tree will affect the reconciliation algorithm because the areNodesEquals() function requires this attribute to compare component nodes. That observation is valid . But you aren't modifying the original props object in the vdom node; you're creating a new one when you use the spread operator:

```
// props is a shallow copy of vdom.props
const { on: events = {}, ...props } = vdom.props
```

The component instance gets a props object without the key attribute, but the props object in the virtual DOM tree still has it. You can convince yourself by running a quick experiment in the browser console.

## 12.2  *Extending the solution to element nodes*

The reconciliation algorithm you wrote in chapters 7 and 8 is powerful enough to handle any kind of change in a list of elements, but it might do much more work than necessary in some cases. Figure 12.3 shows an example in where two <p> elements swap positions inside the same <section> element.

In a list of elements, if all elements have the same tag, the reconciliation algorithm—the arraysDiffSequence() function, to be more precise—will never know that an element has been moved (figure 12.4). Recall that we deem two elements to be equal if they have the same tag, regardless of their contents.

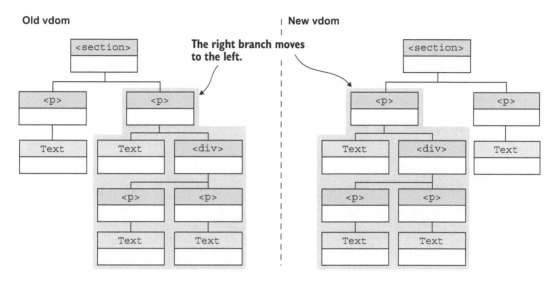

**Figure 12.3  Two elements swapping positions**

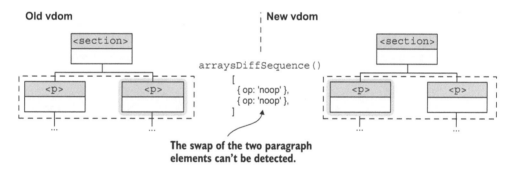

**Figure 12.4  The reconciliation algorithm can't detect the swap of the two paragraph nodes.**

Big portions of the DOM tree might be re-created unnecessarily because the reconciliation algorithm is incapable of detecting that an element has been moved. In the preceding example, all the elements in the <p> elements will be re-created even though they haven't changed—simply moved together with their parent element. To see your reconciliation algorithm do unnecessary extra work, complete exercise 12.1.

## Exercise 12.1

Let's look at the problem of unnecessarily re-creating entire branches of the DOM tree in action. You want to copy/paste the code from your framework into the browser's console. You can use your framework's previous version from unpkg.com or copy/paste it from the bundled file inside your dist/ folder.

When you have all of your framework's code available on the console, copy/paste the following virtual DOM tree:

```
const before = h('ul', {}, [
  h('li', {}, ['Item 1']),
  h('li', {}, ['Item 2']),
  h('li', {}, [
    h('div', {}, [
      h('div', {}, [
        h('div', {}, [
          h('p', {}, ['Item 3']),
        ]),
      ]),
    ]),
  ]),
])
```

This `<ul>` list has three `<li>` elements, the last one containing a nested tree of elements. Mount this view into the body of the current document:

```
mountDOM(before, document.body)
```

You should see the list rendered in the browser. Now paste the following virtual DOM tree, which is the same as the preceding one, but with the last item moved to the middle of the list (highlighted in bold):

```
const after = h('ul', {}, [
  h('li', {}, ['Item 1']),
  h('li', {}, [
    h('div', {}, [
      h('div', {}, [
        h('div', {}, [
          h('p', {}, ['Item 3']),
        ]),
      ]),
    ]),
  ]),
  h('li', {}, ['Item 2']),
])
```

Your challenge is to set a breakpoint inside the `patchDOM()` function to inspect the `diffSeq` calculated inside the `patchChildren()` subfunction. You want to check what set of operations the reconciliation algorithm is going to perform to transform the `before` tree into the `after` tree. When the code you want to debug is code that you pasted into the browser's console, setting a breakpoint is a bit tricky. You may want to do a quick search in your browser of choice to find out how. Then execute the `patchDOM()` function to hit the breakpoint:

`patchDOM(before, after, document.body)`

Explore the flow of execution of the `patchDOM()` function, and try to answer the following questions:

- Did the reconciliation algorithm figure out that it could simply move the last `<li>` element to the middle of the list?
- Did it detect any movement of elements inside the `<ul>`?
- Was the second `<li>` element re-created from scratch?

Find the solution at http://mng.bz/NV82.

Why not extend the `key` attribute to element nodes? With a bit of help from the developer, we can guide the reconciliation algorithm to help it detect when an element has been moved. Figure 12.5 shows the same example as before, but this time, the developer provided a `key` attribute to each element node, and the reconciliation algorithm detects that the element has been moved.

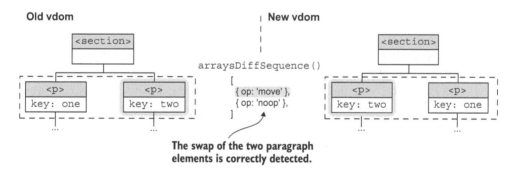

**Figure 12.5   Two elements swapping positions using the `key` attribute**

Let's modify the `areNodesEqual()` function to support the `key` attribute in element nodes. Open the nodes-equal.js file, and add the code shown in bold in the following listing.

**Listing 12.4   Using the `key` attribute to compare element nodes (nodes-equal.js)**

```
export function areNodesEqual(nodeOne, nodeTwo) {
  if (nodeOne.type !== nodeTwo.type) {
    return false
  }
```

```
if (nodeOne.type === DOM_TYPES.ELEMENT) {
  const {
    tag: tagOne,                                        Extracts the first
    props: { key: keyOne },        ◁─                   node's key prop
  } = nodeOne
  const {
    tag: tagTwo,                                        Extracts the second
    props: { key: keyTwo },        ◁─                   node's key prop
  } = nodeTwo

  return tagOne === tagTwo && keyOne === keyTwo    ◁───┐ Compares the
}                                                       │ two key props

if (nodeOne.type === DOM_TYPES.COMPONENT) {
  const {
    tag: componentOne,
    props: { key: keyOne },
  } = nodeOne
  const {
    tag: componentTwo,
    props: { key: keyTwo },
  } = nodeTwo

  return componentOne === componentTwo && keyOne === keyTwo
}

return true
}
```

With this simple change, you can use the `key` attribute to guide the reconciliation algorithm when an element has been moved. Now you need to modify the `mountDOM()` function to use the `extractPropsAndEvents()` function, which is in charge of removing the `key` attribute from the `props` object before passing it to the element. If you didn't do this, your `addProps()` function would attempt to add a `key` attribute to the DOM node, which you don't want to do. The `key` attribute doesn't exist for DOM elements.

> **NOTE**  If the `key` attribute existed in the DOM standard, you'd want to name the prop differently to prevent collisions. Some frameworks prepend their internal props with a dollar sign (`$key`) or two dollar signs (`$$key`). You could also look at Python for inspiration and use dunders (double underscores), as in `__key__`. For simplicity, we'll use `key` as the prop name. The only drawback to this approach is that you won't be able to call `key` a prop in your components because `key` is reserved for the framework.

Open the mount-dom.js file, and modify the code in the `createElementNode()` function as shown in the following listing. You want to remove the part where you destructure the `props` object and pass it to the `addProps()` function. The `addProps()` function will be in charge of extracting the props and events from the vdom node.

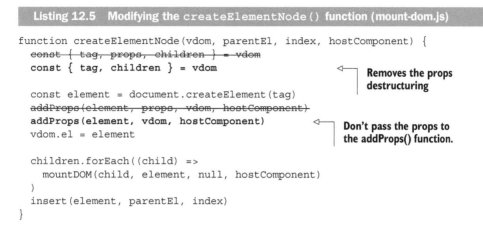

**Listing 12.5   Modifying the `createElementNode()` function (mount-dom.js)**

```
function createElementNode(vdom, parentEl, index, hostComponent) {
  const { tag, props, children } = vdom
  const { tag, children } = vdom                      ◁─┐ Removes the props
                                                         │ destructuring
  const element = document.createElement(tag)
  addProps(element, props, vdom, hostComponent)
  addProps(element, vdom, hostComponent)              ◁─┐ Don't pass the props to
  vdom.el = element                                      │ the addProps() function.

  children.forEach((child) =>
    mountDOM(child, element, null, hostComponent)
  )
  insert(element, parentEl, index)
}
```

Now, inside the `addProps()` function, you need to extract the props and events from the vdom node. For this purpose, you'll use the `extractPropsAndEvents()` function, which you modified to remove the `key` attribute from the `props` object. Modify the `addProps()` function as shown in the following listing.

**Listing 12.6   Modifying the `addProps()` function (mount-dom.js)**

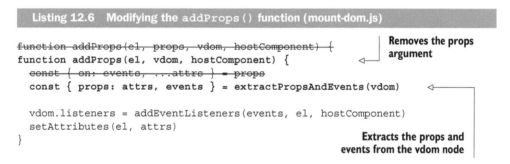

```
function addProps(el, props, vdom, hostComponent) {         ◁─┐ Removes the props
function addProps(el, vdom, hostComponent) {                   │ argument
  const { on: events, ...attrs } = props
  const { props: attrs, events } = extractPropsAndEvents(vdom)   ◁─

  vdom.listeners = addEventListeners(events, el, hostComponent)
  setAttributes(el, attrs)
}                                                  Extracts the props and
                                                   events from the vdom node
```

That's it! You can use the `key` attribute to guide the reconciliation algorithm when an element has been moved. Before you publish the new version of your framework, let's take a little detour to talk about some good practices for using the `key` attribute.

## 12.3   Using the key attribute

The `key` attribute is a powerful tool that helps the reconciliation algorithm detect when an element has been moved, but it's also a tool that can easily be misused. In this section, we'll look at two common mistakes in using the `key` attribute.

### 12.3.1   Mistake 1: Using the index as key

A typical example of misuse occurs when the developer uses the index of the element in the list as the value of the `key` attribute. Why is this approach a bad idea? There's no guarantee that the same elements or components will always be in the same positions in the list, so they won't always have the same index—a problem referred to as *unpredictable reordering*. The key attribute doesn't work unless a node keeps the same key value consistently.

This problem affects only lists of components, not lists of elements. The reconciliation algorithm, as you've already seen, may need to do extra work by re-creating entire view trees, but it always gets the final result right. With components, this isn't the case, because components have their own state, invisible to the virtual DOM. So components can't be re-created; the live instances need to be moved around in the DOM. This situation is why the key attribute is so important for components.

Suppose that you have a list with three `<MyCounter>` components. You decide to use their positions in the list as the value of the key attribute:

```
<div>
  <MyCounter key="0" />
  <MyCounter key="1" />
  <MyCounter key="2" />
</div>
```

Now suppose that the middle component (the one with the key attribute set to 1) is removed from the list:

```
<div>
  <MyCounter key="0" />
  <MyCounter key="1" />
  <MyCounter key="2" />
</div>
```

The component with the key attribute set to 2 will be moved to the position of the component with the key attribute set to 1. Thus, its index changes from 2 to 1:

```
<div>
  <MyCounter key="0" />
  <MyCounter key="1" /> <!-- Wrong! was key="2" -->
</div>
```

By looking at the two virtual DOM trees, the reconciliation algorithm incorrectly assumes that the component with the `key="2"` was removed from the bottom of the list when in reality, the middle component was removed.

Lists of components or elements are typically generated inside a loop, and the index of the element in the list is the index of the loop. Thus, the index of the element might change as things are added, removed, or moved in the list. The developer must make sure that the key attribute is set to a value that doesn't change, even if the index of the element in the list changes.

> **NOTE** The key attribute attached to a component or element must be consistent across renders. The same element or component must have the same key value throughout the whole life cycle of the node.

To see the problem of using indices as keys in action, I recommend that you work on exercise 12.2.

---

**Exercise 12.2**

Create a component called `MyCounter` that consists on a button with a counter. The button increments its counter when it's clicked. Next to this button, create another button with the label `"Remove"` that emits a `'remove'` event when clicked.

Create a second component (you can call it `App`) that has a count of counters as its state. Set its initial state to `3`:

```
const App = defineComponent({
  state() {
    return { counters: 3 }
  },
  render() { ... }
})
```

Make the `App` component render a list of `MyCounter` components, one for each counter in the state. For their key, use the index of the counter in the list. When the `'remove'` event is emitted, update the state to remove one counter. You can follow this example:

```
const App = defineComponent({
  state() { ... },
  render() {
    const { counters } = this.state

    return h(
      'div',
      {},
      Array(counters)
        .fill()
        .map((_, index) => {
          return h(MyCounter, {
            key: index,
            on: {
              remove: () => {
                this.updateState({ counters: counters - 1 })
              },
            },
          })
        })
    )
  }
})
```

Mount the application into the DOM. Next, change the counter in the middle of the list to have a count of `2` and the last counter to have a count of `3`. Click the `"Remove"` button of the counter in the middle (the second one, with a count of `2`). Is the correct counter removed? (You'd expect to have two counters left, with counts `1` and `3`.)

Find the solution at http://mng.bz/D919.

### 12.3.2 *Mistake 2: Using the same key for different elements*

Keys must be unique across the same list. Different lists can have elements with the same key but not the same list. What happens when the same key is assigned to two elements or components in the same list? The reconciliation algorithm can't determine unequivocally which element was moved and might wrongly assume that a node moved when it didn't.

Suppose that you mistakenly assign the same `key` attribute to the two last components in the list, as follows:

```
<div>
  <MyCounter key="abc" />
  <MyCounter key="def" />
  <MyCounter key="def" /> <!-- Wrong! Same key as the previous one -->
</div>
```

Now, if I remove one of the two last components from the list, would you be able to tell me which one I removed?

```
<div>
  <MyCounter key="abc" />
  <MyCounter key="def" />
</div>
```

You can't. Neither can the reconciliation algorithm.

**NOTE** The `key` attribute attached to a component or element must be unique across the same list.

Try exercise 12.3 to see this problem in action.

---

### Exercise 12.3

Use the same `MyCounter` component from the preceding exercise. This time, modify the `App` render function to render all the counters with the same key (using `'abc'` as the key):

```
render() {
  const { counters } = this.state

  return hFragment([
    h('h1', {}, ['Repeated key problem']),
    h('p', {}, [
      'Set a different count in each counter, then remove the middle one.',
    ]),
    h(
      'div',
      {},
```

```
    Array(counters)
      .fill()
      .map(() => {
        return h(MyCounter, {
          key: 'abc',
          on: {
            remove: () => {
              this.updateState({ counters: counters - 1 })
            },
          },
        })
      })
    ),
  ])
}
```

Repeat the same process as in the preceding exercise: set the count of the second counter to 2 and the count of the third counter to 3; then remove the middle counter. Does the correct counter get removed? Can you explain why or why not?

Find the solution at http://mng.bz/lV2M.

## 12.4   *The application instance*

Let's move on to modifying the `createApp()` function to use the new stateful component system. The application instance doesn't need to handle the entire application's state; each component handles its own now. Thus, there's no need to pass the state object and reducers to the `createApp()` function anymore (figure 12.6). You need to pass it only the root component—the component that contains the whole application's view split in subcomponents (figure 12.7).

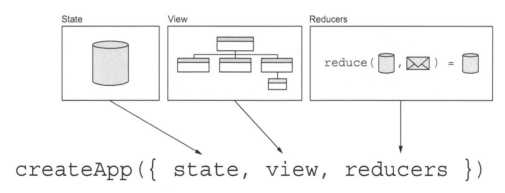

**Figure 12.6   The current framework's application instance requires the global state, reducers, and the root component.**

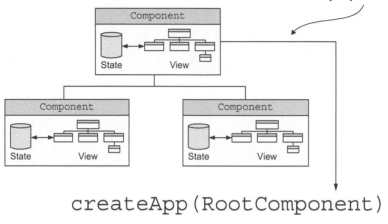

The root component, the one at the top of the hierarchy, is passed to createApp().

# createApp(RootComponent)

**Figure 12.7**   **The new version of the framework's application instance requires only the root component.**

This root component might accept props, so you want to pass the props to the create-App() function as well:

```
function createApp(RootComponent, props = {}) {
  // --snip-- //
}
```

Open the app.js file, and start by removing all the code you wrote; things are going to change a lot. The idea is still the same, though. You want to return an object with two methods: mount() and unmount(). This time, the code is much simpler because each component in the view hierarchy handles its own state. In the app.js file, add the code in the following listing.

**Listing 12.7   The application instance (app.js)**

```
import { mountDOM } from './mount-dom'
import { destroyDOM } from './destroy-dom'
import { h } from './h'

export function createApp(RootComponent, props = {}) {
  let parentEl = null
  let isMounted = false
  let vdom = null

  function reset() {
    parentEl = null
    isMounted = false
    vdom = null
  }
```

Passes the root component and props to the createApp() function

A function to reset the internal properties of the application

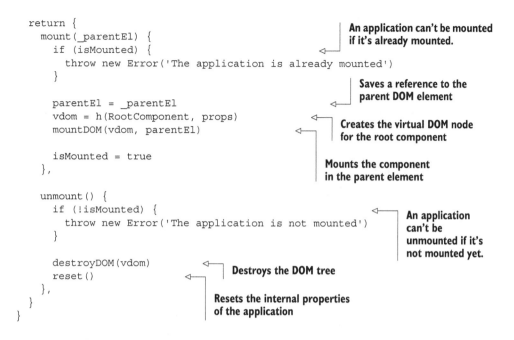

```
    return {
      mount(_parentEl) {
        if (isMounted) {
          throw new Error('The application is already mounted')
        }

        parentEl = _parentEl
        vdom = h(RootComponent, props)
        mountDOM(vdom, parentEl)

        isMounted = true
      },

      unmount() {
        if (!isMounted) {
          throw new Error('The application is not mounted')
        }

        destroyDOM(vdom)
        reset()
      },
    }
}
```

An application can't be mounted if it's already mounted.

Saves a reference to the parent DOM element

Creates the virtual DOM node for the root component

Mounts the component in the parent element

An application can't be unmounted if it's not mounted yet.

Destroys the DOM tree

Resets the internal properties of the application

This code is much simpler, right? To get the framework ready for publication, you want to export the defineComponent() function from your framework's public API, which is as simple as exporting it from the main barrel file, src/index.js. Open that file, and add the line shown in bold in the following listing.

**Listing 12.8   The framework's updated API (index.js)**

```
export { createApp } from './app.js'
export { defineComponent } from './component.js'
export { DOM_TYPES, h, hFragment, hString } from './h.js'
```

Now that the framework's API is ready, let's publish your new version of the framework to NPM.

## 12.5  *Publishing the framework*

To publish version 3.0 of your framework, you need to update the version number in the package.json file. Open this file (remember that it's inside the packages/runtime folder, not the top-level one), and change the version number to 3.0.0:

```
{
  "name": "your-fwk-name",
  "version": "2.0.0",
  "version": "3.0.0",
  ...
}
```

Now you can publish the new version of the framework to NPM. Make sure that your terminal is in the packages/runtime folder, and run the following command:

```
$ npm publish
```

You—and the rest of the world—can install and use the version of your framework that includes stateful components. You'll use this new version in exercise 12.4 to refactor the TODOs application.

> **Exercise 12.4—Challenge**
>
> Using the new version of your framework, refactor the TODOs application to use stateful components.
>
> Find the solution at http://mng.bz/BAKg.

## Summary

- In a list of components, a unique key must be provided to each component so that the reconciliation algorithm can differentiate among them.
- In a list of elements, the key isn't mandatory, but using it improves performance. Without a `key` attribute, the reconciliation algorithm will do more work than necessary.
- The key must be unique and invariant in the list of elements or components.
- Never use the index of the element of component as the key because when an element is removed, added, or moved, the index of the rest of the elements will change.

# The component
# lifecycle hooks
# and the scheduler

**This chapter covers**

- Understanding a lifecycle hook
- Executing code when a component is mounted
- Executing code when a component is unmounted
- Publishing version 4 of the framework

It's not uncommon for a component to execute some code when it's mounted into or unmounted from the Document Object Model (DOM). The classic example is fetching data from a server right after the component is mounted. In that case, the component is already part of the DOM, so it can display a loading indicator while the data is being fetched. When the data is ready, the component updates its view by removing the loading indicator and rendering the newly fetched data.

Your existing framework runs code only when a user-originated event happens, such as clicking a button. (Technically, it could also run code as part of a `setTimeout()` or `setInterval()` callback, but let's omit this possibility for the sake of simplicity in the explanation.) It can't fetch data when a component first shows up, which is a limitation because developers can't make code run before the user interacts with the page.

299

A *lifecycle hook* is a user-defined function that is executed when a component goes through a lifecycle event. Lifecycle events include the creation, mounting, updating, and unmounting of a component. In this chapter, you'll explore how lifecycle hooks fix the aforementioned limitation and how to implement them in your framework.

Lifecycle hooks are often asynchronous, such as when the user uses them to fetch data from a server after a component is mounted. Your mounting process has been synchronous so far, but as soon as you run asynchronous code as part of it, an interesting problem arises. If you `await` the component's hook that executes after the component is mounted, you block the first render of the application: while a component is waiting for the hook to finish, the remaining components have to wait in line to be rendered. That situation isn't what you want; it yields a bad user experience and the sensation that the application is slow (when in reality it's waiting to finish mounting a component before it moves to the next), as depicted in figure 13.1.

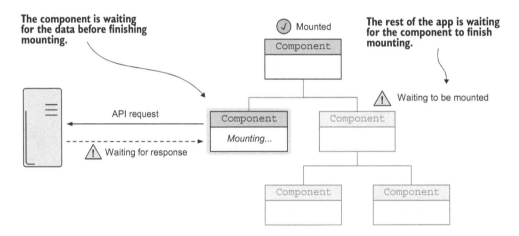

**Figure 13.1   While a component is fetching data from a server, the rest of the application needs to wait to be mounted.**

To avoid blocking the first render of the application, you shouldn't use `await` for the mounted hook to finish. In section 13.3, you'll learn about the *scheduler,* a mechanism that allows the execution of code to be delayed until the current render cycle is finished. With the scheduler, you can schedule asynchronous hooks to run after the application is fully mounted, thus not blocking the first render. In this chapter, you'll publish version 4 of your framework so that you can put lifecycle hooks to use.

**NOTE**   You can find all the listings in this chapter in the listings/ch13/ directory of the book's repository (http://mng.bz/8w7K). The code in this chapter can be checked out from the ch14 label (http://mng.bz/EZRq): `$ git switch --detach ch14`.

**Code catch-up**

In chapter 12, you updated the `areNodesEqual()` function to include the case of two component nodes. This function checks whether the component types are the same and their `key` props—if they have one—are equal. You made a quick modification to the `extractPropsAndEvents()` function to remove the `key` property from the props object so that it doesn't reach the component and isn't mistaken for a prop.

You also included the `key` prop comparison for the case of two element nodes inside the `areNodesEqual()` function. This change required you to modify the `createElementNode()` and `addProps()` functions to use the `extractPropsAndEvents()` function so that the `key` prop is removed from the props object before it reaches the element creation and is mistaken for an HTML attribute.

Last, you rewrote the `createApp()` function and exported it from the runtime package by exporting it from the index.js file.

## 13.1 The component lifecycle

The *lifecycle* of a component is the sequence of events that it goes through from the moment it's created until it gets destroyed. Table 13.1 describes the lifecycle of a component in your framework.

**Table 13.1   The lifecycle of a component**

| Lifecycle event | Code | Explanation |
| --- | --- | --- |
| Creation | `new Component (…)` | When the `mountDOM()` function is passed a component, it instantiates it. |
| Mounting | `component.mount (…)` | Then the `mountDOM()` function calls the component's `mount()` method. This event is when the component is mounted into the DOM and its view first appears onscreen. |
| Updating | `#patch() { … }` | The component remains onscreen until it's removed from the DOM, but it can render itself multiple times when the internal state changes or the external props change. This task is handled by the component's private `#patch()` method. |
| Unmounting | `component.unmount()` | Finally, when the component is removed from the DOM, the `destroyDOM()` function calls the component's `unmount()` method. This event is when the component is unmounted from the DOM and its view disappears from the screen. |

Figure 13.2 shows the lifecycle of a component, which includes the lifecycle events discussed in table 13.1. Starting from the left, the component starts in the *none* state; it's not instantiated yet. Then, after the component is created, it goes to the *created* state,

where you have an instance of your component class, but it's not mounted into the DOM yet. Next is the mount lifecycle event, after which the component is in the *mounted* state. From being mounted, it can take two paths: it can be updated or unmounted. If it's updated, it goes back to the *mounted* state, and the cycle repeats. If it's unmounted, it goes to the *destroyed* state; the instance of the component still exists but is detached from the DOM.

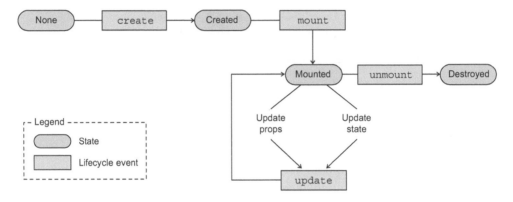

**Figure 13.2   The lifecycle of a component**

Now that you're familiar with how components go through lifecycle events, let's dive into finding out why lifecycle hooks are useful. This feature lets developers who work with your framework run their own code at these specific events. This way, they can customize how their components behave at each stage, tailoring the behavior to suit their application's needs.

Different frameworks have different lifecycle hooks, but creation, mounting, and unmounting are the three most common, used in almost all (if not all) frameworks. Table 13.2 compares the lifecycle hooks of a few popular frameworks.

**Table 13.2   Lifecycle hooks in popular frameworks**

| Framework | Hooks | Comments |
|---|---|---|
| Svelte (v4) | <ul><li>`onMount()`—Executed when the component is mounted into the DOM</li><li>`beforeUpdate()`—Executed before the component is updated</li><li>`afterUpdate()`—Executed after the component is updated</li><li>`onDestroy()`—Executed when the component is unmounted from the DOM</li></ul> | Svelte defines four main lifecycle hooks (https://svelte.dev/docs/ svelte). Svelte also defines a special lifecycle hook called `tick()` that returns a promise that resolves when the "pending changes have been applied." |

**Table 13.2  Lifecycle hooks in popular frameworks** *(continued)*

| Framework | Hooks | Comments |
|---|---|---|
| Vue (v3) | <ul><li>`onBeforeMount()`—Executed before the component is mounted into the DOM</li><li>`onMounted()`—Executed when the component is mounted into the DOM</li><li>`onBeforeUpdate()`—Executed before the component's DOM is updated</li><li>`onUpdated()`—Executed after the component's DOM is updated</li><li>`onBeforeUnmount()`—Executed before the component is unmounted from the DOM</li><li>`onUnmounted()`—Executed when the component is unmounted from the DOM</li></ul> | Vue defines as many as 12 lifecycle hooks (http://mng.bz/NRyE), but these are the most common ones. |
| Angular (v16) | <ul><li>`ngOnInit()`—Executed when the component is initialized</li><li>`ngOnChanges()`—Executed when the component's input properties change</li><li>`ngAfterViewInit()`—Executed after the component's view is initialized</li><li>`ngOnDestroy()`—Executed before the component is destroyed</li></ul> | Angular defines eight lifecycle hooks (http://mng.bz/Ddoy), but these are the most common ones. |
| React (v18) | To execute code when the component is mounted, call the `useEffect()` hook, passing an empty array as the second argument:<br><br>`useEffect(() => {`<br>`  // code to execute when the`<br>`  // component is mounted`<br>`}, [])`<br><br>You can specify the dependencies of the hook by passing them in the array. In that case, the effect would run when the component is mounted and every time one of the dependencies changes. To execute code when the component is unmounted, return a function from the `useEffect()` hook that has an empty array as the second argument:<br><br>`useEffect(() => {`<br>`  // code to execute when the`<br>`  // component is mounted`<br><br>`  return () => {`<br>`    // code to execute when the`<br>`    // component is unmounted`<br>`  }`<br>`}, [])` | React is a bit different. It doesn't define lifecycle hooks, but it does define side effects (http://mng.bz/lMvj) that are executed when the component is mounted, updated, or unmounted. |

**Table 13.2   Lifecycle hooks in popular frameworks *(continued)***

| Framework | Hooks | Comments |
|---|---|---|
| | To execute code when the component is updated (including after being mounted), don't pass the dependencies array as the second argument to the `useEffect()` hook:<br><br>`useEffect(() => {`<br>`  // code to execute every time the`<br>`  // component is updated`<br>`})`<br><br>In this case, the effect would run when the component is mounted and every time the component is updated—that is, when the component's state changes or its props change. | |

You'll implement two lifecycle hooks in your framework:

- `onMounted()`—Allows the developer to run code just after the component is mounted into the DOM
- `onUnmounted()`—Allows the developer to run code just after the component is unmounted from the DOM

These two hooks are depicted in figure 13.3, which is an updated version of figure 13.2.

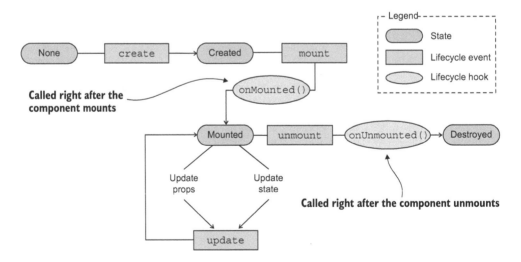

**Figure 13.3   The `onMounted()` and `onUnmounted()` lifecycle hooks**

The process is so straightforward that you may want to take inspiration from other frameworks and implement more lifecycle hooks on your own. Developers most often use the `onMounted()` and `onUnmounted()` lifecycle hooks, which makes them a great starting point.

No more talking. Let's get to work!

## 13.2  Implementing the mounted and unmounted lifecycle hooks

The first step in implementing the `onMounted()` and `onUnmounted()` lifecycle hooks is defining them in the `Component` class. You want to let developers define these lifecycle hooks when they create a new component by using the `defineComponent()` function:

```
defineComponent({
  onMounted() { ... },
  onUnmounted() { ... },

  render() { ... }
})
```

To do so, you need to accept those two new functions in the object that's passed as an argument to the `defineComponent()` function. You want to give developers an empty function as the default value of the new functions so that they can omit those functions. Open the component.js file, and add the code shown in bold in the following listing.

**Listing 13.1  Defining a component with lifecycle hooks (component.js)**

```
const emptyFn = () => {}

export function defineComponent({
  render,
  state,
  onMounted = emptyFn,
  onUnmounted = emptyFn,
  ...methods
}) {
  class Component {
    // --snip-- //
  }
}
```

You need to take two important things into account regarding the passed-in `onMounted()` and `onUnmounted()` functions:

- Hooks asynchronicity
- Hooks execution context

Sections 13.2.1 and 13.2.2 discuss these two concerns in order.

### 13.2.1 Hooks asynchronicity

The functions passed by the developer are quite possibly asynchronous and return a `Promise`. The typical use of the mounted hook is to fetch data from an API, so it's very likely that the function will `await` for a `Promise` to be resolved:

```
async onMounted() {
  const data = await fetch('https://api.example.com/data')
  this.updateState({ data })
}
```

The hooks may be synchronous, but wrapping their result inside a `Promise` doesn't hurt. This approach also has the benefit of allowing you to treat all hooks as though they were asynchronous:

```
Promise.resolve(onMounted())
```

### 13.2.2 Hooks execution context

The second concern is the execution context. As with `state()` and `render()`, the developer expects the context of the `onMounted()` and `onUnmounted()` hooks to be the component instance. Inside the hook functions, the developer should be able to access the component's state and methods:

```
async onMounted() {
  const data = await fetch('https://api.example.com/data')
  this.updateState({ data })
}
```

You already know how to solve this problem. Explicitly bind the functions to the component instance:

```
Promise.resolve(onMounted.call(this))
```

You want to create two new methods in the `Component` class, called the same way as the lifecycle hooks, that wrap the hooks inside a promise and bind them to the component instance.

### 13.2.3 Dealing with asynchronicity and execution context

In the component.js file, add the code shown in bold in the following listing, just below the constructor.

> **Listing 13.2    Wrapping the hooks inside a `Promise` (component.js)**

```
export function defineComponent({
  render,
  state,
  onMounted = emptyFn,
  onUnmounted = emptyFn,
```

```
    ...methods
  }) {
    class Component {
      // --snip-- //

      constructor(props = {}, eventHandlers = {}, parentComponent = null) {
        // --snip-- //
      }

      onMounted() {
        return Promise.resolve(onMounted.call(this))
      }

      onUnmounted() {
        return Promise.resolve(onUnmounted.call(this))
      }

      // --snip-- //
    }

    // --snip-- //
  }
```

Now that you have the onMounted() and onUnmounted() lifecycle hooks defined, you need to call them at the right time. But what is the right time?

## 13.3  *The scheduler*

Mounting the application is a synchronous and fast process (at least, it has been up to now), which is exactly what you want. The application's first render should be as fast as possible. But lifecycle hooks may not be as fast; they might take some time to finish while they fetch data from a server, for example. What would happen if you await for the onMounted() hook to finish before moving to the next component inside the mountDOM() function?

```
async function mountDOM(...) {
  switch (vdom.type) {
  // --snip --//

    case DOM_TYPES.COMPONENT: {
      createComponentNode(vdom, parentEl, index, hostComponent)
      await vdom.component.onMounted()        ◁──┐  Waits for the
      break                                       │  onMounted() hook to
    }                                             │  finish before moving to
                                                  │  the next component
  // --snip --//
  }
}
```

This code would block the first render of the application because the mountDOM() function wouldn't move to the next component until the onMounted() hook is finished—which might take some time. Let's look at an example.

The application whose virtual DOM tree is depicted in figure 13.4 has three components: Header, Main, and Footer. The Main component has an onMounted() hook that fetches data from a server. When the application mounts, the mountDOM() function mounts first the Header component and then the Main component; next, it calls the onMounted() hook of the Main component, which blocks the rendering of the Footer component until the hook is finished. Section 13.3.1 presents a naive solution to this problem.

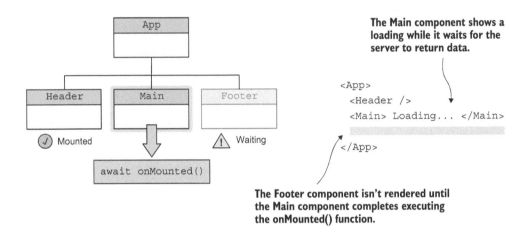

Figure 13.4  **The Main component blocks the rendering of the Footer component.**

### 13.3.1 A simple solution that doesn't quite work

A simple solution is to not await for the onMounted() hook to finish:

```
function mountDOM(...) {
    switch (vdom.type) {
    // --snip --//

    case DOM_TYPES.COMPONENT: {
      createComponentNode(vdom, parentEl, index, hostComponent)
      vdom.component.onMounted()
      break
    }

    // --snip --//
  }
}
```

I'll explain why this solution might be problematic. The code inside onMounted() would execute until the first await is encountered. At this point, a callback would be added to the microtask queue (http://mng.bz/Bd0v). I'll explain shortly. Then the mounting process would continue. The promise's callback would be executed later, when JavaScript's execution call stack is empty—that is, after the `mountDOM()` function is finished. If the `onMounted()` hook of the `Main` component from the preceding example is defined as follows,

```
async onMounted() {
  this.setState({ loading: true })
  const data = await fetch('https://api.example.com/data')
  this.setState({ data, loading: false })
}
```

the first line of the hook, which sets the `loading` state to `true`, would be executed immediately. Then the `fetch()` function would be called, returning a `Promise` whose callback—the rest of the `onMounted()` function's body—would be added to the microtask queue. After that, the mounting process would continue.

Because using `async/await` can be seen as syntactic sugar for handling promises using `then()` and `catch()`, the preceding code can be rewritten as follows:

```
onMounted() {
  this.setState({ loading: true })
  fetch('https://api.example.com/data').then((data) => {
    this.setState({ data, loading: false })
  })
}
```

This example may help you understand why the first line is called synchronously, whereas the rest of the code—the callback passed to `then()`—is moved to the microtask queue. The callback is made to the rest of the `onMounted()` function's body, which includes the final line that sets the `loading` state to `false` and the data received from the server. This approach might work well in most cases, but it leaves unhandled promises in your code, exposing your mounting process to two problems:

- You have no control of the sequencing of the code in the mounting process. An `await` is a blocking operation that prevents some part of the code from executing until a promise is resolved. It ensures that the part of the code that requires the promise to be resolved doesn't run before the promise is resolved. If you don't handle the components' `onMounted()` promises, the user might interact with the component while the `onMounted()` callback is waiting in the microtask queue. This interaction might cause a re-render of the partly mounted component. Then, when the `onMounted()` callback is finally executed, it likely renders the component again, which might cause a race condition. Ideally, a component isn't rendered while it's being mounted.
- If an error occurs while the `onMounted()` hook is executing, the promise is rejected, but you have no way to handle the error. If the developer isn't notified of the error, they might not even know that something went wrong. At least print the error to the console so that the developer can analyze it and fix the problem.

NOTE The typescript-eslint program has a rule called "no-floating-promises" that warns you when you have unhandled promises in your code. Similarly, a plugin for ESLint called "eslint-plugin-no-floating-promise" does the same. Unhandled (or floating) promises expose your code to sequencing and error-handling problems that are complex to track down. As a general rule, avoid unhandled promises in your code.

Instead, you want to mount the entire application synchronously and then execute all the onMounted() hooks in the order in which they were encountered, ensuring that they complete and their errors are handled. Only then should you allow the framework to execute any other code. To accomplish this task, you need to learn how asynchronous code is executed in the browser, so bear with me. If you're familiar with event loops, tasks, and microtask queues, you can skip the next section. In particular, though, you should know about the order in which the event loop processes tasks and microtasks.

### 13.3.2 Tasks, microtasks, and the event loop

When a website loads in a browser, the synchronous JavaScript code executes immediately. The application reaches a point at which there's no JavaScript code left to execute, which is necessary for the website to respond to user interactions—the perks of single-threaded JavaScript. At this point, we say that the *execution stack* is empty. The JavaScript run time doesn't have any code pending to execute.

DEFINITION The *execution stack* (or *call stack*) is a stack data structure that stores the functions currently being executed by the JavaScript run time. When a function is called, it's added to the top of the stack, and when it returns, it's popped from the top of the stack.

The rest of the JavaScript code that runs is triggered by user interactions, such as clicking a button or typing in an input field, or scheduled tasks, such as those scheduled by setTimeout() or setInterval(). If nothing is scheduled to run, or if the user doesn't interact with the application, the JavaScript run time's execution stack is empty.

When the execution stack is empty the *event loop* reads from two queues (the task and microtask queues) and executes the callbacks that are in them. Examples of tasks are the callbacks of the event listeners. When an event is triggered, the callback (the function registered as its event handler) is added to the task queue. Microtasks are mainly the callbacks of promises.

DEFINITION An *event loop* (http://mng.bz/d67D) is a loop that runs continuously in the browser's JavaScript run time and decides what code to execute next. The event loop is responsible for reading from the task and microtask queues and pushing their callbacks to the execution stack.

Why does the browser need two queues instead of one? What's relevant for now is that the event loop handles the tasks and microtasks differently. Understanding these differences is the key to understanding how to schedule asynchronous hooks to run after the application is fully mounted. Let's open the hood of the event loop to see how it reads from the task and microtask queues and pushes their callbacks to the execution stack.

### 13.3.3 *The event loop cycle*

When you know the steps of an event loop cycle (when it reads from the task and microtask queues) and understand how it pushes the callbacks to the execution stack, you'll be able to decide the best way to schedule the execution of the onMounted() and onUnmounted() hooks.

> **NOTE** You can read the execution steps in more detail in the HTML specification (http://mng.bz/rVGg). You can also find a great article explaining the event loop at https://javascript.info/event-loop#event-loop.

The following sections present the simplified steps of an event loop cycle.

#### STEP 1
Execute all the microtasks in the microtask queue in order, even those that were added while executing other microtasks in this same cycle (figure 13.5). While the microtasks are executing, JavaScript's thread is blocked—that is, the browser can't respond to user interactions. (Note that this same situation happens when you execute synchronous JavaScript code.)

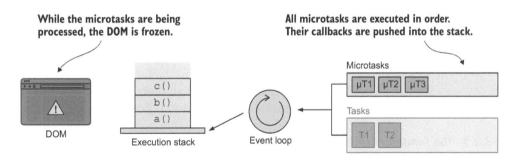

**Figure 13.5  Execute all the microtasks in the microtask queue.**

#### STEP 2
Execute the oldest task in the task queue. Only those tasks that were added to the task queue before the start of this cycle are considered (figure 13.6). While the task is executing, JavaScript's thread is still blocked.

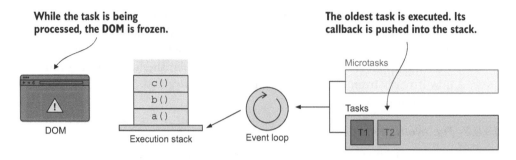

**Figure 13.6   Execute the oldest task in the task queue.**

### STEP 3

Enable the browser to render the DOM if changes are pending (figure 13.7).

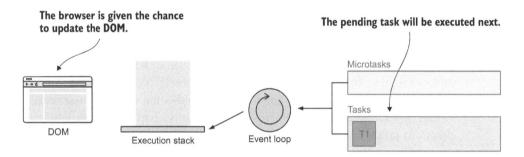

**Figure 13.7   Enable the browser to render the DOM.**

### STEP 4

Go back to step 1 until there are no more tasks in the task queue.

With this knowledge, think about how you can design a scheduler that schedules the onMounted() hooks to run after the application is fully mounted.

### 13.3.4  *The fundamentals of the scheduler*

The mountDOM() function executes synchronously when the application is loaded into the browser. When this code finishes executing, if no more synchronous JavaScript code is left, the execution stack becomes empty. At this point, you want the onMounted() hooks to execute in the order in which they're scheduled, and for this purpose, the microtask queue is perfect (figure 13.8).

The execution order is guaranteed for microtasks, and if those microtasks enqueue more microtasks, all of them will be executed in the same cycle. Think about

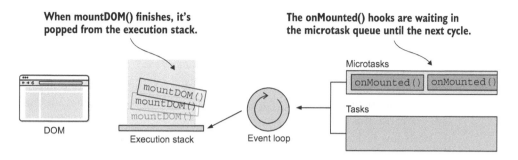

**Figure 13.8** The `onMounted()` **hooks are executed in the order in which they're scheduled.**

how to implement a scheduler based on this idea. You want to collect all the `onMounted()` lifecycle hooks in a queue of pending jobs:

```
const jobs = []

function enqueueJob(job) {
  jobs.push(job)
}
```

Another function processes the jobs. The solution is as simple as dequeuing the jobs and executing them in order:

```
function processJobs() {
  while (jobs.length > 0) {
    const job = jobs.shift()
    job()
  }
}
```

To schedule the `processJobs()` function into the microtask queue so that it runs when the execution stack is empty, you can use the `queueMicrotask()` function (http://mng.bz/VxwX), which is present in the global `Window` object. Be careful that you don't schedule the `processJobs()` function multiple times. To prevent this situation, you can have an `isScheduled` Boolean variable keep track of whether the function is already scheduled:

```
let isScheduled = false

function scheduleUpdate() {
  if (isScheduled) return

  isScheduled = true
  queueMicrotask(processJobs)
}
```

You want to call the `scheduleUpdate()` function every time a job is enqueued:

```
function enqueueJob(job) {
  jobs.push(job)
  scheduleUpdate()
}
```

When the first job is enqueued, the processJobs() function is scheduled to run. All the jobs that are added before processJobs() is executed don't schedule the function again because the isScheduled flag is set to true.

With this task, you have all the fundamentals of the scheduler. Now it's time to implement that feature.

### 13.3.5  *Implementing a scheduler*

You want to implement the scheduling logic in a separate file. Create a new file called scheduler.js inside the src/ folder. In that file, write the code in the following listing.

**Listing 13.3   The scheduler (scheduler.js)**

```
let isScheduled = false                    ◁──┐  Private flag to indicate
const jobs = []                            ◁─┐ │  whether the processJobs()
                                              │    function is scheduled
export function enqueueJob(job) {             │
  jobs.push(job)                           ◁──┘  Private array of jobs
  scheduleUpdate()                         ◁──┐  to execute
}                                             │
                                              │  Enqueues a job
function scheduleUpdate() {                    │
  if (isScheduled) return                      │  Schedules an update

  isScheduled = true
  queueMicrotask(processJobs)              ◁──┐  Queues a microtask to run
}                                             │  the processJobs() function

function processJobs() {
  while (jobs.length > 0) {                ◁──┐  Pops and executes job
    const job = jobs.shift()                  │  functions until the queue
    job()                                     │  is empty
  }

  isScheduled = false                      ◁──┐  Sets the flag to false
}
```

The jobs might be asynchronous, as is the case for the onMounted() and onUnmounted() hooks. Let's do one more thing to prevent floating promises (http://mng.bz/x2B8) in the application: wrap the result of calling each job() function inside a Promise and add callbacks to handle the result or reject the promise. When the promise resolves, you don't want to do anything else, so you can keep that callback empty. When the promise is rejected, you want to log the error to the console so that the developer knows something went wrong. In the scheduler.js file, write the code shown in bold in the following listing.

**Listing 13.4    Handling promises in the scheduler (scheduler.js)**

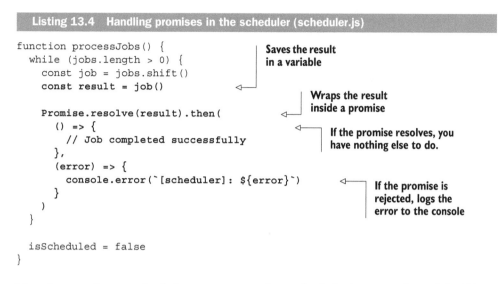

```
function processJobs() {
  while (jobs.length > 0) {
    const job = jobs.shift()
    const result = job()

    Promise.resolve(result).then(
      () => {
        // Job completed successfully
      },
      (error) => {
        console.error(`[scheduler]: ${error}`)
      }
    )
  }

  isScheduled = false
}
```

- Saves the result in a variable
- Wraps the result inside a promise
- If the promise resolves, you have nothing else to do.
- If the promise is rejected, logs the error to the console

Now that you have a scheduler, you can use it to schedule the execution of the lifecycle hooks.

> **Exercise 13.1**
>
> What is the order of the `console.log()` resulting from running the following code?
>
> ```
> console.log('Start')
> setTimeout(() => console.log('Timeout'))
> queueMicrotask(() => console.log('Microtask 1'))
> enqueueJob(() => console.log('Job'))
> queueMicrotask(() => console.log('Microtask 2'))
> console.log('End')
> ```
>
> Try to reason your way to the answer before running the code. Draw a diagram with the task and microtask queues, if that helps.
>
> Find the solution at http://mng.bz/ddmX.

### 13.3.6   *Scheduling the lifecycle hooks execution*

The `mountDOM()` function is the right place to schedule the execution of the `onMounted()` hooks. Right after a component virtual DOM node is created, you want to enqueue the `onMounted()` hook in the scheduler. Open the *mount-dom.js* file, and add the code shown in bold in the following listing.

**Listing 13.5    Scheduling the `onMounted()` method of a component (mount-dom.js)**

```
import { setAttributes } from './attributes'
import { addEventListeners } from './events'
import { DOM_TYPES } from './h'
```

```
import { enqueueJob } from './scheduler'
import { extractPropsAndEvents } from './utils/props'

export function mountDOM(vdom, parentEl, index, hostComponent = null) {
  switch (vdom.type) {
    // --snip-- //

    case DOM_TYPES.COMPONENT: {
      createComponentNode(vdom, parentEl, index, hostComponent)
      enqueueJob(() => vdom.component.onMounted())
      break
    }

    default: {
      throw new Error(`Can't mount DOM of type: ${vdom.type}`)
    }
  }
}

// --snip-- //
```

**Imports the enqueueJob() function from the scheduler**

**Enqueues the component's onMounted() hook in the scheduler**

Let's do the same thing with the `onUnmounted()` hook. This time, the `destroyDOM()` function is the right place to schedule the execution of the `onUnmounted()` hooks, right after the component is removed from the DOM. Open the *destroy-dom.js* file, and add the code shown in bold in the following listing.

> Listing 13.6   Scheduling the `onUnmounted()` method of a component (destroy-dom.js)

```
import { removeEventListeners } from './events'
import { DOM_TYPES } from './h'
import { enqueueJob } from './scheduler'
import { assert } from './utils/assert'

export function destroyDOM(vdom) {
  const { type } = vdom

  switch (type) {
    // --snip-- //

    case DOM_TYPES.COMPONENT: {
      vdom.component.unmount()
      enqueueJob(() => vdom.component.onUnmounted())
      break
    }

    default: {
      throw new Error(`Can't destroy DOM of type: ${type}`)
    }
  }

  delete vdom.el
}
```

**Imports the enqueueJob() function from the scheduler**

**Enqueues the component's onUnmounted() hook in the scheduler**

That's it! The `onMounted()` and `onUnmounted()` hooks are scheduled to run after the application is fully mounted and unmounted (respectively), and they're executed in the order in which they're scheduled. Nevertheless, it's a good idea to use your framework to debug the execution of an application so you can see how the scheduler works and how the hooks are executed at the right time (exercise 13.2).

---

**Exercise 13.2**

Create a component that receives a name as a prop and renders that name. The component should also have an `onMounted()` hook that logs to the console where the component was mounted, including the `name` prop. Your component should look something like this:

```
const NameComponent = defineComponent({
  onMounted() {
    console.log(`Component mounted with name: ${this.props.name}`)
  },
  render() {
    return h('p', {}, [this.props.name])
  }
})
```

Now create an `App` top-level component that includes five `NameComponent` components, each with a different name. Mount the application into the DOM like so:

```
const App = defineComponent({
  render() {
    return hFragment([
      h(NameComponent, { name: 'Alice' }),
      h(NameComponent, { name: 'Bob' }),
      h(NameComponent, { name: 'Charlie' }),
      h(NameComponent, { name: 'Diana' }),
      h(NameComponent, { name: 'Eve' })
    ])
  }
})
```

```
createApp(App).mount(document.body)
```

Instrument the application in the browser, adding a log breakpoint in the `mountDOM()` call inside the application's instance `mount()` method. Set another log breakpoint in the line immediately after the `mountDOM()` call so you'll know when the application has finished mounting.

What is the order in which the operations are logged to the console? Debug the application, setting breakpoints when the `onMounted()` hooks are scheduled and when they're executed. Did the scheduler do what you expected—that is, enqueue the hooks and execute them in order after `mountDOM()` finished executing?

Find the solution at http://mng.bz/rjmZ.

## 13.4    *Publishing version 4 of the framework*

Now let's publish the new version of the framework. In the package.json file, update the version number to `4.0.0`:

```
"version": "3.0.0",
"version": "4.0.0",
```

Remember to move your terminal to the root of the project and run `npm install` so that the package version number in the package-lock.json file is updated:

```
$ npm install
```

Finally, place your terminal inside the packages/runtime folder, and run

```
$ npm publish
```

Congratulations! The new version of your framework is published.

> **Exercise 13.3: Challenge**
> Refactor the TODOs application so that it saves the to-dos in the browser's local storage. Load the to-dos from local storage when the application is mounted, and save them to local storage when they are added, removed, or updated.
>
> Find the solution at http://mng.bz/VRGO.

### *Summary*

- The *lifecycle* of a component is the sequence of events that it goes through from the moment it's created until it's removed from the DOM.
- A *lifecycle hook* is called at a specific moment in the component's lifecycle.
- The *mounted* lifecycle hook is scheduled to run after the component is mounted into the DOM.
- The *unmounted* lifecycle hook is scheduled to run after the component is removed from the DOM.
- The scheduler, which is in charge or running jobs in the order in which they're scheduled, is based on the microtask queue.
- The event loop runs continuously in the browser's JavaScript run time and decides what code to execute next. In every cycle, it executes all pending microtasks first, followed by the oldest task in the task queue; finally, it gives the browser the opportunity to render the DOM.

# Testing asynchronous components

## This chapter covers

- Testing synchronous components
- Testing components with asynchronous behavior
- Implementing the `nextTick()` function

Testing components whose behavior is purely synchronous is straightforward. But components can have asynchronous hooks or event handlers, so testing them becomes a bit more complicated (and interesting) in these cases.

The main question the tester must face is how you know when all the asynchronous jobs have finished executing and the component has re-rendered. In this chapter, you'll implement a `nextTick()` function. This function returns a `Promise` that resolves when all the pending jobs in the scheduler have finished executing. This way, by `awaiting` this `Promise`, you can be sure that the component has re-rendered, and you can check what's in the Document Object Model (DOM).

> **NOTE** You can find all the listings in this chapter in the listings/ch14/ directory of the book's repository (http://mng.bz/y82p). The code in this chapter can be checked out from the ch14 label (http://mng.bz/MZWQ):
> `$ git switch --detach ch14`.

> ### Code catch-up
>
> In chapter 13, you defined two new functions that can be passed as arguments to the `defineComponent()` function: `onMounted()` and `onUnmounted()`. You implemented two new methods in the `Component` class, also called `onMounted()` and `onUnmounted()`, that wrap those two functions inside a `Promise` and bind them to the component instance.
>
> Then you implemented a simple scheduler to run the hooks asynchronously. The scheduler's API consists of one function: `enqueueJob()`, which queues a job to be executed asynchronously.
>
> The scheduler uses two more functions internally:
>
> - `scheduleUpdate()`—Queues the `processJobs()` function to be executed as a microtask
> - `processJobs()`—Runs all the jobs in the scheduler
>
> Last, you modified the `mountDOM()` and `destroyDOM()` functions to enqueue the `onMounted()` and `onUnmounted()` hooks, respectively, as jobs in the scheduler.

## 14.1   Testing components with asynchronous behavior: nextTick()

If you build an application with your own framework, you want to unit-test it—as you normally do (because you *do* test your applications, right?). Before you introduced asynchronous hooks, testing components was straightforward. Let's look at an example.

> **NOTE**   I'm using the Vitest testing library (https://vitest.dev) for the examples—the same one I used in the repository of the project. Its API is very similar to Jest's (https://jestjs.io), so if you're familiar with Jest, you'll feel right at home.

Suppose that you have a component called `Counter`, consisting of a button that increments a counter when clicked. If you render the component into the DOM, you get something like this:

```
<span data-qa="counter">0</span>
<button data-qa="increment">Increment</button>
```

After the button is clicked, the counter is incremented and the DOM is updated:

```
<span data-qa="counter">1</span>
<button data-qa="increment">Increment</button>
```

You can test this simple component as follows (and note that I'm using `data-qa` attributes to select the elements in the DOM):

```
import { test, expect, beforeEach, afterEach } from 'vitest'
import { createApp } from 'fe-fwk'
import { Counter } from './counter'

let app = null

beforeEach(() => {
  app = createApp(Counter)
  app.mount(document.body)
})

afterEach(() => {
  app.unmount()
})

test('the counter starts at 0', () => {
  const counter =
    document.querySelector('[data-qa="counter"]')
  expect(counter.textContent).toBe('0')
})

test('the counter increments when the button is clicked', () => {
  const button = document.querySelector('[data-qa="increment"]')
  const counter = document.querySelector('[data-qa="counter"]')

  button.click()

  expect(counter.textContent).toBe('1')
})
```

Creates an application and mounts it into the DOM before each test

Unmounts the application after each test

Selects the counter element

Checks that the counter starts at 0

Clicks the increment button

Checks that the counter is 1

But what if the component has an onMounted() hook that fetches data from a server asynchronously? Then you can't assume that right after mounting the application, the components have already updated their state or re-rendered their view.

In this case, your framework needs to give the developer a function—typically called nextTick()—to return a Promise that resolves when all the pending jobs in the scheduler have finished executing. This function would wait for all components to run their onMounted() hooks, as follows:

```
test('the component loads data from a server', async () => {
  const app = createApp(MyComponent)
  app.mount(document.body)

  // At this point, the component has gone through its first render, but
  // the onMounted() hooks haven't finished executing.

  await nextTick()

  // At this point, MyComponent's onMounted() hook has finished executing.
  // You can safely check what is rendered in the DOM.
})
```

Let's look at a realistic example with a loading state so that this concept is clearer. For the example, we'll assume that the `nextTick()` function already exists in your framework, but you won't implement it until section 14.1.3.

### 14.1.1  *Testing a component with an asynchronous onMounted() hook*

Suppose that you have a component called `TodosList`, which loads a list of to-dos from a server when it's mounted. While the data is being loaded, the component renders a loading indicator. You might use the following code to implement such a component:

```
export const TodosList = defineComponent({
  state() {
    return {
      isLoading: true,
      todos: [],
    }
  },

  async onMounted() {
    const todos = await fetch('https://api.example.com/todos')
    this.updateState({ isLoading: false, todos })
  },

  render() {
    const { isLoading, todos } = this.state

    if (isLoading) {
      return h('p', {}, ['Loading...'])
    }

    return h('ul', {}, todos.map((todo) => h('li', {}, [todo])))
  }
})
```

The first thing you'd naturally do is mock the `fetch()` function to return a promise that resolves with the data you want to test:

```
import { vi } from 'vitest'

// Mock the fetch API
global.fetch = vi.fn().mockResolvedValue({
  json: vi.fn().mockResolvedValue([
    'Feed the cat',
    'Mow the lawn',
  ]),
})
```

That code had a little trick in it: `fetch()` returns a promise that resolves with a response object that has a `json()` method that returns a promise that resolves with the data. That sentence is a mouthful, but the concept isn't complicated. In any case, you've already mocked the call to the server. To test that the loading indicator is rendered while the data is being fetched, you can do the following:

```
test('Shows the loading indicator while the todos are fetched', () => {
  // If nextTick() isn't awaited for, the onMounted() hooks haven't run,
  // so the loading should be displayed.

  expect(document.body.innerHTML).toContain('Loading...')
})
```

It's that easy! If you don't await for the nextTick() function, the onMounted() hook hasn't run yet, so the loading indicator is displayed. But at some point after the test has finished, the DOM will be updated and the loading indicator will disappear. You want to clean up the DOM after each test so that the next test starts with a clean DOM. The only thing you need to do is await for the nextTick() function before unmounting the application, as shown in bold in the following snippet:

```
afterEach(async () => {
  await nextTick()        ◁——————  Waits for the nextTick() function
  app.unmount()                    before unmounting the application
})
```

Note that if you had onUnmounted() asynchronous hooks, you'd also want to await for the nextTick() function after unmounting the application:

```
afterEach(async () => {
  await nextTick()
  app.unmount()
  await nextTick()
})
```

To test that the list of to-dos is rendered after the data is fetched, you can do the following:

```
test('Shows the list of todos after the data is fetched', async () => {
  // The nextTick() function is awaited for, so the onMounted() hooks
  // have finished running, and the list of todos is displayed.

  await nextTick()                                                    ◁—————

  expect(document.body.innerHTML).toContain('Feed the cat')
  expect(document.body.innerHTML).toContain('Mow the lawn')
})
```

**Waits for the nextTick() for the data to be fetched and the component to re-render**

A much better approach would be to add data-qa attributes to the elements in the DOM so that you can select them easily and then check their text content. But this example is simplified to show how to test components with asynchronous hooks.

The same `nextTick()` function could test components that have asynchronous event handlers, such as a button that loads more data from a server when clicked, so you may wonder how you implement the `nextTick()` function. I'm glad you asked! Let's implement it. Make sure that you have a clear understanding of event loops, tasks, and microtask queues, because that knowledge is key to understanding what comes next. Buckle up!

### 14.1.2   *The fundamentals behind the nextTick() function*

The `nextTick()` function might appear to be magical, but it's based on a solid understanding of the event loop's mechanics. Some of the big frameworks implement similar functions, which are widely used for testing components with asynchronous behavior, so I'm positive that implementing your own function will help you understand how it works and when to use it.

> ### The `nextTick()` function in some libraries
>
> The `nextTick()` function defined in Vue can be used both in production code and in tests. Its usefulness resides in the fact that the code that you run after `awaiting` for the `nextTick()` function is executed after the component has re-rendered, when you know that the DOM has been updated. This function is documented at https://vuejs.org/api/general.html#nexttick. You can also check how it's implemented in the runtime-core package, inside the scheduler.ts file, at http://mng.bz/7va4.
>
> Node JS implements a `process.nextTick()` function that's used to schedule a callback to be executed on the next iteration of the event loop. You can find the documentation for it at http://mng.bz/aE4j. I recommend that you give this documentation a read because it's short and well explained.
>
> Svelte defines a `tick()` function that returns a `Promise` that resolves when the component has re-rendered. Its use is similar to that of the `nextTick()` function in Vue. This function is documented at https://svelte.dev/docs/svelte#tick. You can check its implementation in the runtime.js file inside the internal/client/ folder at http://mng.bz/mjP0.

The `nextTick()` function returns a `Promise` that resolves when all the pending jobs in the scheduler have finished executing. So the question is how you know when all the pending jobs in the scheduler have finished executing. First, you want to call the `scheduleUpdate()` function to make sure that when the `nextTick()` function is called, the `processJobs()` function is scheduled to run:

```
export function nextTick() {
  scheduleUpdate()
  // ...
}
```

If you remember from chapter 13, when the execution stack empties, the event loop executes all the microtasks first; then it executes the oldest task in the task queue, lets the DOM render, and starts over. You've queued the `scheduleUpdate()` function to run as a microtask, so you know that as soon as the execution stack is empty, the `processJobs()` function will be executed (figure 14.1).

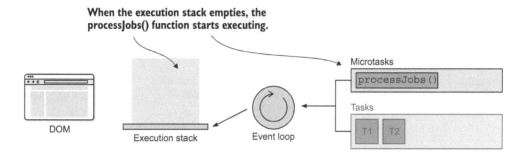

**Figure 14.1** The `processJobs()` function is scheduled to run as a microtask.

All the jobs in the scheduler are asynchronous because even if they weren't originally, you've wrapped them inside a `Promise` and set up a `then()` callback to handle the result or rejection of the promise. As a result, the `processJobs()` function will queue more microtasks as it runs jobs (figure 14.2).

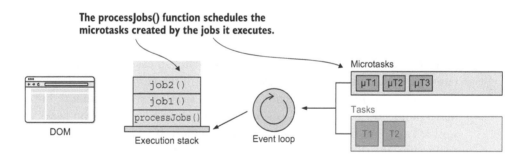

**Figure 14.2** The `processJobs()` function queues more microtasks.

The event loop won't take the next task until all microtasks have been executed, including the microtasks that are queued by the `processJobs()` function. So to make sure that you resolve only the `Promise` returned by the `nextTick()` function when all the pending jobs in the scheduler finish executing, you need to schedule a task whose callback resolves the `Promise` returned by the `nextTick()` function. You can use `set-Timeout()` to schedule a new task:

```
new Promise((resolve) => setTimeout(resolve))
```

By scheduling the created `Promise` in the task callback, you're forcing the event loop to go through at least another cycle before resolving the `Promise` because the `resolve()` function inside a `Promise` is scheduled as a microtask. So if the microtask is queued only when a task is executed, the event loop needs to process all pending microtasks, process the task that resolves the `Promise`, and then process all the pending microtasks until that `resolve()` is executed. Only then does `awaiting` for the `Promise` returned by the `nextTick()` function resolve (figure 14.3).

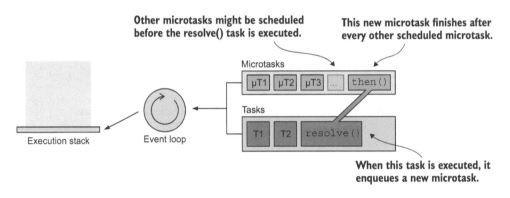

**Figure 14.3  The `Promise` returned by the `nextTick()` function resolves when all the pending jobs in the scheduler have finished executing.**

This process of scheduling a microtask via a task is commonly referred to as *flushing promises*. Many frontend and testing frameworks include a function to flush pending promises, mostly for testing purposes, so that you can easily write your unit tests without worrying about the asynchronous behavior of the components.

I know that this concept might be hard to wrap your head around, but you must understand how the event loop works to understand how the `nextTick()` function works. Take your time processing this information. If you need to, read this chapter again, draw the diagrams yourself, and experiment with the browser's console. In section 14.1.3, I'll ask you to do just that.

### 14.1.3  *Implementing the nextTick() function*

You should understand how the `nextTick()` function works by now, so you're ready to implement it. Inside the scheduler.js file, add the code in listing 14.1.

**Listing 14.1  `nextTick()` and `flushPromises()` (scheduler.js)**

```
export function nextTick() {
  scheduleUpdate()
  return flushPromises()
}
```

```
function flushPromises() {
  return new Promise((resolve) => setTimeout(resolve))
}
```

Before publishing the framework's next version—version 4.1, including the `next-Tick()` function—I want you to complete exercise 14.1. It challenges you to guess what the order of some `console.log()` calls will be—a classic JavaScript interview question—and will help you understand the principle behind the `flushPromises()` function.

### Exercise 14.1

Open the browser's console, and write this slightly modified version of the `flush-Promises()` function:

```
function flushPromises() {
    return new Promise((resolve) => {
        console.log('setTimeout() with resolve() as callback...')
        setTimeout(() => {
            console.log('About to resolve the promise...')
            resolve(42)
        })
    })
}
```

Note the two console logs:

- One inside the `Promise` body, before the `setTimeout()` function is called
- One inside the `setTimeout()` callback, right before the `resolve()` function is called

Now write this `doWork()` function, which schedules both microtasks and tasks and then `await`s for the `Promise` returned by the `flushPromises()` function:

```
async function doWork() {
    queueMicrotask(() => console.log('Microtask 1'))
    setTimeout(() => console.log('Task 1'))
    queueMicrotask(() => console.log('Microtask 2'))
    setTimeout(() => console.log('Task 2'))

    const p = flushPromises()

    queueMicrotask(() => {
      console.log('Microtask 44')
      queueMicrotask(() => console.log('Microtask 45'))
    })
    setTimeout(() => console.log('Task 22'))

    const value = await p
    console.log('Result of flush:', value)
}
```

**(continued)**

Can you guess the order in which all these `console.log()` calls will be executed when you execute the `doWork()` function? Draw a diagram with the task and micro-task queues to help you figure it out. Then run the `doWork()` function and compare the result with your expectations.

Find the solution at http://mng.bz/xjGY.

## 14.2  *Publishing version 4.1 of the framework*

Let's publish the new version of the framework. First, you want to include the `next-Tick()` function as part of the public API of the framework. Including it allows developers to use this function inside their unit tests, as you saw in section 14.1. In the *index.js* file, add the import statement shown in bold:

```
export { createApp } from './app.js'
export { defineComponent } from './component.js'
export { DOM_TYPES, h, hFragment, hString } from './h.js'
export { nextTick } from './scheduler.js'
```

Then, in the package.json file, update the version number to `4.1.0`:

```
"version": "4.0.0",
"version": "4.1.0",
```

Remember to move your terminal to the root or the project. Then run `npm install` so that the package version number in the package-lock.json file is updated:

```
$ npm install
```

Finally, place your terminal inside the packages/runtime folder, and run

```
$ npm publish
```

The new version of your framework, which includes the `nextTick()` function, is published.

## 14.3  *Where to go from here*

Congratulations on reaching the final chapter of the book! By now, you've achieved an impressive learning milestone. Your grasp of how frontend frameworks work surpasses that of 99 percent of developers in this field. Even more remarkable, you've not only delved into the theory, but also mastered the practical aspect of frontends by building your own framework.

You may be eager to continue enhancing your skills. Consider adding a router to enable seamless transitions among pages and incorporating a template compiler into your build process. Perhaps you're even contemplating creating a Chrome/Firefox extension to debug applications written with your framework. These features are common in frontend frameworks, and understanding how to implement them can further elevate your expertise. Originally, I intended to cover these topics in the book, but due to the book's length constraints, they had to be omitted.

Nevertheless, I wanted to cover this material, so I had two options: write an extra part for this book or publish the material online. The second option seemed to be a better idea, so I've published some extra chapters in the wiki section of the book's code repository (http://mng.bz/gvYe). I suggest that you continue your learning journey by reading the chapters in the wiki; they follow a similar structure to the chapters in this book, so you should feel right at home. The material covered in the wiki is more advanced, however, so be ready to embrace the challenge.

When you've finished reading the advanced extra chapters in the wiki, you'll have a nice frontend framework of your own—one that you can try in your next project. Build your portfolio with it, or create that side project you've been thinking about for a while. When you use your framework in a medium-size project, you'll see its shortcomings. Maybe it isn't as convenient to use as the big frameworks, for example, or it may be missing some features. Reflect on what features you could add to fix those shortcomings and then try to implement them. The process will be challenging (and fun). You'll want to open the source code of other frameworks, read their documentation, and debug their code, which is how you learn.

The GitHub repository's discussions section is a forum where you can propose new features for the framework, ask questions, and get help from the community so that we can learn from one another. If you have a great idea for a feature but don't know how to implement it, or if you have several options but want help from the community to evaluate its tradeoffs, this section is the place to go. You can find it at http://mng .bz/0GWp.

As in any other public forum where people with all levels of experience participate and ask for directions, please be respectful and kind. I know that you are a kind person with a big heart and willingness to help, so I don't think you need to be reminded of this point. Also, value other people's time, and don't expect them to do your work for you. Take the time to do your research and pose your questions in a way that makes it easy for others to help you. You can read more about these guidelines in the "how to ask" section of Stack Overflow (https://stackoverflow.com/help/ how-to-ask).

After reading this book, completing the advanced topics in the wiki, and building a project with your framework, you can go a step further and try the following:

- *Innovate*—Do you have an idea for a new feature that would make your framework stand out from the rest? What's stopping you from implementing it?
- *Collaborate in the development of a well-established framework such as Vue, React, Angular, or Svelte*—These projects are open source, and they're always looking for new contributors. You'll need to get acquainted with the codebase first, but you have many of the core concepts already covered.

- *Improve the performance of your framework*—Do you need inspiration? Check out Inferno JS (https://www.infernojs.org/about). Start by measuring the performance of the operations in your framework; you might need to look for some tooling. Then find the bottlenecks and think about how to get rid of them.
- *Write another framework from scratch*—Make all the decisions yourself, weigh the tradeoffs, and learn from your mistakes. You can always come back to this book for reference, but this time, you'll be the one making the decisions.

I hope you've enjoyed reading this book as much as I enjoyed writing it. This chapter is a goodbye from me, but I hope to see you in the discussions section of the repository or the issues section if you find a bug in the code. I wish you all the best in your learning journey, in your professional career, and, above all, in your life.

## Summary

- To test components with asynchronous hooks or event handlers, you need to `await` for the `nextTick()` function before checking what's in the DOM.
- The `nextTick()` function returns a `Promise` that resolves when all the pending jobs in the scheduler have finished executing.
- To implement the `nextTick()` function, you need to schedule a task whose callback resolves the `Promise` returned by the `nextTick()` function.

# appendix
## Setting up the project

Before you write any code, you need to have an NPM project set up. In this appendix, I'll help you create and configure a project to write the code for your framework.

I understand that you might not configure an NPM project from scratch with a bundler, a linter, and a test library, as most frameworks come with a command-line interface (CLI) tool (such as create-react-app or angular-cli) that creates the scaffolding and generates the boilerplate code structure. So I'll give you two options to create your project:

- *Use the CLI tool I created for this book.* With a single command, you can create a project and can start writing your code right away.
- *Configure the project from scratch.* This option is more laborious, but it teaches you how to configure the project.

If you want to get started with the book quickly and can't wait to write your awesome frontend framework, I recommend that you use the CLI tool. In this case, you need to read section A.8. But if you're the kind of developer who enjoys configuring everything from scratch, you can follow the steps in section A.9 to configure the project yourself.

Before you start configuring your project, I'll cover some basics: where you can find the code for the book and the technologies you'll use. These sections are optional, but I recommend that you read them before you start configuring your project. If you can't wait to start writing code, you can skip them and move on to sections A.8 and A.9. You can always come back and read the rest of the appendix later.

331

## A.1   *Where to find the source code*

The source code for the book is publicly available at http://mng.bz/lVO8. I recommend that you clone the repository or download the zip archive of the repository so you can follow along with the book. The archive contains all the listings that appear in the book (in the listings folder), sorted by chapter. I'm assuming that you're familiar with Git and know how to clone a repository and checkout tags or branches. If the previous sentence looks like nonsense to you, don't worry; you can still follow along. Download the project as a zip archive by clicking the <> Code button in the repository and then clicking the Download ZIP button.

> **WARNING**   The code you'll find in the repository is the final version of the framework—the one you'll have written by the end of the book. If you want to check the code for each chapter, you need to check out the corresponding Git tag, as explained in the next section. You can also refer to the listings directory in the repository, which contains all the listings from the book sorted by chapter.

### A.1.1   *Checking out the code for each chapter*

I tagged the source code with the number of each chapter where a new version of the framework is available. The tag name follows the pattern *chX*, where *X* is the number of the chapter. The first working version of the framework appears in chapter 6, for example, so the corresponding code can be checked out with the following Git command:

```
$ git checkout ch6
```

Then, in chapters 7 and 8, you implement the reconciliation algorithm, resulting in a new version of the framework with enhanced performance. The corresponding code can be checked out as follows:

```
$ git checkout ch8
```

By checking out the code for each chapter, you can see how the framework evolves as we add features. You can also compare your code by the end of each chapter with the code in the repository. Note that not all chapters have a tag in the repository—only those that have a working version of the framework. I also wrote unit tests for the framework that I won't cover in the book, but you can look at them to find ideas for testing your code.

> **NOTE**   If you're not familiar with the concept of Git tags, you can learn about them at https://git-scm.com/book/en/v2/Git-Basics-Tagging. For this book, I assume that you have basic Git knowledge.

I recommend that you avoid copying and pasting the code from the book; instead, type it yourself. If you get stuck because your code doesn't seem to work, look at the code in the repository, try to figure out the differences, and then fix the problem yourself. If you write a unit test to reproduce the problem, so much the better. I know that this approach is more cumbersome, but it's the best way to learn, and it's how you'd probably want to tackle a real-world bug in your code. You can also refer to the listings/ directory in the repository, which contains all the listings from the book sorted by chapter.

You can find instructions for running and working with the code in the README file of the repository (http://mng.bz/BAp8). This file contains up-to-date documentation on everything you need to know about the code. Make sure to read it before you work with the code. (When you start working with the code in an open source repository, reading the README file is the first thing you should do.)

### A.1.2   *A note on the code*

I didn't write the code to be the most performant and safest code possible. Many code snippets could use better error handling, or I could have done things in a more performant way by applying optimizations. But I emphasized writing code that's easy to understand, clean, and concise—code that you read and immediately understand.

I pruned all the unnecessary details that would make code harder to understand and left in only the essence of the concept I want to teach. I went to great lengths to simplify the code as much as possible, and I hope you'll find it easy to follow. But bear in mind that the code you'll find in the repository and the book was written to teach a concept efficiently, not to be production-ready.

### A.1.3   *Reporting problems in the code*

As many tests as I wrote and as many times as I reviewed the code, I'm sure that it still has bugs. Frontend frameworks are complex beasts, and it's hard to get everything right. If you find a bug in the code, please report it in the repository by opening a new problem.

To open a new problem, go to the issues tab of the repository (http://mng.bz/ ZR1O), and click the New Issue button. In the Bug Report row, click the Get Started button. Fill in the form with details on the bug you found, and click the Submit New Issue button.

You'll need to provide enough information that I can easily reproduce and fix the bug. I know that it takes time to file a bug report with this many details, but it's considered to be good etiquette in the open source community. Filing a detailed report shows respect to the people who maintain a project, who use their free time to create and maintain it for everyone to use free of charge. It's good to get used to being a respectful citizen of the open source community.

### A.1.4   *Fixing a bug yourself*

If you find a bug in the code and know how to fix it, you can open a pull request with the fix. Even better than opening a problem is offering a solution to it; that's how open source projects work. You may also want to look at bugs that other people reported and try to fix them. This practice is a great way to learn how to contribute to open source projects, and I'll be forever grateful if you do so.

If you don't know what GitHub pull requests are, I recommend that you read about them at https://docs.github.com/en/pull-requests. Pull requests enable you to contribute to open source projects on GitHub, and also many software companies use them to add changes to their codebase, so it's good to know how they work.

## A.2  Solutions to the exercises

In most chapters of this book, I present exercises to test your understanding of the concepts I've explained. Some may seem to be straightforward, but others are challenging. If you want to absorb the concepts in the book, I recommend doing the exercises. Only if you get stuck or when you think you've found the solution should you check the answers. I've included the answers to all the exercises in the wiki of the repository:

http://mng.bz/27Pd

In the wiki, you'll find a page for the solutions to the exercises in the book by chapter:

http://mng.bz/PRl9

The wiki includes extra chapters that cover advanced topics. These chapters didn't make it into the book because the book would've been too long.

## A.3  Advanced topics

When you finish this book, you'll have a decent frontend framework—one that wouldn't be suitable for large production applications but would work very well for small projects. The key is for you to learn how frontend frameworks work and have fun in the process. But you may want to continue learning and improving your framework. So I've written some extra chapters on advanced topics, which you can find in the repository's wiki (section A.2). In these chapters, you'll learn to

- Add Typescript types to your framework bundle.
- Add support for server-side rendering.
- Write the templates in HTML and compile them to render functions.
- Include external content inside your components (slots).
- Create a browser extension to inspect the components of your application.

I hope that you enjoy these chapters, but you have to learn the basics first, so make sure that you finish this book with a solid understanding of the topics it covers.

## A.4  Note on the technologies used

There are heated discussions in the frontend ecosystem about the best tools. You'll hear things like "You should use Bun because it's much faster than Node JS" and

"Webpack is old now; you should start using Vite for all your projects." Some people argue about which bundler is best or which linter and transpiler you should be using. I find blog posts of the "top 10 reasons why you should stop using X" kind to be especially harmful. Apart from being obvious clickbait, they usually don't help the frontend community, let alone junior developers who have a hard time understanding what set of tools they "should" be using.

> ### A cautionary tale on getting overly attached to tools
>
> I once worked for a startup that grew quickly but wasn't doing well. Very few customers used our app, and every time we added something to the code, we introduced new bugs. (Code quality wasn't a priority; speed was. Automated testing was nowhere to be found.) Surprisingly, we blamed the problem on the tools we were using. We were convinced that when we migrated the code to the newest version of the framework, we got more customers, and things worked well from then on. Yes, I know that belief sounds ridiculous now, but we made it to "modernize" the tooling. Guess what? The code was still the same: a hard-to-maintain mess that broke if you stared at it too long. It turns out that using modern tools doesn't make code better if the code is poorly written in the first place.
>
> What do I want to say here? I believe that **your time is better used writing quality code than arguing about what tools will make your application successful. Well-architected and modularized code** with a great suite of automated tests that, apart from making sure that the code works and can be refactored safely, also serves as documentation, **beats any tooling**. That isn't to say that the tools don't matter because they obviously do. Ask a carpenter whether they can be productive using a rusty hammer or a blunt saw.

For this book, I tried to choose tools that are mature and that most frontend developers are familiar with. Choosing the newest, shiniest, or trendiest tool wasn't my goal. I want to teach you how frontend frameworks work, and the truth is that most tools work perfectly well for this purpose. The knowledge that I'll give you in this book transcends the tools you choose to use. If you prefer a certain tool and have experience with it, feel free to use it instead of the ones I recommend here.

### A.4.1  Package manager: NPM

We'll use the NPM package manager (https://docs.npmjs.com) to create the project and run the scripts. If you're more comfortable with yarn or pnpm, you can use them instead. These tools work very similarly, so you shouldn't have any problem using the one you prefer.

We'll use NPM workspaces (https://docs.npmjs.com/cli/v7/using-npm/workspaces), which were introduced in version 7. Make sure that you have at least version 7 installed:

```
$ npm --version
8.19.2
```

Both yarn and pnpm support workspaces, so you can use them as well. In fact, they introduced workspaces before NPM did.

### A.4.2   Bundler: Rollup

To bundle the JavaScript code into a single file, we'll use Rollup (https://rollupjs.org), which is simple to use. If you prefer Webpack, Parcel, or Vite, however, you can use it instead. You'll have to make sure that you configure the tool to output a single ESM file (as you'll see).

### A.4.3   Linter: ESLint

To lint the code, we'll use ESLint (https://eslint.org), a popular linter that's easy to configure. I'm a firm believer that static analysis tools are musts for any serious project in which code quality is important (as it always is).

ESLint prevents us from declaring unused variables, having unused imports, and doing many other things that cause problems in code. ESLint is super-configurable, but most developers are happy with the default configuration, which is a good starting point. We'll use the default configuration in this book as well, but you can always change it to your liking. If you deem a particular linting rule to be important, you can add it to your configuration.

### A.4.4   (Optional) Testing: Vitest

I won't be showing unit tests for the code you'll write in this book to keep its size reasonable, but if you check the source code of the framework I wrote for the book, you'll see lots of them. (You can use them to better understand how the framework works. When they're well written, tests are great sources of documentation.) You may want to write tests yourself to make sure that the framework works as expected and that you don't break it when you make changes. Every serious project should be accompanied by tests, which serve as a safety net as well as documentation.

I've worked a lot with Jest (https://jestjs.io), which has been my go-to testing framework for a long time. But I recently started using Vitest (https://vitest.dev) and decided to stick with it because it's orders of magnitude faster. Vitest's API is similar to Jest's, so you won't have problems if you decide to use it as well. But if you want to use Jest, it'll do fine.

### A.4.5   Language: JavaScript

Saying that we'll use JavaScript may seem to be obvious, but if I were writing the framework for myself, I'd use TypeScript without hesitation. TypeScript is fantastic for large projects: types tell you a lot about the code, and the compiler will help you catch bugs before you even run the code. (How many times have you accessed a property that didn't exist in an object using JavaScript? Does `TypeError` sends shivers down your spine?) Nontyped languages are great for scripting, but for large projects, I recommend having a compiler as your companion.

Why, then, am I using JavaScript for this book? The code tends to be shorter without types, and I want to teach you the principles of how frontend frameworks work—principles that apply equally well to JavaScript and TypeScript. I prefer to use JavaScript because the code listings are shorter and I can get to the point faster, thus teaching you more efficiently.

As with the previous tools, if you feel strongly about using TypeScript, you can use it instead of JavaScript. You'll need to figure out the types yourself, but that's part of the fun, right? Also, don't forget to set up the compilation step in your build process.

## A.5 Read the docs

Explaining how to configure the tools you'll use in detail, as well as how they work, is beyond the scope of this book. I want to encourage you to go to the tools' websites or repository pages and read the documentation. One great aspect of frontend tools is that they tend to be extremely well documented. I'm convinced that the makers compete against one another to see which one has the best documentation.

If you're not familiar with any of the tools you'll be using, take some time to read the documentation, which will save you a lot of time in the long run. I'm a firm believer that developers should strive to understand the tools they use, not just use them blindly. (That belief is what encouraged me to learn how frontend frameworks work in the first place, which explains why I'm writing this book.)

One of the most important lessons I've learned over the years is that taking time to read the documentation is a great investment. Reading the docs before you start using a new tool or library saves you the time you'd spend trying to figure out how to do something that the documentation explains in detail. The time you spend trying to figure things out and searching StackOverflow for answers, is (in my experience) usually greater than the time you'd have spent reading the documentation up front.

*6 hours of debugging can save you 5 minutes of reading documentation*

—Jakob (@jcsrb) Twitter

Be a good developer; read the docs. (Or at least ask ChatGPT a well-structured question.)

## A.6 Structure of the project

Let's briefly go over the structure of the project in which you'll write the code for your framework. The framework that you'll write in this book consists of a single package (NPM workspace): runtime. This package is the framework itself.

> **NOTE** The advanced chapters you can read in the repository's wiki add more packages to the project. For this reason, you want to structure your project by using NPM workspaces. It may seem silly to use workspaces when the project consists of a single package, but this approach will make sense when you add packages to the project.

**TIP**   If you're not familiar with NPM workspaces, you can read about them at https://docs.npmjs.com/cli/v9/using-npm/workspaces. It's important to understand how they work so that the structure of the project makes sense and you can follow the instructions.

The folder structure of the project is as follows:

```
examples/
packages/
    └── runtime/
```

When you add packages (advanced chapters in the repository), they'll be inside the *packages* directory as well:

```
examples/
packages/
    ├── compiler/
    ├── loader/
    └── runtime/
```

Each package has its own package.json file, with its own dependencies, and is bundled separately. The packages are effectively three separate projects, but they're all part of the same repository. This project structure is common these days; it's called a *monorepo*. The packages you include will define the same scripts:

- *build*—Builds the package, bundling all the JavaScript files into a single file, which is published to NPM.
- *test*—Runs the automated tests in watch mode.
- *test:run*—Runs the automated tests once.
- *lint*—Runs the linter to detect problems in your code.
- *lint:fix*—Runs the linter and automatically fixes the problems it can fix.
- *prepack*—A special lifecycle script (http://mng.bz/Jdj0) that runs before the package is published to NPM. It's used to ensure that the package is built before being published.

**WARNING**   The aforementioned scripts are defined in each of the three packages' package.json files (packages/runtime, for example), not in the root package.json file. Bear this fact in mind in case you decide to configure the project yourself because there will be two package.json files total, plus one package that you add to the project.

## A.7   *Finding a name for your framework*

Before you create the project or write any code, you need a name for your framework. Be creative! The name needs to be one that no one else is using in NPM (where you'll be publishing your framework), so it must be original. If you're not sure what to call it, you can simply call it *<your name>-fe-fwk* (your name followed by *-fe-fwk*). To make sure

that the name is unique, check whether it's available on npmjs.com (https://www
.npmjs.com) by adding it to the URL, as follows:

www.npmjs.com/package/ *<your framework name>*

If the URL displays the `404-not found` error page, nobody is using that name for a
Node JS package yet, so you're good to go.

> **NOTE**  I'll use the *<fwk-name>* placeholder to refer to the name of your frame-
> work in the sections that follow. Whenever you see *<fwk-name>* in a command,
> you should replace it with the name you chose for your framework.

Now let's create the project. Remember that you have two options. If you want to configure things yourself, jump to section A.9. If you want to use the CLI tool to get
started quickly, read section A.8.

## A.8   Option A: Using the CLI tool

Using the CLI tool I created for the book is the fastest way to get started. This tool will
save you the time it takes to create and configure the project from scratch, so you can
start writing code right away. Open your terminal, move to the directory where you
want the project to be created, and run the following command:

```
$ npx fe-fwk-cli init <fwk-name>
```

With npx, you don't need to install the CLI tool locally; it will be downloaded and executed automatically. When the command finishes executing, it instructs you to `cd` in to
the project directory and run `npm install` to install the dependencies:

```
$ cd <fwk-name>
$ npm install
```

That's it! Go to section A.10 to learn how to publish your framework to NPM.

## A.9   Option B: Configuring the project from scratch

> **NOTE**  If you created your project by using the CLI tool, you can skip this
> section.

To create the project yourself, first create a directory for it. On the command line, run
the following command:

```
$ mkdir <fwk-name>
```

Then initialize an NPM project in that directory:

```
$ cd <fwk-name>
$ npm init -y
```

This command creates a package.json file in the directory. You need to make a few edits in the file. For one, you want to edit the `description` field to something like

```
"description": "A project to learn how to write a frontend framework"
```

Then you want to make this package private so that you don't accidentally publish it to NPM (because you'll publish the workspace packages to NPM, not the parent project):

```
"private": true
```

You also want to change the name of this package to *<fwk-name>-project* to prevent conflicts with the name of your framework (which you'll use to name the runtime package you create in section A.10). Every NPM package in the repository requires a unique name, and you want to reserve the name you chose for your framework for the runtime package. So append *-project* to the `name` field:

```
"name": "<fwk-name>-project"
```

Finally, add a `workspaces` field to the file, with an array of the directories where you'll create the packages that comprise your project (so far, only the runtime package):

```
"workspaces": [
  "packages/runtime"
]
```

Your package.json file should look similar to this:

```
{
  "name": "<fwk-name>-project",
  "version": "1.0.0",
  "description": "A project to learn how to write a frontend framework",
  "private": true,
  "workspaces": [
    "packages/runtime"
  ]
}
```

You may have other fields—`author`, `license`, and so on—but the ones in the preceding snippet are the ones that must be there. Next, let's create a directory in your project where you can add example applications to test your framework.

### A.9.1   *The examples folder*

Throughout the book, you'll be improving your framework and adding features to it. Each time you add a feature, you'll want to test it by using it in example applications. Here, you'll configure a directory where you can add these applications and a script to serve them locally. Create an examples directory at the root of your project:

```
$ mkdir examples
```

TIP While the examples folder remains empty—that is, before you write any example application—you may want to add a .gitkeep file to it so that Git picks up the directory and includes it in the repository. (Git doesn't track empty directories.) As soon as you put a file in the directory, you can remove the .gitkeep file, but keeping it doesn't hurt.

To keep the examples directory tidy, create a subdirectory for each chapter: examples/ch02, examples/ch03, and so on. Each subdirectory will contain the example applications using the framework resulting from the chapter, which allows you to see the framework become more powerful and easier to use. You don't need to create the subdirectories now; you'll create them as you need them in the book.

Now you need a script to serve the example applications. Your applications will consist of an entry HTML file, which loads other files, such as JavaScript files, CSS files, and images. For the browser to load these files, you need to serve them from a web server. The http-server package is a simple web server that can serve the example applications. In the package.json file, add the following script:

```
"scripts": {
  "serve:examples": "npx http-server . -o ./examples/"
}
```

NOTE This script is the only one you need to add to the project root package.json file. All the other scripts will be added to the package.json files of the packages you'll create in the following sections. You won't add any other script to the root package.json file.

The project doesn't require the http-server package to be installed, as you're using npx to run it. The -o flag tells the server to open the browser and navigate to the specified directory—in the case of the preceding command, the examples directory. Your project should have the following structure so far:

```
<fwk-name>/
    ├── package.json
    └── examples/
        └── .gitkeep
```

Great. Now let's create the three packages that will make up your framework code.

## A.9.2 Creating the runtime package

As I've said, your framework will consist of a single package: runtime. In the advanced chapters published in the repository's wiki (section A.2), you'll add packages to the project, but for now, you'll create only the runtime package.

Before you create the package, you need to create a directory where you'll put it: the packages directory you specified in the workspaces field of the package.json file. Make sure that your terminal is inside the project's root directory by running the pwd command:

```
$ pwd
```

The output should be similar to this (where *path/to/your/framework* is the path to the directory where you created the project):

```
path/to/your/framework/<fwk-name>
```

If your terminal isn't in the project's root directory, use the cd command to navigate to it. Then create a packages directory:

```
$ mkdir packages
```

### THE RUNTIME PACKAGE
Let's create the runtime package. First, cd into the *packages* folder:

```
$ cd packages
```

Then create the folder for the runtime package and cd into it:

```
$ mkdir runtime
$ cd runtime
```

Next, initialize an NPM project in the runtime folder:

```
$ npm init -y
```

Open the package.json file that was created for you, and make sure that the following fields have the right values (leaving the other fields as they are):

```
{
  "name": "<fwk-name>",
  "version": "1.0.0",
  "main": "dist/<fwk-name>.js",
  "files": [
    "dist/<fwk-name>.js"
  ]
}
```

Remember to replace *<fwk-name>* with the name of your framework. The main field specifies the entry point of the package, which is the file that will be loaded when you import the package. When you import code from this package as follows,

```
import { something } from '<fwk-name>'
```

JavaScript resolves the path to the file specified in the main field. You've told NPM that the file is the dist/*<fwk-name>*.js file, which is the bundled file containing all the code for the runtime package. Rollup will generate this file when you run the build script you'll add to the package.json file in the next section.

   The files field specifies the files that will be included in the package when you publish it to the NPM repository. The only file you want to include is the bundled file, so you've specified that in the files field. Files like README, LICENSE, and package.json are automatically included in the package, so you don't need to include them. Your project should have the following structure (the parts in bold are the ones you just created):

```
<fwk-name>/
    ├── package.json
    ├── examples/
    │   └── .gitkeep
    └── packages/
        └── runtime/
            └── package.json
```

### INSTALLING AND CONFIGURING ROLLUP

Let's add Rollup to bundle the framework code. Rollup is the bundler that you'll use to bundle your framework code; it's simple to configure and use. To install Rollup, make sure that your terminal is inside the runtime package directory by running the pwd command:

```
$ pwd
```

The output should be similar to

```
path/to/your/framework/<fwk-name> packages/runtime
```

If your terminal isn't inside the packages/runtime directory, use the cd command to navigate to it. Then install the rollup package by running the following command:

```
$ npm install --save-dev rollup
```

You also want to install two plugins for Rollup:

- rollup-plugin-cleanup—To remove comments from the generated bundle
- rollup-plugin-filesize—To display the size of the generated bundle

Install these plugins with the following command:

```
$ npm install --save-dev rollup-plugin-cleanup rollup-plugin-filesize
```

Now you need to configure Rollup. Create a rollup.config.mjs file in the runtime folder. (Note the .mjs extension, which tells Node JS that this file should be treated as an ES module and thus can use the import syntax.) Then add the following code:

```
import cleanup from 'rollup-plugin-cleanup'
import filesize from 'rollup-plugin-filesize'

export default {
  input: 'src/index.js',        ◁── Entry point of the framework code
  plugins: [cleanup()],         ◁── Removes comments from the generated bundle
  output: [
    {
```

```
    file: 'dist/<fwk-name>.js',        ◁         Name of the
    format: 'esm',                   ◁           generated bundle
    plugins: [filesize()],         ◁
  },
 ],
}
```

**Displays the size of the**  **Formats the bundle**
**generated bundle**  **as an ES module**

The configuration, explained in plain English, means the following:

- The entry point of the framework code is the src/index.js file. Starting from this file, Rollup will bundle all the code that is imported from it.
- The comments in the source code should be removed from the generated bundle; they occupy space and aren't necessary for the code to execute. The plugin-rollup-cleanup plugin does this job.
- The generated bundle should be an ES module (using import/export syntax, supported by all major browsers) that is saved in the dist folder as *<fwk-name>*.js.
- We want the size of the generated bundle to be displayed in the terminal so we can keep an eye on it and make sure that it doesn't grow too much. The plugin-rollup-filesize plugin does this job.

Now add a script to the package.json file (the one inside the runtime package) to run Rollup and bundle all the code, and add another one to run it automatically before publishing the package:

```
"scripts": {
  "prepack": "npm run build",
  "build": "rollup -c"
}
```

The prepack script is a special script that NPM runs automatically before you publish the package (by running the npm publish command). This script makes sure that whenever you publish a new version of the package, the bundle is generated. The prepack script simply runs the build script, which in turn runs Rollup.

To run Rollup, call the rollup command and pass the -c flag to tell it to use the rollup.config.mjs file as configuration. (If you don't pass a specific file to the -c flag, Rollup looks for a rollup.config.js or rollup.config.mjs file.)

Before you test the build command, you need to create the src/ folder and the src/index.js file with the following commands:

```
$ mkdir src
$ touch src/index.js
```

**NOTE**   In Windows Shell, touch won't work; use call > filename instead.

Inside the src/index.js file, add the following code:

```
console.log('This will soon be a frontend framework!')
```

Now run the `build` command to bundle the code:

```
$ npm run build
```

This command processes all the files imported from the src/index.js file (none at the moment) and bundles them into the dist folder. The output in your terminal should look similar to the following:

```
src/index.js → dist/<fwk-name>.js...
```

```
┌─────────────────────────────────┐
│                                 │
│   Destination: dist/<fwk-name>.js │
│   Bundle Size:   56 B           │
│   Minified Size:   55 B         │
│   Gzipped Size:   73 B          │
│                                 │
└─────────────────────────────────┘
```

```
created dist/<fwk-name>.js in 62ms
```

Recall that instead of *<fwk-name>*, you should use the name of your framework. That rectangle in the middle of the output is the rollup-plugin-filesize plugin in action. It's reporting the size of the generated bundle (56 bytes, in this case), as well as the size it would be if the file were minified and gzipped. We won't be minifying the code for this book, as the framework is going to be small, but for a production-ready framework, you should do that. A browser can load minified JavaScript faster and thus improve the Time to Interactive (TTI; http://mng.bz/wjNq) metric of the web application that uses it.

A new file, dist/*<fwk-name>*.js, has been created in the dist folder. If you open it, you'll see that it contains only the `console.log()` statement you added to the src/index.js file.

Great! Let's install and configure ESLint.

### INSTALLING AND CONFIGURING ESLINT

ESLint is a linter that helps you write better code; it analyzes the code you write and reports any errors or potential problems. To install ESLint, run the following command:

```
$ npm install --save-dev eslint
```

You'll use the ESLint recommended configuration, which is a set of rules that ESLint enforces in your code. Create the .eslintrc.js file inside the packages/runtime directory with the following content:

```
module.exports = {
  env: {
    browser: true,
    es2021: true,
  },
  extends: 'eslint:recommended',
  overrides: [],
```

```
  parserOptions: {
    ecmaVersion: 'latest',
    sourceType: 'module',
  },
  rules: {},
}
```

Finally, add the following two scripts to the package.json file:

```
"scripts": {
  "prepack": "npm run build",
  "build": "rollup -c",
  "lint": "eslint src",
  "lint:fix": "eslint src --fix"
}
```

You can run the lint script to check the code for errors and the lint:fix script to fix some of them automatically—those that ESLint knows how to fix. I won't show the output of the lint script in the book, but you can run it yourself to see what it reports as you write your code.

### INSTALLING VITEST (OPTIONAL)

As I've mentioned, I used a lot of tests while developing the code for this book, but I won't be showing them in the book. You can find them in the source code of the framework and try to write your own as you follow along. Having tests in your code will help you ensure that things work as expected as you move forward with the development of your framework. We'll use Vitest to run the tests. To install Vitest, run the following command:

```
$ npm install --save-dev vitest
```

Tests can run in different environments, such as Node JS, JSDOM, or a real browser. Because we'll use the Document API to create Document Object Model (DOM) elements, we'll use JSDOM as the environment. (If you want to know more about JSDOM, see its repository: https://github.com/jsdom/jsdom.) To install JSDOM, run the following command:

```
$ npm install --save-dev jsdom
```

With Vitest and JSDOM installed, you can create the vitest.config.js file with the following content:

```
import { defineConfig } from 'vitest/config'

export default defineConfig({
  test: {
    reporters: 'verbose',
    environment: 'jsdom',
  },
})
```

This configuration tells Vitest to use the JSDOM environment and the *verbose* reporter, which outputs a descriptive report of the tests.

You should place your test files inside the src/__tests__ folder and name them *.test.js so that Vitest can find them. Create the src/__tests__ folder:

```
$ mkdir src/__tests__
```

Inside, create a sample.test.js file with the following content:

```
import { expect, test } from 'vitest'

test('sample test', () => {
  expect(1).toBe(1)
})
```

Now add the following two scripts to the package.json file:

```
"scripts": {
  "prepack": "npm run build",
  "build": "rollup -c",
  "lint": "eslint src",
  "lint:fix": "eslint src --fix",
  "test": "vitest",
  "test:run": "vitest run"
}
```

The test script runs the tests in watch mode, and the test:run script runs the tests once and exits. Tests in watch mode are handy when you're working with test-driven development, as they run every time you change the test file or the code you're testing. Try the tests by running the following command:

```
$ npm run test:run
```

You should see the following output:

```
 ✓ src/__tests__/sample.test.js (1)
   ✓ sample test

 Test Files  1 passed (1)
      Tests  1 passed (1)
   Start at  15:50:11
   Duration  1.47s (transform 436ms, setup 1ms, collect 20ms, tests 3ms)
```

You can run individual tests by passing the name or path of the test file as an argument to the test:run and test scripts. All the tests that match the name or path will be run. To run the sample.test.js test, for example, issue the following command:

```
$ npm run test:run sample
```

This command runs only the sample.test.js test and produces the following output:

```
✓ src/__tests__/sample.test.js (1)
  ✓ sample test

Test Files  1 passed (1)
     Tests  1 passed (1)
  Start at  15:55:42
  Duration  1.28s (transform 429ms, setup 0ms, collect 32ms, tests 3ms)
```

Your project structure should look like the following at this point (the files and folders that you've created are in bold):

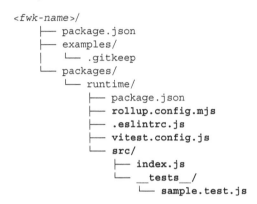

```
<fwk-name>/
    ├── package.json
    ├── examples/
    │    └── .gitkeep
    └── packages/
         └── runtime/
              ├── package.json
              ├── rollup.config.mjs
              ├── .eslintrc.js
              ├── vitest.config.js
              └── src/
                   ├── index.js
                   └── __tests__/
                        └── sample.test.js
```

Your runtime package is ready for you, and you can start writing code. Next, let's see how you can publish it to NPM.

## A.10   Publishing your framework to NPM

As exciting as it is to develop your own framework, it's even more exciting to share it with the world. NPM allows us to ship a package with one simple command:

```
$ npm publish
```

But first, you need to create an account on NPM and log in to it from the command line. If you don't plan to publish your framework, you can skip the next section.

### A.10.1   Creating an NPM account

To create an NPM account, go to https://www.npmjs.com/signup and fill out the form. It's simple, and it's free.

### A.10.2   Logging in to NPM

To log in to NPM in your terminal, run the command

```
$ npm login
```

and follow the prompts. To make sure that you're logged in, run the following command:

```
$ npm whoami
```

You should see your username printed in the terminal.

### A.10.3 Publishing your framework

To publish your framework, you need to make sure that your terminal is in the right directory, inside packages/runtime:

```
$ cd packages/runtime
```

Your terminal's working directory should be packages/runtime (in bold):

```
<fwk-name>/
    ├── package.json
    ├── examples/
    │   └── .gitkeep                    Your terminal's
    └── packages/                       working directory
        ├── runtime/        ⭠          should be here.
        ├── compiler/
        └── loader/
```

> **WARNING** Make sure that you're not in the root folder of the project. The root folder's package.json file has the `private` field set to `true`, which means that it's not meant to be published to NPM. The runtime package is what you want to publish to NPM.

> **NOTE** Remember that the runtime package is the code for the framework (what you want to publish), and the root of the project is the monorepo containing the runtime and other packages (not to be published to NPM).

With your terminal in the runtime directory, run the following command:

```
$ npm publish
```

You may wonder what gets published to NPM. Some files in your project always get published: package.json, README.md, and LICENSE. You can specify which files to publish in the `files` field of the package.json file. If you recall, the `files` field in the package.json file of the runtime package looks like this:

```
"files": [
  "dist/<fwk-name>.js"
],
```

You're publishing only the dist/*<fwk-name>*.js file, the bundled version of your framework. The source files inside the src/ folder are not published.

The package is published with the version specified in the package.json file's `version` field. Bear in mind that you can't publish a package with the same version twice. Throughout the book, we'll increment the version number every time we publish a new version of the framework.

## A.11   *Using a CDN to import the framework*

After you've published your framework to NPM, you can create a Node JS project and install it as a dependency:

```
$ npm install <fwk-name>
```

This approach is great if you plan to set up an NPM project with a bundler (such as Rollup or Webpack) configured to bundle your application and the framework together, which you typically do when you're building a production application with a frontend framework. But for small projects or quick experiments that use only a few files—like those you'll work on in this book—it's simpler to import the framework directly from the dist/ directory in your project or from a *content-delivery network* (CDN).

One free CDN that you can use is unpkg (https://unpkg.com). Everything that's published to NPM is also available on unpkg.com, so after you've published your framework to NPM, you can import it from there:

```
import { createApp, h } from 'https://unpkg.com/<fwk-name>'
```

If you browse to https://unpkg.com/fwk-name, you'll see the dist/*<fwk-name>*.js file you published in NPM, which the CDN serves to your browser when you import the framework from there. If you don't specify a version, the CDN serves the latest version of the package. If you want to use a specific version of your framework, you can specify it in the URL:

```
import { createApp, h } from 'https://unpkg.com/<fwk-name>@1.0.0'
```

Or if you want to use the last minor version of the framework, you can request a major version:

```
import { createApp, h } from 'https://unpkg.com/<fwk-name>@1'
```

I recommend that you use unpkg with the versioned URL so you don't have to worry about changes in the framework that might break your examples as you publish new versions. If you import the framework directly from the dist folder in your project, every time you bundle a new version that's not backward-compatible, your example applications will break. You could overcome this problem by instructing Rollup to include the framework version in the bundled filename, but I'll be using unpkg in this book.

You're all set! It's time to start developing your framework. You can turn to chapter 2 to start the exciting adventure that's ahead of you.

# *index*